Bottleneck

D1617070

Bottleneck

Moving, Building, and Belonging in an African City

CAROLINE MELLY

The University of Chicago Press
Chicago and London

The University of Chicago Press, Chicago 60637
The University of Chicago Press, Ltd., London
© 2017 by The University of Chicago
Published 2017
Printed in the United States of America

26 25 24 23 22 21 20 19 18 17   1 2 3 4 5

ISBN-13: 978-0-226-48887-5 (cloth)
ISBN-13: 978-0-226-48890-5 (paper)
ISBN-13: 978-0-226-48906-3 (e-book)
DOI: 10.7208/chicago/9780226489063.001.0001

Library of Congress Cataloging-in-Publication Data
Names: Melly, Caroline, author.
Title: Bottleneck : moving, building, and belonging in an African city /
    Caroline Melly.
Description: Chicago ; London : The University of Chicago Press, 2017. |
    Includes bibliographical references and index.
Identifiers: LCCN 2017003727 | ISBN 9780226488875 (cloth : alk. paper) |
    ISBN 9780226488905 (pbk. : alk. paper) | ISBN 9780226489063 (e-book)
Subjects: LCSH: Social mobility—Senegal—Dakar. | Dakar (Senegal)—Social
    conditions.
Classification: LCC HN829.D3 M455 2017 | DDC 305.5/1309663—dc23
    LC record available at https://lccn.loc.gov/2017003727

♾ This paper meets the requirements of ANSI/NISO Z39.48-1992
(Permanence of Paper).

CONTENTS

ACKNOWLEDGMENTS

It is in writing a book that one truly comes to appreciate authorship as a deeply collaborative process. This book belongs as much to the people and institutions I thank here as it does to me.

Above all, this book would not have been possible without the insights, encouragement, and *teranga* (hospitality) offered by countless residents of Dakar, many of whom I cannot mention here by name. One of the great joys of conducting research in Dakar is that urban residents are typically quite eager to engage in vigorous debate and probing discussion, even with people they do not know. This book has benefited enormously from these brilliant encounters, and I am grateful to the many anonymous urbanites who shared their encouragement, critique, and perspectives with me. My deepest debts, perhaps, are owed to our Parcelles Assainies "family," who made Dakar home for me and my husband and who eagerly accepted us as part of their lives. Our time with them gave me an extraordinary glimpse into the dynamics of migration, gender, and household in contemporary Dakar. Without the patient explanations and extensive networks of "Maman," the dynamic matriarch of the all-female household, my research would not have gotten off the ground. I am grateful, too, to "Yaye" and "Aïda," as I have called them in this book, for their friendship, good humor, and seemingly endless patience with their American "sister." I cherish Fatima and Yacine, who made our days so warm and memorable. Deep gratitude is owed to the fantastic Faye family, who likewise took us in as family and taught us so much about what it means to live in a global Dakar. We are so fortunate to count them as friends. I am grateful to my colleagues at L'Agence Nationale Chargée de la Promotion d'Investissement et des Grands Travaux (APIX), most especially "El Hadji" and another office mate, for their interest in and support of my research. I am deeply indebted to "Ousseynou," "Baba," and many other taxi drivers, whose keen perspectives and vibrant hopes are at the very heart of this book. My thanks to Saliou Sall and his lovely wife, Cousson, who offered lodging, friendship, and a sounding board for ideas in the early stages of this project. Moutarou Diallo's passion for Senegal and his linguistic expertise have left an indelible mark on this book. I thank him for being such a patient Wolof teacher and for discussing many of the arguments presented in this book with me. Fellow *anthropologue* Emilie Venables made fieldwork more pleasurable and Senegal more enchanting. The pages that follow bear the traces of many fruitful conversations with Emilie over gin and tonics and a Scrabble board.

I was so fortunate to be at UC Irvine at a time of spectacular intellectual renaissance. While there, I had the great fortune of working with many innovative and dedicated scholars who were as generous and student-centered as they were brilliant. Victoria Bernal's passion for African studies and attentive ethnography continues to inspire and guide me. I thank Michael Montoya for his support and guidance. Tom Boellstorff has provided invaluable feedback and sage advice at every stage of my career. Inderpal Grewal has been an exceptional mentor, and her perspectives have deeply shaped my writing and teaching. I thank Bill Maurer for his steadfast support, both scholarly and personal, and for his enthusiasm for my ideas and approaches. This project would never have taken shape without him.

At Irvine, I had the privilege of living, thinking, and writing alongside a collegial and inspiring group of graduate students. I am especially thankful to Nanao Akanuma, Jesse Cheng, Allison Fish, Sylvia Martin, Connie McGuire, Erin Moran, Guillermo Narváez, Joanne Randa Nucho, SeoYoung Park, Rob Phillips, Kathy Quick, Priya Shah, Erica Vogel, Neha Vora, and various others who have left their mark on this book.

My anthropology colleagues at Smith College have been unwavering in their support and enthusiasm for this project. Sincere gratitude is owed to Fernando Armstrong-Fumero, Elliot Fratkin, Suzanne Gottschang, Pinky Hota, Don Joralemon, and Liz Klarich for fostering an environment where critical scholarship and innovative teaching go hand in hand. I have also benefited from the collegial support and insights of members of the African studies programs both at Smith and in the Five Colleges. Being part of this dynamic community of scholars has enriched this book in ways I could never have imagined. I am thankful, too, to Debbora Battaglia, Catharine Newbury, Margaret Sarkissian, and Tina Wildhagen, each of whom has helped make this book a reality in some way.

My students at Smith College have been critical interlocutors in this project, helping me to sharpen my arguments and clarify my writing. In particular, students in my Globalization in Africa, Citizenship and Belonging, and Urban Anthropology courses contributed in important ways. Working with Dongyoung Kim and Prim Devakula has been especially rewarding and generative, and their feedback and encouragement have been indispensable.

My thanks to Victoria Beckley and Jon Caris at Smith's Spatial Analysis Lab for producing the map that appears in the introduction to this book. Deep gratitude is owed to the talented Fally Sene Sow, whose artwork appears on the cover.

This book has benefited from the perceptive insights and suggestions of many readers over the years. I thank especially Jonathan Anjaria, Chris Dole, Vincent Foucher, Britt Halvorson, Pinky Hota, Serin Houston, and Katherine Lemons. It has been a pleasure working with Kathryn Wright; her work has enriched my understandings of the economic, political, and social contributions of Senegalese diaspora. I have also profited from excellent feedback at numerous conferences and workshops. Among these, the organizers and attendees of the Mellon-funded "Gender and Diaspora" workshop at Vassar in 2010 deserve special mention. I am particularly grateful to Ben Page, whose invitation to participate in the "Migration and Homes" workshop at the University College of London in June of 2014 came at a crucial time in the manuscript process.

Working with the University of Chicago Press staff has been a remarkable experience. I had the great fortune of working with not one but two outstanding editorial teams. I am thankful to David Brent for seeing value in this project and for his patience with my writing process and with the unforeseen obstacles I faced along the way. Thank you to Ellen Kladky for her quick responses to my queries and for her keen attention to detail. Priya Nelson brought great energy to the project at a very crucial time. Dylan Montanari was heroic in his quests to acquire permissions and attend to last minute details. I cannot imagine working with a more supportive, responsive, and knowledgeable group. I am grateful, too, to Daniel Jordan Smith and two other anonymous reviewers, whose careful and generous readings of the manuscript helped strengthen this book and clarify its stakes.

This book would not have materialized without the "village" that has helped to raise my children over the past six years. I would like to thank the staff of Williston Children's Center, especially Blair Aiello, Charlene Cross, and Keira Durrett, for their commitment to my family and kind friendship over the years it took to complete this book. I am particularly grateful to Blair Aiello, who provided care during those crucial summer months so that I could focus on writing.

Deepest gratitude is owed to my parents, Stephen and Catherine Melly, who believed in this research and in my future more ardently than anyone.

Thank you to my sister Kristyn and brothers Stephen and Gregory, whose support was constant and whose good humor has kept me sane. My thanks, too, to my mother-in-law, Marilyn Wright, and my brothers- and sisters-in-law for their encouragement. I thank Jill Smink and Colleen Feller for their lasting friendship and for their patient faith in me, especially when I doubted myself, and to the many other friends who have endured the book writing process with grace. I am most grateful to my dear little boy Adrien, whose insistence on an elaborate home-cooked meal each night and whose utter disinterest in "the book"—until he learned his name would appear here in the acknowledgments anyway—always helped to ground and refresh me after a long day of writing. And thank you to our newest addition, Lionel, whose remarkable resilience and joyful spirit have carried me through toughest of times to finish this project.

This book is dedicated to two marvelous partners in this scholarly journey. Thank you to Neha Vora for her unwavering insistence that I focus, quite simply, on telling the truth. It is an extraordinary gift to write alongside such a talented and generous scholar. It was through our writing partnership that this book took form, and she deserves much of the credit for its completion. And finally, deep gratitude and admiration is owed to Doug Wright, amateur ethnographer and committed partner, whose shared passion for Senegal, social justice, and life in general has sustained and inspired me through the years. So many of the ideas and arguments I present in these pages were inspired by our conversations and experiences together, and I am sincerely grateful for his sharp perspective and faithful companionship through this journey. *Dëgg-laa.*

Financial support for this research was provided by the National Science Foundation; the Fulbright-Hays Doctoral Dissertation Research Abroad Award; the Department of Anthropology and the School of Social Sciences at the University of California, Irvine; and Smith College.

Some of the material in the following chapters first appeared in print elsewhere. My thanks to the editorial staffs at *American Ethnologist, Comparative Studies in Society and History*, and *Africa* for giving me permission to reprint these portions here. Several anonymous reviewers for these journals offered constructive feedback that has shaped and strengthened this book project, and I thank them as well.

Introduction: *Embouteillage*

It was a sweltering morning in May 2006, and the stagnant air, the taxicab in which I sat, and my research agenda stood motionlessly on the streets of Dakar, Senegal. My taxi driver (*taksimann*) that day, who called himself Vieux, had launched a friendly but heated debate about who should be held responsible for the worsening traffic jams, called *embouteillages*, that threatened to destroy both of our livelihoods. I spoke with him through a handkerchief, which I had begun to carry with me on my daily journeys to help filter the exhaust that built up as we sat in traffic. While traffic jams were nothing new in the cramped peninsular city, they had proliferated and intensified over the past three months. During this time, President Abdoulaye Wade had initiated two separate road projects as part of a broader effort to revitalize the African capital city. Funded by multinational investment partnerships and overseen by the state, these ambitious infrastructural schemes aimed to facilitate movement within the densely inhabited metropolitan area, home to an estimated two and a half million people, and to better connect it with the country's vast interior. In the short term, however, the projects further strained circulations, prompting road closures, creating a bewildering labyrinth of sanctioned detours and illicit routes, and disrupting economic exchange and urban rhythms. The commencement of these projects had coincided with the start of my internship at Senegal's national investment promotion agency, APIX,[1] a key partner in one of these schemes. It

---

1. L'Agence Nationale Chargée de la Promotion d'Investissement et des Grands Travaux (APIX) is a quasi-state body that is charged both with promoting large-scale investment and with overseeing major public works projects, including the national autoroute. I focus on this organization more closely in chapter 4.

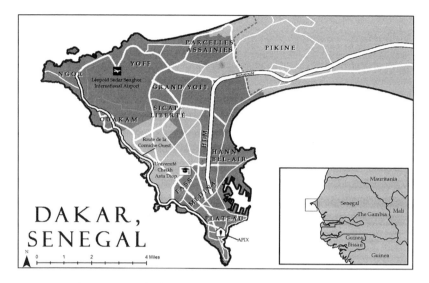

Figure 1. Map of Dakar. Courtesy of Victoria Beckley and Jon Caris, Smith College Spatial Analysis Lab.

was at APIX where I was to chronicle the state's efforts to transform remitting migrants into market-savvy entrepreneurs. Now, the roughly eight-mile commute from my apartment in the city's northern extremities to APIX's offices in Dakar's southern administrative district took nearly two hours each way.

That morning, which was to be a particularly hectic one at my downtown office, the commute was worse than ever before, as traffic patterns were altered again and additional side roads were barricaded. Sensing my increasing frustration and concerned for his income, Vieux spontaneously spun the cab around and headed down a side street. For the remainder of our journey, he carved his own path, winding through oncoming traffic, through deep gullies along the side of the road, alongside makeshift markets, and through neighborhoods unfamiliar to me. As we navigated through a dense network of unpaved residential streets, Vieux returned to his assessment of the city's bottlenecked roads. President Wade cared only for foreign investors and tourists, he griped, for whom he was building these roads; he had no concern for taxi drivers and other urban residents whose livelihoods he was destroying. As he spoke, Vieux gestured to the half-finished villas that cast shadows onto the street. Often built with capital earned by transnational migrants living abroad, these structures were, for him and many others, indisputable evidence that things were moving elsewhere. He had dreamed of migrating for years, Vieux explained, as it was his only hope for establishing a family of his own and securing his future in the city. Now that these construction projects had begun and his income was dwindling, he was more desperate than ever to find a way to leave. Over the course of nearly an hour, Vieux wove together critiques of international migration regulations, free market ideologies, local Senegalese politics, urban development schemes, and the rising cost of living in Dakar. As we finally neared my downtown office, Vieux ended the conversation with a deep sigh and a confident claim: somehow, he'd find a way through these *embouteillages* and onto Europe.

After offering Vieux a few words of encouragement and paying my fare, I slipped out of the cab and through APIX's marble flanked entryway, past larger-than-life investment banners extolling Senegal's limitless potential. When I first began my position at APIX, the agency's grand headquarters had seemed a refuge from the city's traffic-clogged streets. Weary from my long commute, it was a relief to settle into my daily routine as a *stagiaire* (intern): observing office interactions, attending meetings, translating promotional materials, sorting paperwork, assembling PowerPoint files, and gathering information about other countries' efforts to woo transnational

Figure 2. A taxi moves along the emergent autoroute. Through the windshield, houses under construction can be seen.

migrants to invest at "home." In stark contrast to the sputtering cabs and overcrowded buses that delivered me to my downtown destination each morning, APIX's spacious interior was air conditioned, smartly furnished, and flooded with light. Meetings began on time, and deadlines were considered firm. This was the face of a new Senegal, officials declared, one in which barriers to investment were removed and capital circulated, where plans for *grands travaux* (public works projects) and financial infrastructures were drafted and celebrated—all with the hopes of transforming the everyday lives of people like Vieux. Here at APIX, my colleagues beamed, *things were moving*.

But as I moved between Vieux's heaving cab and my makeshift desk at APIX that May morning, I began to see my environs and my research project quite differently. I came to realize that the bottlenecks that I had wanted so desperately to escape were in fact *central* to the story I was trying to tell. Indeed, everyday practice inside this cutting-edge bureaucracy was as marked by uncertainty and snarled plans as the streets outside. Despite decades of structural adjustment reforms and triumphant claims about the country's imminent economic emergence, Senegal's economy was sluggish at best. Daily routines at APIX revolved around anticipating and alleviating bureaucratic *embouteillages*, as they were called, and designing "road maps" to help ease the journeys of investors unfamiliar with Senegal's economic terrain. Staff members spent much of their days attending to the investor dossiers that piled up on their desks, worrying about the lags investors encountered as they tried to start businesses, and working to forge new alliances with private and public sector offices that might lead to fruitful collaborations in the future. The migrant-investor program I had come to study was particularly prone to bottlenecks, I quickly learned, and the program remained stuck in the planning stages for the duration of my work there.

In the early days of my research, I worried deeply that postponed meetings, delayed documents, traffic jams, and long lines would distract me from the "real" work of studying migration and development. Like generations of scholars before me, I was lured to Dakar because of its reputation as a cosmopolitan crossroads and by its long and vibrant histories as a critical node in regional and global migratory flows.[2] In a country with relatively few profitable resources, transnational migration has played a fundamental role in keeping national and household budgets afloat, particularly in the

---

2. There is robust literature on Dakar's (and Senegal's) cosmopolitan past and present. Particularly notable is Diouf's (2000) notion of "vernacular cosmopolitanism." Scheld (2007) offers a useful summary of the concept and this literature.

decades following structural adjustment. But even in precolonial and colonial times, migratory circuits were fueled by more than economic deprivation or colonial coercion; instead, mobility has been a constitutive feature of community life and kinship networks for many generations (Manchuelle 1997; see also Lambert 2002; Diop 2008). I was interested, then, in studying how institutions, communities, and individuals in Senegal weathered economic uncertainty through their connections to the country's vast diaspora. I wanted to understand how mobility became a personal and national value of sorts, and how this helped to bring about new conceptions of belonging and urban presence. And I wanted to develop tools for thinking about urban belonging and governance after the institution of structural adjustment reforms that might help push against academic and popular diagnoses of "crisis," disconnection, and failure in contemporary Africa.

To my surprise, however, circumstances of *embouteillage* proved to be critical opportunities to pursue precisely these lines of inquiry. It was in moving through and talking about bottlenecks of all sorts, I began to realize, that residents were grappling most urgently and intimately with the changing nature of citizenship and governance in the structurally adjusted capital city. What they confronted was a critical paradox, one that would come to define the trajectory of my research: *to be mobile* was a cultural imperative in Dakar, a coveted way of being and belonging, and a critical means of securing the future, especially for young men. Both state agendas and conceptions of belonging and effective presence were seen as contingent on movements of capital, goods, labor, and ideas. Indeed, mobility was increasingly configured as a social value and as a resource in itself: it was *through mobility* that one was able to stake claim to urban permanence and social presence. At the very same time, both global and local mobilities were increasingly regulated, constricted, interrupted, and rendered impossible, particularly in the wake of changes wrought by 9/11, economic slowdowns in Europe, and political shifts in Senegal and beyond. In other words, both the state and citizen found themselves "caught" in bottlenecks of all sorts—wedded to mobile agendas that they could not likely pursue. I quickly came to see that these circumstances and spaces were neither exceptional nor aberrant. Quite to the contrary, the *embouteillage* was a constitutive site of urban sociality.

A Concept in Motion

Inspired by the keen insights and everyday struggles of urban residents, this book claims the bottleneck as both an ethnographic point of departure and as a theoretical lens for making sense of belonging and governance in urban

Africa and beyond. To do so, this book borrows and reshapes a culturally significant concept to think about life and policy in contemporary Dakar. Of French provenance, the word *embouteillage* is best translated as "bottling" and typically refers to the traffic jams and bottlenecks that plague city streets. Talk of the city's worsening traffic jams was omnipresent during the time of my research: It spilled beyond the spaces of congested streets and stalled vehicles, into bureaucratic offices and spaces of cosmopolitan consumption, into radio programs and popular songs, through pulsing neighborhoods and into family homes. In these spaces, urbanites shared wisdom about areas of the city to avoid and the best times of day to travel. They planned daily visits, errands, and commutes to coincide with lulls in traffic. They complained of flat tires, missed appointments, tense encounters with angry motorists, respiratory problems caused by the oppressive heat and exhaust fumes, lost income, and clothing soiled by accumulating dust. And they gossiped about the poor planning efforts and questionable motives of government leaders, who seemed more attentive to the needs of foreign investors than to the circumstances of the city's residents. *Embouteillage* even infused daily greetings. Sandwiched between formulaic questions about another's wives and children, the weather, or work, urbanites asked each other about their experiences with gridlock: "Ana waa kër ga? Ça va? Et les embouteillages?" (How is your family? Is everything going well? And the bottlenecks?)[3]

In these kinds of exchanges, however, people were talking about more than just the city's insufferable traffic jams. *Embouteillage* was in fact as much a vibrant, indigenous term as it was a global import from the language of the former colonizer. Dakarois often pronounced the word with a hard *z* sound rather than a softer *zh*, as it would be in Parisian French. This seemingly subtle shift places the word within the realm of what scholars call "Dakar Wolof," a hybrid and dynamic dialect that has helped forge and celebrate a distinct urban culture and identity in the capital city (McLaughlin 2001; see also Irvine 1995).[4] Not only did the term acquire new linguistic

3. Urbanites would use the term *embouteillage* in greetings in various ways; this string of questions gives just one typical example. While French is the official language of Senegal, Wolof is more widely spoken, even by those who are not ethnically Wolof. In everyday practice in Dakar, however, the boundaries between these languages are far from discrete, as this particular multilingual greeting makes clear.

4. Fiona McLaughlin (2001) has described how this urban brand of Wolof developed amidst the political tumult of the 1990s, which I describe in greater detail in chapter 1. Dakar Wolof signals the emergence of a distinct urban identity that very purposefully borrows and adapts words and phrases. McLaughlin describes how these borrowings "undergo phonological changes that

sounds as it moved through the city, it accumulated new points of reference and new meanings. In governing spaces, for instance, *embouteillage* was a means of describing the trickle of investment funds or foreign travel visas,[5] the sluggish pace of regulatory change, and official papers piled high in dusty boxes, waiting to be approved or sorted or archived. Urbanites also sometimes employed the term to refer to tedious bureaucratic lags that left people waiting for necessary permits, licenses, and records. Hopeful migrants sometimes used the word to index long lines and delays at embassies. And residents often described overcrowded neighborhoods, electricity and water shortages, patchy Internet connections, and even the growing capital city itself as bottlenecked.

Embouteillage was thus a slippery term, one that enabled people to speak about various circumstances of narrowed passage and restricted flow and the effects these processes had on everyday lives, policies, and landscapes. In this way, it provided a compelling framework for thinking about one's place in a rapidly changing city and world. Writing about other African contexts, scholars have likewise explored how people have harnessed Pentecostalism and Charismatic Christianity (Meyer 2004; Shaw 2007; Smith 2014; Comaroff and Comaroff 2001) and beliefs about witchcraft, sorcery, and the occult (Meyer 1998; Comaroff and Comaroff 1999; Geschiere 1997) in order to make sense of the paradoxes of contemporary life. These frameworks share an attention to the seemingly opaque and arbitrary nature of global capitalism, to the swift and unsettling pace of social and moral change, and to the murky boundaries between success and failure, inclusion and exclusion, accumulation and loss. Dakarois likewise turn to Islam, *maraboutage* (divination practices), and beliefs about *jinne* (spirits) to make sense of the shifting worlds they inhabit and shape. *Embouteillage* offered a different (and at times complementary) perspective, one firmly embedded not in otherworldly relationships but in concrete landscapes and everyday encounters.

---

adapt their pronunciation to the sound patterns of Wolof," though these are very variable, dependent primarily on a speaker's command of French and Wolof (162–63). Moreover, urbanites often move between French and Wolof in everyday speech, as this greeting suggests. Although I use the French spelling of *embouteillage* in this book, I want to underscore the broad continuum of pronunciations—dependent on a speaker's education, class, global experiences, and interlocutor—that characterizes this word. My use of the term *embouteillage* throughout this text is meant to encompass and foreground this diversity and complexity, not to obscure or resolve it.

5. In her article on motorbike usage in Ho Chi Minh City, Allison Truitt similarly notes that the word people use to describe traffic jams is also used to describe being "financially blocked." For urban Vietnamese, the city's traffic congestion is a sign of the paradoxes of the country's economic development (2008, 12).

Through their engagements with bottlenecks of all sorts, urban residents and bureaucrats laid bare the myriad mundane forces—from road surfaces and paper pile-ups to migration regulations and economic reforms—that helped pave urban and global itineraries.

What realities come into view when, following the cue of urbanites, we take seriously the bottleneck as an analytic device and an ethnographic field site? And how might this concept reinvigorate and refocus broader scholarly discussions of migration, citizenship, statecraft, and urban life in an era of economic, political, and social predicament? Drawing on nearly twenty months of ethnographic research in Dakar, the majority of which I conducted in 2006 and 2007, I seek to tease out the complex meanings that the term evoked for people living in the city. I also work to expand and develop *embouteillage* as a scholarly framework that might help us think differently about what it means to live in and govern the city after structural adjustment. In many ways, "bottleneck," which typically refers to a particular site of congestion or disruption, is a rather lackluster English approximation of the vibrant concept I am working to develop here. As I hope will become clear in the discussion that follows, *embouteillage* in fact indexes a much more complex array of urban experiences, processes, and realities. I nonetheless use the two terms relatively interchangeably throughout this book for the ease of the reader. As it is absorbed into this anthropological study, the term takes on new layers of significance, new associations, and new possibilities for drawing otherwise incommensurable experiences of mobility and suspension into the same ethnographic frame. What results is a synthetic conceptual device, one forged through the complex interaction between urban residents and ethnographer. It is a framework that is attentive to the specificity of urban life in Dakar but that also opens up ways of speaking about and theorizing life in other parts of the world.

Framing my everyday work around the concept of *embouteillage* fundamentally changed the way I moved through, engaged with, and inhabited the city as a researcher. It enabled me to see the deep and consequential connections between three seemingly distinct spheres of urban life. First, as an intern at APIX, I navigated each day through a constellation of state, nongovernmental organizations (NGOs), and international organizations (IOs). It was within these bureaucratic offices—largely but not exclusively located in the city's southern extremities—that "mobility" was (ostensibly) monitored, managed, packaged, and exploited as a national value. Secondly, I both inhabited and moved through Dakar's burgeoning residential neighborhoods, particularly those situated in the city's northern reaches, where everyday life and household budgets were deeply impacted both by the ongoing infrastructural projects and diasporic movements of labor and capital. Finally, I spent a good deal of time on the roads themselves, navigating the complex system of emergent highways and neglected side roads that linked north and south, residential neighborhoods and bureaucratic buildings, state and citizen.

As I moved through these spheres, I connected with a remarkably diverse group of people engaged in a wide range of seemingly bottlenecked initiatives; these actors led me, in turn, to other informants, sites, and questions I could not have anticipated at the outset of my research. I conducted interviews in Wolof and French, frequently moving between the two languages, and employed both semistructured and unstructured formats. Many of these more informal interviews took place in transit, as I accompanied colleagues to meetings, navigated traffic with cab drivers, sat stranded with fellow bus passengers, or meandered through neighborhoods with hopeful migrants. This ethnographic approach means that that the city itself—its spaces, institutions, vocabularies, and materiality—has become inextricable from the data I collected. As a result of these methodological decisions, this book is as much about what it means to be part of, to move through, to inhabit, and to construct an African city as it is about the desire and imperative to mobilize labor, capital, and knowledge on national and global scales. It is as attentive to the perspectives, projects, and expertise generated by the city's taxi drivers, unemployed youth, and failed migrants—not typical subjects for a study of migration or economic development—as it is to those of state bureaucrats and international officials. "Mobility" emerges in this study as an enduring and elusive collective value, as a differentially distributed resource, as an intensely embodied expectation, and as a complex, contested, and often futile process that exceeds binaristic geographies of arrival and departure. Mobility is not just an abstract imaginary (see Fouquet 2007, Willems 2014), sensibility, or goal to which urban residents and bureaucrats aspire, but rather a materially unstable reality that has profound and quite visible effects on urban lives and spaces.

My daily routines, commitments, and scholarly preoccupations have shaped this ethnography in profound ways. Had I arrived in the city a year earlier or later, rented a more centrally located apartment, been interested primarily in women's economic endeavors, or secured a position at another state institution, a somewhat different picture of life and policy in Dakar would surely have emerged, and the bottleneck may not have figured so centrally in my analysis. Indeed, it is not the case that nothing moves with ease in or beyond the city; there are plenty of instances where plans are effectively carried out, connections are made with relative ease, projects are completed on time, and resources are quickly channeled. What *embouteillage* in fact afforded was a very particular ethnographic vantage point, one that brought into view certain perspectives, experiences, and engagements while obscuring others. As Donna Haraway has persuasively argued, it is only by claiming a situated, embodied, and partial perspective that we are able to recuperate some sort of objective vision as ethnographers (1988, 583). The ethnography that results is resolutely feminist in its approach. It does not strive to be exhaustive or encompassing in its treatment of transnational migration, citizenship and governance, or urban life. Instead, the concept of *embouteillage* cuts across conventional scholarly domains of study, offering an ethnographic "depth" that is, perhaps, more horizontal than vertical. In the pages that follow, I am particularly attentive to the narratives and experiences of state workers and urban men, two groups of actors whose sense of authority and belonging is imagined to be "in crisis" in structurally adjusted Senegal. By juxtaposing their perspectives with powerful counternarratives offered by women, other governing organizations, migrants, and other urban actors, I also pay close attention to how these gendered and partial narratives are interrupted, disputed, and endlessly reinterpreted.

Bottleneck makes two primary arguments. First, I argue that that the *embouteillage* is a defining feature of life and policy in Dakar and in many other "structurally adjusted" cities. At once mundane and volatile, the bottleneck is the most tangible and potent sign of an era, one in which urban and global mobilities are both intensely valorized and increasingly regulated, restricted, and deferred. *Embouteillage*, then, indexes the complex patterns of suspension, exclusion, uncertainty, and opportunity that this moment produces. It is, in other words, the concrete manifestation of very abstract, often diffuse changes taking place in the city and elsewhere in the world—from infrastructural renovations to regulatory shifts that govern the movement of migrants and capital.

At the same time, the *embouteillage* does more than just describe or reflect the conditions of life and policymaking in Dakar and beyond—it is in fact *the very means through which* both citizen and state are constituted in this contemporary era. Unpredictable and wildly generative, the bottleneck is a critical urban force that often exceeds management, planning, and intervention. It is a once a problem to solve, a circumstance to avoid, and a site and resource to be exploited. It is here within the spaces and circumstances of *embouteillage*, I argue, that the city, its relations, and its possibilities are incessantly reconstituted. I pay careful attention to the urban landscapes, temporalities, and modes of gendered belonging and governance that take shape amidst and through conditions of *embouteillage*. I examine how diverse actors harness bottlenecks of all sorts to cultivate projects, networks, and identities that help them lay claim to the city and its future.

Infrastructures Overwhelmed

To speak of *embouteillage* is an effort in "thinking infrastructurally," as Julie Chu (2014, 353) has described it.[6] Infrastructures are the "materiality of [the] in-between" (Simone 2012). They are the channels through which people, resources, goods, knowledge, and capital are circulated and exchanged across time and space. In contemporary Dakar, it is infrastructure that makes mobility *matter*—that gives it material substance and ideological weight—as a public and personal value. At once material and semiotic, technical and ideological, infrastructures express mobile visions while also offering platforms for realizing these visions. Centralizing infrastructures and their effects brings into sharper view the patterns and practices of inclusion and exclusion, access and authority, that define social worlds. "Thinking infrastructurally" thus sheds light on the ways in which citizenship and governance become articulated in the contemporary world.

When we think of infrastructures, we typically imagine the systems of highways, pipes, cables, and virtual networks that undergird and facilitate our everyday lives. During the time of my research in Dakar, there was intensified financial, moral, and political investment in developing precisely these kinds of physical infrastructures.[7] The city's road projects were perhaps

6. In recent years, there has been a significant scholarly investment in reinvigorating our conceptualizations of infrastructures and in better understanding the social, material, ideological, and technological work that they do. These conversations began primarily within the interdisciplinary field of science and technology studies (see, e.g., Graham and Marvin 2001) but have since gathered a great deal of momentum within anthropology. For an excellent overview of this emergent literature, see Larkin 2013. Other notable examples include Anand 2011, 2012; Appel 2012a, 2012b; Carse 2014; Chalfin 2014; Chu 2014; Elyachar 2010; Fisch 2013; Fischer 2005; Gürsel 2012; Hetherington 2014; Larkin 2008; Mains 2012b; Schnitzler 2008, 2013.

7. Contemporary Africa is typically perceived as critically "lacking" reliable infrastructure (see Foster and Briceño-Garmendia 2010). The continent's aging and insufficient infrastructures are typically cast as a symptom of the failure of state governance, and they are signaled as a primary factor in many countries' poor economic growth. In recent years, then, IOs, foreign governments, transnational investment and engineering firms, and African states have designed, financed, and launched various infrastructural projects, alone and through partnerships, to bridge this assumedly cavernous gap "in between" Africa and the rest of the world. In many ways, these contemporary projects—and the discourses about African lack, disconnection, and intervention that accompany them—are deeply reminiscent of colonial and independence-era strategies of governance, which saw infrastructural development as critical to civilizing and modernizing missions. But this new spate of projects also expresses a remarkably different vision of African futures, one contingent on economic liberalization and the "free" movement of people,

the most conspicuous and controversial of these efforts, and they serve as a concrete point of departure for this book. But these urban projects were also complexly and explicitly linked to a spate of other, much less visible efforts to facilitate mobility and to regulate it as a public good.[8] Indeed, as I moved through the city each day—through bustling neighborhoods, along emergent highways and neglected side streets, into bureaucratic office spaces—a dizzying array of projects came into view. Economic development and state policy, for instance, had become a matter of building and maintaining financial infrastructures that could "channel" and "canalize" (primarily foreign) capital into Senegal. Among these financial infrastructures were the migrant-investor schemes that had brought me to intern with APIX in the first place. These state-sanctioned schemes were modeled on and tapped into existent "informal" investment networks that funneled capital into, through, and out of Dakar—and these investment networks in turn were entangled with legal infrastructures and clandestine networks that kept migrants, documents, and capital in motion.

It was not just me, the ethnographer, who regarded these infrastructures as complexly entangled. Quite to the contrary, thinking infrastructurally was precisely what Dakarois were doing each day and what they were urging me to do as well. Vieux drew remarkably explicit connections between his experiences navigating the city's roads, his desires and inability to migrate abroad, and the politics of neoliberal reform in Senegal. At APIX, too, officials explicitly described migration policy, investment programs, and road development as complexly linked channels that helped determine the flow of capital and expertise. For those with whom I lived and worked, roads were not merely "like" migratory routes or investment channels; instead, these local and global infrastructures were complexly tangled, and these entanglements had real, material impacts on people's everyday lives. As Dakarois knew well, infrastructures, whether concrete structures or clandestine social networks, are inherently unstable configurations; they are prone to constant breakdown, cooptation, and reconfiguration. The work of making mobility

---

goods, ideas, and capital. Officials insisted that new roads and highways, hydroelectric dams, fiber optic cables, and airports would open Africa to the world and spark long-awaited, large-scale economic and political change. For an excellent critical reflection on this assumption of "lack," see Simone 2004a, 2004b, 2006.

8. In this way, I join other scholars in working to open up the concept of infrastructure itself to include things that are not generally considered to be "infrastructures" in the strictest sense of the term. This move, I argue, gives us a better understanding of the relations that underpin everyday movements. Two prominent examples of this effort to rework the term include Simone (2004a, 2004b, 2006); and Elyachar (2010).

matter is thus necessarily fraught and always ongoing (see Larkin 2008). It involves bringing together a complex and geographically dispersed constellation of actors, materials, expertise, labor, and ideologies. To "think infrastructurally," then, requires attending "to the resonance of things unfolding on other planes, and, in turn, to the distributive forms of agency drawing efficacy from links to elsewhere and elsewhen" (Chu 2014, 353).

The *embouteillage* is, put most simply, a condition of infrastructural overload. It occurs when infrastructures cannot accommodate the pressure placed on them—because demand is too high, or because paths have been narrowed, degraded, or obstructed. Traffic is thus limited or rerouted, but it is not entirely cut off; some people and things are able to move and connect. Dakar's bottlenecks were not a sign of infrastructural failure or disconnection but rather of the intense force with which people tried to connect and the building sense of momentum these efforts generated. The condition of strained passage I am describing here was by no means "new" in Dakar. Lured by Dakar's reputation as a vital crossroads and a place of relative tolerance, people from around the world have long come to Dakar to seek short- and long-term opportunities. This was particularly the case as structural adjustment reforms were put into place, as rural dwellers devastated by the removal of agricultural subsidies fled to Senegal's capital seeking work. But adjustment policies had eroded public-sector employment and social safety nets in the city, too. What these diverse newcomers found, then, was a congested city built on a narrow peninsula with little room for growth and with scant opportunities. Drawing on data collected more than a decade before I arrived in Dakar, Michael Lambert described the city in astonishingly similar terms to those I am using here: "People are funneled from the rural hinterland to Dakar where they find themselves at a *bottleneck*—not having found what they were in search of, yet unable to move forward to more promising destinations" (2002, xxi; emphasis added).

By the time I arrived in the city in 2006, however, infrastructures of all sorts faced mounting pressures, and bottlenecks had proliferated. Steady population growth, intensified patterns of consumption, and the growth of private car ownership overwhelmed the city's already outdated and limited infrastructures. This sparked traffic jams, water shortages, and blackouts. Many of the city's renewal projects, including the road projects, were aimed at addressing these circulatory problems. In the short term, however, these efforts only exacerbated matters, as urban roads were blocked or rerouted. Unemployment persisted, and making ends meet was as difficult as ever. At the very same time—and in deeply connected ways, as this book aims to show—many of the global routes into and out of the city were narrowed, too. In response to political movements and economic circumstances half-way around the world, infrastructures that facilitated international migration, capital transfers, foreign aid, and citizenship were revised, restricted, monitored, or blocked. Transnational migration, already an impossibility for many, became much more difficult; remittance and other capital flows became less dependable. In other words, seemingly abstract policy changes made halfway around the world resonated and effected change, often in deeply personal ways, on the city's traffic clogged streets, in its bustling bureaucratic spaces, and in its vibrant residential neighborhoods.[9]

Nearly all of the city's residents—including my APIX colleagues, taxi drivers like Vieux, and myself as ethnographer—found themselves caught up in some way in circumstances of *embouteillage*. Indeed, these were highly complex occurrences that were exceedingly difficult to predict, avoid, or contain. They were the product of human intervention but also revealed the limits of human agency. Some of my colleagues at APIX even went so far as to proclaim the city's traffic jams as a "democratizing" force in the city (see also Melly 2013), as they brought urban residents from all walks of life together in the same spaces. It was nonetheless quite clear that *embouteillages* produced a remarkably uneven urban terrain. Local and global traffic was never entirely cut off; rather, circulations were dramatically constricted.[10] Many residents thus found themselves "stuck" in various circumstances, their daily routines and movements interrupted, their incomes threatened, their long-distance connections strained, and their hopeful itineraries indefinitely postponed. Meanwhile, some urban residents were better able to weather dramatic infrastructural shifts, relying on generators, payoffs and bribes, air-conditioned vehicles, diasporic connections, entrepreneurial pluck, salaried jobs, or old-fashioned good luck to buffer themselves and their families from the acute hardships of life in the city (see also Melly 2013). What resulted was a profoundly volatile and uneven social landscape, one characterized by frenzied movement and repressive stasis, by persistent anticipation and deepening inequality. While many of these inequalities and exclusions fell along predictable lines like class, many others were quite surprising, challenging any

9. To focus on *embouteillage* is to pull various kinds and scales of mobility into the same ethnographic frame. It is to insist on theorizing stalled vehicles and stalled plans for migration abroad as profoundly, sometimes paradoxically, interconnected. This move places this book in a stream of recent developments in the anthropology/sociology of mobilities. Most prominent within this emergent scholarship is the journal *Mobilities* and the work of John Urry, alone and in collaboration with others (see, e.g., Urry 2007; Sheller and Urry 2006; Featherstone, Thrift, and Urry 2007). Other notable examples include Chu 2010; Salazar 2010; Coutin 2007.

10. There are resonances here with Anand's (2012) discussion of abjection and infrastructure.

simplistic dichotomy of wealth and dispossession, inclusion and exclusion that tends to characterize discussions of cities in the global·south (see also Anand 2011). In this way, *embouteillage* not only ordered urban life and relations but also gave residents opportunities to debate and push against this ordering.

The constant narrowing and rerouting of local and global infrastructures also shaped the city's built environment in profound ways. All across Dakar, projects and structures remained in various stages of construction and decay as people waited for *embouteillages* to dissipate. This produced a very particular urban aesthetic that came to define the city during the time of my research. *Bottleneck* explores this aesthetic and its complex effects. For instance, my movements through the city with Vieux offer a glimpse of the migrant-built houses that have come to define Dakar's landscape. Many of these houses linger unfinished and even uninhabited for many years, as capital flows connecting Senegal and the diaspora become bottlenecked for various reasons. This book investigates the aesthetic that these remarkable structures install in the city, and it asks what it means to live amongst these half-built houses in an era when migration abroad has become increasingly impossible. Through an ethnographic examination of these houses and other stalled projects, I argue that moving through and inhabiting a landscape marred by *embouteillages* of all sorts has produced very particular ways of seeing and inhabiting the city, while foreclosing others.

Quite remarkably, it was here—amidst overburdened infrastructures, languishing urban projects, and dramatic exclusions—that mobility was publicly reaffirmed as both a mark of privilege and status (see also Chu 2010) and as a critical means of claiming presence in the city. Bottlenecks did not reveal transnational migration as a bankrupt endeavor, as one might expect. Rather, the impossibility of migration seemed only to spur migratory plans and expectations, centralizing the transnational migrant as a critical public actor in an era of *embouteillage*. This book explores this tension and its everyday effects. Moreover, at the very same time that bottlenecks strained flows and limited mobility, they also held the promise of future movement. They were, by their very nature, transitory phenomena. Though they left powerful and very material traces on urban lives and spaces, producing inequalities and exclusions, they also shifted, dissipated, and dematerialized with time. To speak of *embouteillage*, then, was to emphasize one's expectations for a resolution of impasse, for renewed movement, and for future inclusion. In this sense, the bottleneck was an instance of potential energy. This fact shaped urban perspectives in profound ways, as I demonstrate in the chapters that follow. At the very same time that many Dakarois described themselves as excluded from urban belonging and global flows, they also continually carved out a space for future presence. It was in fact through the city's bottlenecked projects and structures—through the very landscape that they described as exclusionary—that urbanites worked to fashion the city a habitable space. Vieux's parting words are particularly illustrative here, and they are echoed in different ways throughout the book. As he moved through the city, Vieux blasted the road projects and spoke of his social im-mobility. But he also ended our journey with a bold claim, one that seemed unsettling to me at the time: that he'd find his way through *embouteillage* and that he'd migrate abroad. In this way, I argue, citizenship is itself bot-tlenecked: though it appears as highly exclusionary in the present tense, it holds, too, the radical promise of future belonging and presence. *Bottleneck* thus engages with a rich scholarly literature on the changing nature of citi-zenship in cities of the global south to explore urban belonging as a set of claims and practices that are always volatile, often paradoxical, and com-prised of multiple temporalities.[11]

Predicament and Possibility in the Structurally Adjusted City

The experiences of suspension and postponement I am describing were not entirely new. Rather, people were grappling with the deepening sense of eco-nomic, political, and social predicament that had come to grip life in the structurally adjusted city. Instituted in the late 1970s, structural adjustment reforms were conceived as a series of technical and temporary interventions to "open up" Senegal's economy to the world. This involved a rigorous plan for deregulating, privatizing, and diversifying Senegal's economy; devalu-ing the regional currency; and redefining the role and reach of the state in this new economy. As many scholars have documented, these liberalization measures did not produce the economic growth and social stability that the international community had anticipated. Instead, countries like Senegal found themselves in a state of "permanent transition" (Clark 2005), crippled by what were supposed to be short-term side effects like unemployment, stag-nant private sector growth, and skyrocketing prices, and prone to unrelenting

---

11. This book is in conversation with a number of scholars working to theorize the shifting relationship between citizenship and the city, particularly in the global south. See Appadurai and Holston 1996, Caldeira 2000, Diouf 1996, Holston 1999, 2008; Lefebvre 1991, Simone 2004a, 2004b; Nguyen 2010; and Lukose 2009.

adjustment measures. With few viable economic opportunities and without the social safety nets long provided by the state, Senegalese turned to various assumedly short-term strategies for "getting by." As I describe in greater detail in the next chapter, it was in response to the destabilizations of structural adjustment that transnational migration, long part of the national imaginary, became an indispensable means of making ends meet.

I arrived in Dakar in 2006 to find that everyday lives and governing policies were as marred by uncertainty and constant adjustment as they had been in previous decades. Although structural adjustment had ended—or at least the term had fallen into disuse—no sturdy alternative logic had replaced it. In this postadjustment era, austerity and privatization endured as guiding economic, political, and social principles, even though decades of aggressive liberalization had failed to produce any lasting change. Foreign direct investment, still championed as the "cure" to Senegal's dire economic woes, remained scant. Unemployment persisted, and making ends meet was as difficult as ever. Urban residents, I realized, had become accustomed to living in these circumstances—to anticipating and planning for grand, far-off futures while navigating perpetual uncertainty in the present tense (see Guyer 2007). But the tactics on which they had long relied to get through these difficult times—including transnational migration—were increasingly out of reach. What had once appeared as a situation of acute crisis brought on by structural adjustment had become instead a routine way of life in places like Dakar, Senegal.[12]

Embouteillage offered urban residents and bureaucrats a powerful means of rendering visible and debatable this enduring sense of predicament. The term was part of a larger vocabulary that probed the changing nature of urban life. Most notably, young urban men frequently expressed deep concern about being forced to "just sit" (*toog rekk*) during the time of my research. In everyday conversation, the Wolof verb *toog* has long carried quite positive connotations. A host, for instance, might persuade guests to *toogal waay*, to sit and linger over a shared meal or good conversation. But during the time of my research, young men frequently employed the word *toog* to describe their failures to migrate abroad and their gendered anxieties about their prospects in life. This newer colloquial usage of *toog* expressed a certain restlessness and apprehension about the future, a reluctant and disorienting sense of emplacement in the city (see Englund 2002) and yet of exclusion

---

12. For more on the routinization of crisis, see Mbembe and Roitman 1995. Their argument also overlaps in interesting ways with that made by Guyer 2007.

from its possibilities. To "just sit" signaled a lack of opportunity and a limit to one's masculine agency—an inability, for instance, to pursue paths toward social adulthood, fulfill commitments to kin and repay debts, find meaningful or lucrative work, and make a more permanent home for oneself in the city. Rich with local meanings, these ways of speaking about predicament nonetheless bear a striking resemblance to vocabularies and logics have surfaced throughout the world as people grapple with economic, political, and social transformation.[13] As various scholars have shown, narratives of being stuck, stranded, bored, or immobile offer crucial insights into contemporary experiences of temporality, belonging, and social change.[14]

My theorization of *embouteillage* also finds resonance in the scholarly literature on "precariousness"—on the sudden sense of uncertainty, dispossession, and social alienation that accompanies intensified neoliberal reforms.[15] This expanding body of work has paid particular attention to the bodily, social, and economic disruptions produced by the post-Fordist shift toward increasingly informal, temporary, and casual labor arrangements.[16] Together, these diverse literatures probe the historical specificity of contemporary

13. In Ethiopia, for instance, young men worry about "simply sitting" and see migration as a "spatial fix" for their current predicaments (Mains 2007, 2012a); in urban India, youth find themselves "just waiting" for promised political, social, and economic change and opportunity (Jeffrey 2010); and in Guinea, young people seek alternatives to "just sitting around" (Fioratta 2015).

14. On the subject of "stuckedness" and strandedness, see Hage 2009. Hage argues that strandedness is immanent to mobility, not merely its opposite (4). Also relevant is Harms's (2013) theorization of "eviction time" in urban Vietnam as a kind of enforced waiting and Bayart's (2007) discussion of the preponderance of waiting in an increasingly globalized world. Jeffrey (2010), Fioratta (2015), Mains (2007; 2012a), and Masquelier (2013) likewise write of the boredom, disappointment, and waiting that accompany economic and social transformation for young men living in the urban global south.

15. Explicit in their use of the term precariousness are Allison 2013; Cross 2010; Millar 2014; Molé 2010; and Muehlebach 2013. Writing on neoliberalism and heightened uncertainty and modern anxieties more broadly are Besnier 2011; Harvey 2005; Sassen 1988, 2003; Tsing 2004; and Verdery 2000.

16. "Post-Fordism" played out differently in Senegal, a country that was never "industrial" to begin with. Industrial growth in Europe and elsewhere made the global redistribution of labor necessary. Senegalese migrants have long been part of this global traffic in labor. Over the past few decades, Senegalese have headed in increasing numbers to countries like Italy, Spain, and Portugal. As Donald Carter (1997) has noted about Italy, the arrival of these migrants was perceived as indicative of a society in "crisis," and African migrants were often met with hostility and suspicion. African migrants' experiences in these countries have become more difficult over the past few years amidst these states' implementation of rigorous neoliberal reforms—reforms quite similar to those implemented in Africa decades before, which impelled migration from Senegal in the first place. Post-Fordism thus has had an impact on African economies, but not a direct one.

uncertainty (Guyer 2007) and the sense of deferment, uselessness, and exclusion that such conditions often generate. Many of these scholars reflect in particular on the gendered dynamics of this uncertainty, critically analyzing the "crisis of masculinity" that neoliberal modes of governance often produce.[17] Situated at the confluence of these literatures, *Bottleneck* explores how seemingly abstract, apolitical shifts in regulations and policy are experienced in profoundly personal and embodied ways. Amidst unrelenting economic austerity and chronic uncertainty, urban men struggle to find effective ways to participate and to mark their social presence. This is particularly the case in an era when transnational migration, a critical means of achieving masculine social status and providing for a family, is made more impossible. Their circumstances are exacerbated by consequential shifts in development policy: while large-scale, state-led projects of previous decades tended to favor men's endeavors in sectors like agriculture, today's microcredit-focused initiatives, governed by NGOs, IOs, and state partnerships, are much more likely to target women as arbiters of economic development (see also Buggenhagen 2012). Informed by feminist theory and methodology, this book is deeply invested in underscoring the gendered dimensions of citizenship amidst volatile economic and social transformation.[18] In doing so, I critically engage with debates about the crisis of masculinity, paying particularly careful attention to the work that these "crisis" narratives do.

This book also departs from these scholarly accounts of suspension and precarity in a crucial way. Part of what made *embouteillage* such a compelling ethnographic concept was that it insistently brought state and citizen into the same frame of analysis, blurring the assumed distinction between projects and ideologies imposed "from above" and those assembled "from below."[19] In other words, the "crisis" of meaningful presence and participation that gripped everyday lives after adjustment also gripped the state, both

---

17. Scholars critically engaging with the concept of "crisis of masculinity" include Perry (2005) on rural Senegal; Lane (2009) on male unemployment in the United States; and McDowell (2000) on men in the UK. Also relevant for their discussion of gendered coming-of-age dilemmas are Cole and Durham 2007; Cole 2005, 2010; and Johnson-Hanks 2006, 2007.

18. In this way, the book complements work being done by scholars like Babou (2002, 2008), Bouilly (2008), Buggenhagen (2009, 2012), and Venables (2008) on the gendered dimensions of transnational migration from Senegal.

19. The mobility-focused projects I describe in this book cannot easily or neatly be categorized as state-sanctioned "schemes" (Scott 1998) or "grands travaux" (à la APIX) launched "from above" by authorities, nor as "tactics" (Certeau 1984) and or infrastructures (Simone 2004b) assembled "from below." They are neither examples of grand state plans nor are they instances of resistance to these plans.

as an institution and as an aspiration.[20] While much of the literature on precarity and suspension attends to the withdrawal or failure of the state amidst militant neoliberalization, these accounts do not typically offer an ethnographic consideration of the state itself but instead take for granted its detachment from people's everyday lives. In contrast, attending to *embouteil-lage* as a contemporary condition offers a means of probing this detachment and the sense of crisis it is thought to reflect and produce. As my movements through APIX's headquarters make clear, state practice and routines were mired in bottlenecks of all sorts. *Embouteillages*, I argue, are in fact an inevitable part of governing in "structurally adjusted" countries around the world. Decades of structural adjustment reforms had stripped the state of many of its postcolonial duties and powers, reconfiguring it as an impartial arbiter of economic liberalization. But wooing investors to the resource-poor country proved to be a much more difficult task than anticipated. As a result, contemporary state governance in Senegal (and elsewhere) was defined by uneasy "partnerships" forged with IOs and foreign interests, and by constant and often abrupt shifts of priorities, conceptualizations, and regulations in the hopes of (finally) producing lasting economic change.[21] By focusing on the bottlenecks that proliferate across different spheres of urban life, *Bottleneck* gives us a glimpse into the complex and tenuous relationship between state and citizen after structural adjustment.

Yet at the same time that urban men and public officials expressed deep concern about the impacts of tightened regulations and narrowed opportunities—about "crises" of state and masculine citizenship—they kept busy hatching plans, forging networks, and crafting identities. They cast future-focused claims that gave them immediate and visible traction in the city, and they collaborated on projects that insist on the possibility of presence. Indeed, in an effort to claim legitimacy, legibility, and relevance, both state and citizen harnessed uncertainty in fascinating ways.[22] In this way, the city's varied *embouteillages* did not just signal a profound sense of predicament, disconnection, or exclusion from public life; they also opened up opportunities to overcome these conditions. They brought into being a vibrant sphere

20. In theorizing the state after structural adjustment, this book draws in particular on the work of Hibou (2004), Clark (2005), and an edited volume by Delgado and Jammeh (1991).

21. For more on international policy and Senegal, see Ralph 2015.

22. Here, I echo points made by Janet Roitman in *Fiscal Disobedience* (2005): that it is at the margins and shadow zones of the state that its authority is reconstituted. See also Das and Poole 2004.

of social, political, and economic engagement.[23] The chapters that follow move between formal state offices, NGO and IO headquarters, gridlocked streets, and densely populated neighborhoods to examine how policy and practice are shaped through the conditions of *embouteillage*. In doing so, this book configures the bottleneck as a nexus of exchange and theft, where visions, strategies, and vocabularies are trafficked among unexpected allies. In these moments and spaces of volatile predicament, new approaches are generated and circulated, informal strategies give way to formal approaches and vice versa, and dubious or illegal actions are temporarily excused or legitimized.[24] At APIX, for instance, officials used institutional bottlenecks as a platform upon which to tinker with new program ideas, extend networks, and reconceptualize the role and reach of the state after structural adjustment. In doing so, these workers cast the African state as newly relevant, active, and future-focused. In a similar way, taxi drivers like Vieux used traffic jams as opportunities to insert themselves into potentially useful networks in the city, engage in various types of worthwhile transactions, and position themselves as future transnational migrants. And even when they were unsuccessful, clandestine migration voyages opened up possibilities for self- and state-making. What might appear at first glance as moments of "crisis," then, turn out to be critical opportunities for forging new institutions, networks, identities, and futures.

Writing the World from *Embouteillage*

In their essay "Writing the World from an African Metropolis," Achille Mbembe and Sarah Nuttall reflect on the persistent scholarly tendency to "describe Africa as an object *apart from the world*, or as a failed and incomplete example of something else" (2004, 348; original emphasis). Wedded to outdated empirical frameworks and stale concepts, much of the literature on Africa is poorly equipped to make sense of the uncertainty and multiplicity that characterizes everyday life on the continent, the authors contend. These works typically fail to acknowledge Africa's worldliness—to

23. My point here falls in line with Chalfin's observation that the management of public toilets in Ghana "substantiates a public realm that may not pronounce or envision itself as political yet consistently orients urban collective life" (2014, 103).

24. In this way, this book is in conversation with Simone (2004a, 2004b), who examines the vibrant informal infrastructures and economies that undergird African cities. In contrast to Simone's approach, however, I want to further trouble the assumed boundary between formal and informal, state and citizen.

understand it as not merely similar to or different from other places, but as complexly and consequentially linked to various "elsewheres" on the continent and beyond.[25] Coming to terms with the richness and multiplicity of contemporary African life means locating "sites within the continent, entry and exit points not usually dwelt upon in research and public discourse, that defamiliarize commonsense readings of Africa" (352) and that emphatically resituate Africa as *part of the world*.

Embouteillage, I suggest, offers precisely this sort of entry point. In their daily encounters with bottlenecks of all sorts, Dakarois elaborated an emergent geography, one in which relationships and experiences of proximity and distance, of similitude and difference, were endlessly debated and reworked. As they moved through the city, for instance, drivers and passengers frequently compared and contrasted the city's traffic problems to the experiences of residents living in other cities, particularly New York and Paris (two popular destinations for Senegalese migrants), underscoring global alignments that were at once historically rooted and newly forged. In state offices, too, bureaucrats described stalled processes or bottlenecked documents as important indicators of Dakar's complicated relationship to the rest of the world. Accounts of *embouteillage* were remarkably diverse and frequently incompatible: While some urbanites interpreted these patterns of suspension as indicative of Dakar's modernity, of its resemblance to other global cities, others articulated these conditions as evidence of Dakar's failure to be global, of the unbridgeable distance between this African city and the ostensibly modern, developed, and mobile West.

This irresolvable tension about Dakar's place in the world—what scholars might call its "cityness"—is made visible, tangible, and speakable through the *embouteillage*.[26] For many urbanites, bottlenecks were evidence of Dakar's long histories of connection and cosmopolitanism even as they spoke to urbanites' everyday experiences of disconnect, exclusion, and provincialism. They were a sign of modernity's arrival, of its absences and failures, of its promises and possibilities, and of its deep ambivalences. They offered a means of orienting and situating discussions about the world, the city, and one's very located place within both. Rather than seeking to resolve the

---

25. For theorizations of the diaspora as "elsewhere," see Fouquet 2007.

26. For various scholars, the concept of "cityness" emerges as a means of speaking about African and other cities of the global south without relying on Western vocabularies and logics of cosmopolitanism, planning, consumption, development, and governance. To speak of "cityness" is to understand urban Africa on its own terms. It is to highlight the everyday relations, practices, and imaginaries that characterize and shape African cities. See Simone 2004a, Mbembe and Nuttall 2004, McFarlane 2008, Pieterse 2010, Robinson 2002.

discrepancies in these narratives and experiences—that is, rather than arguing that Dakar is globally connected *or* disconnected, that it is modern *or* not, for instance—this book instead centralizes these incongruities and their everyday effects.[27]

In dramatic contrast to many theorizations of "global cities" (see Sassen 1991, 2001), which typically emphasize high-speed connection and unfettered mobility (of capital, expertise, labor) as prerequisites for global inclusion, this book claims the *embouteillage* as a basis for a different geography of global connection, movement, and proximity. Far from marginal to theorizations of global processes and flows (Ferguson 2006), Dakar and other "bottlenecked" cities like it are instead critical sites where the global is relentlessly unraveled, debated, produced, and engaged, albeit in frequently ambivalent and contradictory ways. It offers a strategy not only for defamiliarizing readings of urban Africa but also for thinking in more nuanced ways about life in cities like New York City, Bangkok, Jeddah, Rio de Janeiro, or Beijing. In this way, this book works to turn conventional urban theory on its head by developing a concept from the global south to think about urban life throughout the world (see also Comaroff and Comaroff 2012; Myers 2011; Simone 2004a, 2004b). What would it mean to write Africa—or even the world—from *embouteillage*? And what might be gained from an exercise in global remapping, one that centralizes Dakar as a site where the global is made? These questions inspire much of the ethnography that follows and are taken up explicitly in the conclusion.

Mapping Narrative Moments

The structure of this book echoes my own winding travels through the peninsular city over the course of twenty months of ethnographic research, conducted primarily in 2006 and 2007, with shorter research stints in 2004 and 2010. It was on the campus of Université de Cheikh Anta Diop (UCAD) where I first gained my footing as a fledgling anthropologist in 2004, and it is here where chapter 1 takes off. Situated just north of the city's administrative and economic heart, UCAD has long been considered one of Africa's most prestigious institutions of higher learning, attracting students not only from Senegal but from across the region and beyond the continent. It is well known, too, as a hotbed of political activism, and student demonstrations and strikes frequently punctuate the academic year. Chapter 1 opens

27. There are echoes here of Ferguson's (2006) argument about Africa's simultaneous connection and disconnection from the global. See also Ferguson 1999.

as youth clash with Senegalese *gendarmes* on the storied campus, their skirmish reportedly fueled by officers' taunting reminders that the students' credentials were of little value if not earned abroad. By situating this heated encounter—and the questions it raises about migration, citizenship, and governance in contemporary Dakar—within both urban space and historical context, I argue that urbanites' preoccupations with mobility and *embouteillage* are at once enduring and newly urgent. Throughout the chapter, I touch down at key historical moments to highlight how conceptions of citizenship became entangled through time with experiences of urban and global mobility, the built environment, and shifting forms of authority, thus setting the scene for the chapters that follow.

As my encounter with Vieux suggests, it was on the city's traffic clogged streets where the contours of this book first began to take shape in 2006. Accompanying cab drivers as they move along the city's emergent highways and neglected side roads, chapter 2 considers what citizenship and governance look like for many urban residents in an era of infrastructural impasse. I argue that the traffic bottleneck indexed deep concerns about the suspension of lives and itineraries, but it also offered unexpected strategies and occasions for recuperating the meantime—for elaborating networks, hatching plans, revising legitimate practices, and claiming identities that helped bridge the inescapable present with far-off, mobile futures. In doing so, I position taxi drivers' experiences and perspectives as normative rather than derivative, alternative, or contrary to official visions for the city. I work toward developing the *embouteillage* as a critical ethnographic framework for thinking about the paradoxes of contemporary urban belonging in Dakar more broadly.

Moving from the streets into Dakar's lively residential neighborhoods, chapter 3 employs the lens of *embouteillage* to consider another seemingly stalled urban project: the construction of concrete houses and villas. Often funded by diasporic Senegalese, these ambitious structures are typically built slowly, brick by brick, as money becomes available. Though they are intended for private occupation or to rent for profit, these languishing structures nonetheless became hyperpublic spaces, prone not only to the elements and natural decay but also to intense scrutiny and rumor, political debate, and trespassing and vandalism. While scholarly literature would be inclined to see these often "empty" houses as evidence of the incapacity of the adjusted state and the failure of neoliberalism, this was not how Dakarois typically described these projects and spaces to me. This chapter uses ethnographic work with returned migrants, families with loved ones abroad, state workers, and residents "stuck" in the city to instead conceptualize Dakar's bottlenecked houses as sites and signs of mobility's dramatic potential to transform both the city and citizenship. I pay close attention to the vibrant economies these structures make visible and to the licit and illicit traffic of goods, capital, and labor they generated and sustained. I also explore the ways these controversial constructions dramatically altered the contours of urban belonging and presence. Dakar's bottlenecked houses created rare opportunities and spaces in the city for rural residents who came to work as laborers in the construction sector, tend to vacant properties, or squat in unoccupied structures while looking for work in the city. Despite their evident erosion, I argue, these structures also enabled urban residents to make particular kinds of future-oriented claims on the city, thereby shaping conceptions of citizenship in the future tense.

The next chapter brings us away from the din of the city's streets and residential quarters and into APIX's elegantly appointed downtown headquarters, situated just a short walk from the presidential palace. Drawing on my experiences as an intern with this elite, quasi-state organization, in chapter 4 I examine bottlenecks of an institutional variety. Faced with sluggish foreign investment rates, APIX administrators worked to construct a program that would transform Senegal's remitting migrants into large-scale investors in the nation's "emergent" economy. The hopeful project reflected both global trends in development and local strategies for linking transnational migrants and the communities they left behind. What was particularly striking about APIX's Diasporic Entrepreneur program was that it remained in the planning stages for many years, without enrolled investors, caught between the grim economic realities of the present moment and its ambitious future goals. Rather than theorizing APIX employees' efforts as indicative of the failure, emptiness, or dysfunction of the African state, chapter 4 uses the logic of the *embouteillage* to examine how various institutional actors used the stalled project as a platform upon which to build alliances, exchange ideas, and redefine the contours of legitimate economic intervention. In doing so, APIX officials cast the African state as newly relevant and future-focused and as present through its strategic and purposeful of absence. Moreover, architects of the Diasporic Entrepreneur program institutionalized new visions of the productive citizen, casting the affluent, absent—and indeed *mythical*—migrant as a spectacularly present leader of a new era.

Returning to the city's neighborhoods and moving along sandy shorelines, chapter 5 focuses on the most tragic of Dakar's bottlenecked flows: in 2006 alone, tens of thousands of clandestine migrants, the vast majority of whom were men, departed from West Africa's shores aboard rickety fishing boats called pirogues, headed for "Europe"—despite the well-known fact that nearly all of these voyages ended in repatriation or death. As bodies washed ashore in my neighborhood and informants confided in me their desires to migrate at any cost, I found myself deeply troubled. Why participate in a voyage—one that required a steep financial investment—that was almost certain to end in failure and loss? At first glance, these doomed voyages may appear to be evidence of the state's or neoliberalism's failure or, seen from another perspective, as the epitome of entrepreneurial risk taking and casino capitalism. Taking a different approach, this chapter uses the concept of *embouteillage* to analyze the vibrant if volatile economies, identities, and programs that pirogue voyages produce. It pays specific attention to the lively rumor and storytelling conventions that publicly criticized and celebrated clandestine migration. These everyday efforts to come to terms with and manage "crisis," I argue, in fact query the utility of that term in the first place, drawing attention instead to the modes of self- and state-making made possible by these failed voyages.

Finally, the conclusion to this book considers the adaptability and utility of the concept of *embouteillage* in the years after my research concluded. I first briefly consider the analytical possibilities the concept offers even after the road projects are complete and the traffic has eased. I then move beyond the confines of Dakar to ask how the concept of *embouteillage* might help us understand predicaments of governance, authority, and belonging unfolding on other terrains. Focusing in particular on bottlenecked lives and landscapes in the United States in the time of the Great Recession, this chapter considers *embouteillage* as a framework that is at once expressly Senegalese and surprisingly flexible and adaptable. In doing so, the conclusion explores the generative possibilities that are opened up when insights gathered in Dakar are centralized as a normative and productive standard for understanding life lived elsewhere.

ONE

Making Mobility Matter

Just as Dakar's infrastructural projects were beginning to roar to life in early 2006, a series of street-based protests further strained traffic circulation in the city. Students at UCAD had launched a series of demonstrations and sit-ins aimed at drawing attention to the deteriorating learning and living conditions at the overcrowded university. Public protests of this sort are nothing unusual in postcolonial cities like Dakar, where strikes frequently disrupt the school year and students often struggle to complete their studies in a reasonable amount of time due to *années blanches*, entire academic years "lost" to strike.[1] Indeed, this public protest reflected a long legacy of UCAD students demanding accountability, dialogue, and political change in Senegal. This particular demonstration, national newspapers claimed, had been sparked by the discovery of expired meat lingering in a dining hall refrigerator and by the government's failure to disburse scholarly stipends as scheduled. Outraged students accused the government of neglecting its obligations to the nation's youth and took to the street in angry protest.

I found myself unexpectedly caught up in this commotion one February afternoon as I traveled via cab from my downtown office to an important interview in the city's Liberté section. After cursing the university students for their laziness and the state for its failure to provide, the cab driver reached into the backseat, opened my door, and announced with an air of bitter resignation that I'd have better luck heading to my destination on foot. Unsure of what to do next, I followed a small crowd of other urban residents past long lines of stalled vehicles toward the university—only to find the campus tightly patrolled and restricted by the Senegalese *gendarmerie*. A

---

1. For more on the history of university strikes and student activism in Senegal, see Blum 2012; Zeilig 2009; Zeilig and Ansell 2008.

more complete picture of the day's events emerged that evening, when television news programs aired images of students, the vast majority of whom were men in their late teens and early twenties, clashing with military police officers who had been called in to quell the uprisings. This unexpectedly violent demonstration, the news anchors explained, had prompted the city to barricade roads and limit movement around the campus. In the days and weeks that followed this highly publicized conflict, urban residents struggled to make sense of this violent skirmish in a city known for its relative peacefulness. Rumors soon circulated that tensions had escalated when students of the prestigious university confronted the officers, demanding that the police treat them with respect. After all, they shouted, they were the country's future leaders. Police officers scoffed in reply, according to the rumors, insisting instead that UCAD students were only second tier: *after all, everyone knew that Senegal's future leaders were all educated abroad.*

At first glance, this scuffle between military police and university students might appear to be a straightforward symptom of globalization and its malcontents, a relatively recent effect of neoliberal ideologies and practices that emphasize the redistribution of labor, the restructuring of African economies, and globalized modes of consumption. But a closer look at the historical linkages between transnational migration, authority, and belonging in Dakar quickly suggests otherwise. "Senegalese have always been migrants," was the constant refrain I heard during my research. "It's who we are as a people." Indeed, since at least the colonial era, global mobility has been a mark of belonging, success, and authority in Dakar. All four of Senegal's presidents studied at some point in France, for instance, and top positions in government and the private sector have long been awarded to candidates who were educated abroad. In a country with few profitable natural resources—fishing and peanut cultivation have been Senegal's economic mainstays for more than a century—transnational labor migration has brought relative stability to household budgets and has enabled productive investments and exchanges that would otherwise not have been possible. Even the city itself is narrated as a centuries-old, strategically positioned crossroads shaped by regional and global movements of slaves, goods, currencies, and beliefs.[2] Seen from this perspective, the officers' alleged rebuke of the UCAD protestors is not entirely "new" but is instead a reflection of "trajectories of extraversion" (*trajectoires d'extraversion*) that have linked Africa with the West for centuries (Fouquet 2007, expanding on Bayart 2000).

2. See, e.g., Gellar 1995.

Though concerns about transnational migration and meaningful urban participation are at the heart of this encounter, there is also more to the story. I have carefully framed this confrontation between state emissaries and university students as part of a much more complex urban landscape, one marked by growing concerns about urban mobility, ostentatious construction projects, government accountability, and substantive presence in Dakar. As students and officers wrestled with questions about leadership and migration, residents elsewhere struggled to navigate a city in constant flux, eke out a living, and make sense of an increasingly hostile political and economic landscape. This widened ethnographic lens brings into view the dense entanglements between differently positioned urban residents as well as different kinds and scales of mobility. I argue that students' anxieties about their place in the city are inextricable from state efforts to assert presence through large-scale construction projects, from rumors of government corruption and mismanagement of resources, and from public apprehension about detours, bottlenecks, and rising prices.

This chapter has two primary aims. First, I put contemporary Senegalese preoccupations with global mobility into historical context. To do so, I offer a brief overview of Dakar's colonial, postcolonial, and structural adjustment years. Touching down at key moments in the city's history, I pay close attention to how migration was historically articulated with practices and ideologies of secular governance, gendered citizenship, and urban development. I also attend to the ways that urban construction projects have been used at different points in time to make mobility "matter." The remainder of the chapter identifies a new moment in Dakar's contemporary history, one that is characterized by a steadfast commitment to "mobility" despite—and at times because of—its elusiveness as a goal and strategy. As grand mobility-focused projects and expectations clash with the grim realities of the urban present, there emerge new debates about what it means to live in, belong to, and govern the city.

The Colonial Era: The *Originaire* and the Mark of Mobility

Situated at the westernmost point of the African continent, Dakar has long been narrated as a cosmopolitan crossroads and as a city in perpetual motion.[3] Long before the arrival of European settlers, vast trade networks that

---

3. These conceptualizations of Dakar as a critical global crossroads stand in stark contrast to many popular and scholarly representations of Africa, which too frequently cast the continent

spanned the Sahara regularly stopped along the peninsula, bringing currencies, goods, and Islam from North Africa and beyond into the region. Cap-Vert was later incorporated into transatlantic slave trade circuits and then into the French colonial empire. By the latter half of the nineteenth century, Dakar had emerged as one of four key urban centers, called *Quatres Communes* (Four Communes), in French West Africa.[4] Within the Four Communes, colonial officials built and extended rail and port systems, military installations, and migratory and commercial networks. They also experimented with "assimilationist" modes of citizenship and governance born of French revolutionary thought. By the 1860s, French colonial policies had produced two classes of state subjects in the Senegambia region: a cohort of African elite urban men, called *originaires*, who claimed special privileges and were accorded a status that approximated French citizenship in exchange for their "assimilation" to French cultural norms;[5] and an unassimilated majority "African" population that was confined to peripheral areas and provided labor, paid taxes, and required permission to travel between the urban center and its peripheries. Unequal access to forms of mobility, codified in law, was at the very heart of the distinction between *originaires* and other African subjects. In addition to their ability to move freely within the commune, *originaires* were granted access to the metropole itself, in particular to pursue educational opportunities that would help them cultivate identities as *évolué* (evolved) French citizens. At least as early as the colonial period, then, urban and global mobility emerged as the visible mark and privilege of an elite, male citizen-subject.

Spatial divisions and urban constructions helped to concretize the distinctions between colonial subjects. While intensive French investment in infrastructural development was, in many ways, a practical necessity aimed at better accessing, exploiting, and funneling raw materials to the colonial metropole (Cooper 1996; see also Gellar 1976), Dakar's broad boulevards and paved roads also provided expatriates and *originaires* with modern,

---

and its diverse communities as disconnected, stagnant, or somehow outside of "the global" (See Mbembe and Nuttall 2004; Ferguson 2006; Simone 2001; Piot 1999). My task in this book, then, is not so much to write Dakar as mobile and global but rather to develop a more nuanced and ethnographically attentive framework for thinking about *how* and *in what ways* it is mobile and global, when it is *not*, and—perhaps most importantly—to what effect.

4. The Four Communes included St. Louis (the colonial capital until 1902), Dakar, Gorée, and Rufisque.

5. Whether *originaires* were French citizens or subjects afforded special rights was a topic of great debate in the late nineteenth and early twentieth centuries. For a more thorough discussion of the distinctions between French citizenship and the status of Senegal's *originaires*, see Lambert 1993.

orderly spaces for consumption and leisure that resembled the boulevards of Paris and that clearly demarcated European quarters of the city from so-called African settlements (see Whittlesey 1948). These two spheres were further distinguished through housing construction practices; while European-style concrete structures characterized "Dakar" proper, Africans lived precariously on the city's margins in impermanent structures without running water or other modern amenities. In this way, urban construction and development practices helped to give weight to the French Empire's assimilationist goals and to make visible and tangible colonial visions of society and governance (see Ralph 2005). What emerges from this quick sketch of assimilationist policies and colonial urban landscapes is a sense that mobility, construction, and urban presence and governance have been tethered together in some way since at least the colonial era. Moreover, it was through the construction and regulation of infrastructures, both global and local, that abstract colonial categories and visions were made tangible and visible to ordinary urban dwellers.

The *originaire*/African distinction was not as fixed as these spatial divisions might suggest, however. In reality, the category of *originaire* was an impossibly narrow one, and it only became more exclusive and elusive with time (Gellar 1976; Coquery-Vidrovitch 2001). Even those who claimed *originaire* status did not necessarily identify with French cultural values, particularly those concerning monogamous marriage and religion, and their claims were thus frequently dismissed by the French metropole (Lambert 1993). Nonetheless, *originaires* themselves were keenly aware of the potency of this political category (243) and actively policed its limits, dismissing newcomers to the city as outsiders whose rights and claims to urban presence they found dubious (Johnson 1971; Gellar 1976). The deeply contested category of *originaire* was thus shaped as much by the colonial government as it was by unequal relations among colonial subjects themselves. It was as much a vague assertion of global identity as it was a very grounded claim to the city itself.

Moreover, the *originaire*/African distinction was not the only one of social or political import in colonial Dakar; instead, it was one of many ways to configure success and social status. For instance, occupation-based class hierarchies in colonial Senegal valued work within bureaucratic and administrative offices over work in other sectors (Gellar, Charlick, and Jones 1980, 14). These colonial-inspired conceptions of status and social participation also existed in productive tension with indigenous configurations of authority and presence rooted in Islamic piety and practice and in precolonial modes of governance and social organization. Throughout the colonial era, there was a remarkable resistance among rural-based members of the Murid Sufi order to French models and values—a resistance that would, with time, shape and infuse modes of urban and transnational belonging and social status (Diouf 2000). Emphasizing the spiritual value of hard work, Muridism catalyzed alternative conceptions of belonging that gravitated around agricultural labor, centralized the relationship between religious teachers (called *marabouts*) and adherents, and extended membership opportunities to the masses.[6]

My point is not that contemporary ideas and debates about mobility, construction, and identity map neatly onto colonial policies of assimilation. Nor do I want to suggest that these were the only formulations legible or available to those who lived in colonial Dakar and its periphery. Colonial categories and values were vigorously and relentlessly replaced, debated, reinterpreted, and rejected, undermining the power of the colonial state to authoritatively define and shape African identities and itineraries. What I am suggesting instead is that the contemporary link between mobility and urban presence that appears, at first, so new has instead a longer and more complex history. Indeed, as early as the mid- to late nineteenth century, both urban and global mobility were seen as a means of achieving masculine presence and as a public confirmation of these claims to the city and to citizenship. Within this context, private dwellings and public infrastructures emerged as powerful signs of belonging and exclusion and as technologies for sorting, restraining, excluding, connecting, and abandoning differently positioned bodies. In turn, these assimilationist landscapes further distinguished urban centers like Dakar from the rural hinterlands—a distinction that persists in contemporary Senegal despite the constant traffic that continues to link rural and urban regions.

The Early Independence Era: The Salaried Man and the Construction of the New African Nation

In his report on the 1966 UNESCO-supported First World Festival of Negro Arts, John Povey (1966) writes of the spectacular infrastructural and architectural improvements made by the host city of Dakar in anticipation of this international gathering of artists, intellectuals, and tourists. Describing his arrival by plane in the "fresh, attractive, sophisticated city" (4), the author appears as dazzled by the modern, urban landscape as he is by the

---

6. For more on Muridism during colonialism, see Buggenhagen 2001; Diouf 2000; and Babou 2005.

artistic presentations and productions that were the intended focus of the festival. Povey marvels at the "handsome if flamboyant" new immigration office at the airport, at the legion of comfortable taxis that await disembarking passengers, at the city's fresh white cement and stunning new N'gor Hotel, and at the spectacular views afforded by the Route de la Corniche as one heads into the heart of the city. He recalls strolling past fountains and orderly squares in the city's center, through new downtown museums, theaters, and government buildings. These grand structures and spaces were built to preserve Senegal's cultural heritage and to promote a fantastic vision of the future inspired by the dominant ideologies of *négritude,* a truly global movement that valorized the proud aesthetic and intellectual traditions of Africans living on the continent and throughout the diaspora.[7] Meanwhile, Povey briefly notes, the nagging poverty and inequality that characterized this former colonial capital was carefully contained, deliberately and "neatly shrouded from visitors' view by stretches of rush matting or corrugated iron" (4).

What Povey encountered was a postcolonial capital city in remarkable flux. Between 1946 and his arrival in 1966, Dakar's population had swelled from 190,000 to 480,000 (Lambert 2002, 104), and an increasing number of migrant workers had arrived, seeking seasonal opportunities or permanent residence. These newcomers typically joined other disenfranchised urbanites living in informal settlements on the city's margins, much like they would have during colonialism. These precarious spaces contrasted sharply with Dakar's revitalized urban center, called Plateau, where new museums, galleries, public squares, and bureaucratic complexes hosted a global elite. Just a short drive north of Plateau, the UCAD (then the Université de Dakar, still affiliated with the University of Paris and the University of Bordeaux at that time) was quickly emerging as the city's intellectual heart and one of the most prestigious centers for higher education in West Africa. Through the pouring of concrete and the christening of new institutions, President Léopold Sédar Senghor and his allies worked to establish Dakar as a critical hub of the global *négritude* movement, one that was dedicated to nurturing and displaying Africa's thriving intellectual and artistic spirit. These new structures also housed a highly centralized postcolonial state responsible for distributing resources, overseeing economic and urban development schemes, and defining national priorities and belonging (Diouf 1998). What emerged in the early independence era, then, was a capital city whose

---

7. For more on *négritude,* an ideology popularized in particular by Senegal's first president, see Senghor 1966.

character was defined in direct opposition to colonial privileges and practices even as it was built on and often indistinguishable from them. It was a
city animated as much by modern conventions of governing and building
as it was by claims to a distinctly African intellectual and aesthetic legacy.

Against this backdrop of continuity and change, the "salaried man"—the
postcolonial functionary who helped to construct the nation while providing for the needs of his family—rose to public prominence (Banégas and
Warnier 2001; see also Mbembe and Roitman 1995). Revered as a model of
success, this esteemed urbanite typically achieved his position by attaining a
coveted *diplôme* and exploiting familial and social connections in ways that
echoed patterns of colonial privilege. His monthly salary—a fixed sum of
money delivered (ideally) in a rhythmic, steady, and dependable manner—
became an enviable mark of urban success and offered him a particular kind
of purchase on the capital city. The salaried man was imagined to move each
day along French-built boulevards, past public squares celebrating independence, into newly constructed modernist offices. Here, he effected social change through his collaboration with a cohort of similarly positioned
and privileged men and through displays of his proficient understanding of
French language and bureaucratic customs. At the end of the day, the salaried
man would perhaps retire to his neat and tidy government-built dwelling in
one of the newly incorporated sections of the city. Constructed in the 1950s
and 1960s, these concrete units were built by state organizations like Office
des Habitations à Loyer Modéré (OHLM) and Société Immobilière du Cap-
Vert (SICAP) and were aimed at providing affordable housing options to
government functionaries and their (nuclear) families (Bugnicourt 1983).
These opportunities and spaces contrasted sharply with the relative instability of life in the city's informal settlements, where basic infrastructures were
lacking, neighborhoods were densely settled, and frequent resettlement initiatives sent residents packing.

What comes into view through this analysis is a vision of the postcolonial nation as reborn through its rapidly transforming capital city. This new
urban center was imagined as open to the world, a space where African arts,
histories, and intellectual legacies were revitalized and displayed to an ad-
miring global public. Despite its claims to inclusiveness and optimism, the
new postcolonial capital was also riven with spatial and social divisions that
echoed but did not duplicate colonial distinctions and practices. The esteem
achieved by the "salaried man" in postcolonial Dakar was owed, in part, to
colonial formulations of urban status that privileged bureaucratic work and
that employed techniques of spatial segregation to emphasize and enforce
hierarchies and exclusions. The urbanite's claims to the city were contingent

in particular on his ability to acquire an education, harness personal connections, obtain a monthly salary, and secure permanent housing. As the scuffle between UCAD's students and police officers makes clear, these marks of distinction remain culturally important in contemporary Dakar.

The Generation of Structural Adjustment: The Migrant and the Besieged State

By the late 1970s, the grand theaters, highways, bureaucratic complexes, and modern family dwellings of the independence era had become worn with age, and so had the spirit of African renaissance that had inspired these projects in the first place. Collective optimism was replaced with nagging concerns about recurrent droughts in Senegal's agricultural hinterlands, mounting international debt, global price fluctuations, and economic recession. Western experts blamed Senegal's predicament on its overly regulated economy and its "bloated" and inefficient postcolonial bureaucracy.[8] This diagnosis ushered in what Elyachar (2005) has called the "generation of structural adjustment": a period of intense Western "technical" intervention that sought in particular to "open" Africa's economies to the global economy and to redefine the role and reach of the state. It was a vision fueled by mantras of good governance and by the language of economic diversification, deregulation, decentralization, and privatization (see also Hibou 2004).

In many ways, Senegal was a primary testing ground for structural adjustment policy, as World Bank interventions there date back to 1967, when it approved its first loan to the Senegalese government. It is quite telling that one of the earliest World Bank–sponsored programs in Senegal focused on housing construction. In 1971 and 1972, the bank worked with the Senegalese state to create Parcelles Assainies, a new approach to affordable housing that offered land ownership opportunities at the margins of the city to lower-income urban residents (Tall 1994). This program conceptualized private land ownership as a crucial component of a stable democracy and liberalized economy, and it reflected a broader commitment within policy circles to cultivating individual "responsibility" through the logics

8. While the rains were plentiful and the peanut economy thrived in the years following independence, a drought that would span several decades began in 1968 (Berthélemy, Seck, and Vourc'h 1996, Delgado and Jammeh 1991, Sharp 1994, Somerville 1991). In 1979, these circumstances prompted Senegalese officials, led by then prime minister (and future president) Abdou Diouf to approach multilateral financial institutions for help (Delgado and Jammeh 1991).

of ownership and debt repayment. This early experiment was followed in the 1980s and 1990s by a flurry of liberalizing schemes that slashed government social programs, payrolls, agricultural subsidies, and other public expenditures; sold off parastatal agencies; and devalued the region's currency (CFA franc), tied at that time to the French franc.[9]

These drastic cuts brought very concrete changes to everyday urban lives. No longer symbols of the state's vision or commitment, the city's languishing infrastructures instead told of government neglect and urban disarray. The costs for basic necessities rose suddenly and unpredictably, particularly in the wake of devaluation, wreaking havoc on household budgets (see Bendech et al. 1997; Makhtar Diouf 1992). Urban unemployment skyrocketed as public sector opportunities dwindled and many private-sector firms closed or made staff cuts. The prestigious national university became overenrolled and underfunded, and the once-treasured *diplôme* no longer guaranteed government work (see Cruise O'Brien 1996).[10] As the public sector withered, the Senegalese state launched a program in 1983 and 1984 called Opération Maitrisards, which aimed to use low interest loans to lure university graduates into private sector enterprise. Though this program was estimated to have generated about 200 enterprises and 1,800 jobs, a large proportion of these initiatives were thought to have failed (Makhtar Diouf 1992, 75). In essence, the "salaried man" so revered in the early independence years became a mythical figure. At the same time, seasonal and permanent migration to the capital city intensified as villagers escaped the effects of economic austerity and ecological ruin in the agricultural hinterlands. These newcomers arrived to find a city with few dependable opportunities, scant affordable housing, and few public resources.

What structural adjustment policies brought about, then, was a "freezing of social stratification" (Bayart 2009, 69) rather than increased social mobility. Deep concerns about "crisis"—of the state, of youth, of social reproduction—came to supplant postcolonial optimism (Buggenhagen 2012; Perry 2005, 2009; Mamadou Diouf 1992). Senegalese leaders and other authorities frequently accused the nation's youth—and their participation in delinquent, often violent, behavior—of contributing to a larger social crisis and an erosion of moral values (Diouf 1996). But youth them-

9. For more on structural adjustment policy in Senegal, see Benoit-Cattin 1991; Boone 1990; Delgado and Jammeh 1991; Gersovitz 1987; Markovitz 1991; and Mbodji 1991; and Waterbury and Gersovitz 1987.

10. What I describe here—the erosion of the value of university diplomas and the evaporation of salaried opportunities—coincides with similar changes elsewhere in the world. See, e.g., Jeffrey 2010; Lukose 2009; Mains 2012b; Masquelier 2013.

selves tended to see things quite differently, placing the blame for the country's social and economic crisis squarely on national leaders themselves. In the 1980s and 1990s, university students, political party adherents, street vendors, and many others took to Dakar's streets to protest funding cutbacks, living or working conditions, currency devaluation, new government restrictions, and controversial elections. Perhaps most notable among these street-oriented dramas was the *Set/Setal* ("clean up") movement of the 1990s, in which disaffected youth confronted the state and the ruling class, declared public spaces to be their own, and struggled to install new visions of morality and political accountability (Bugnicourt and Diaollo 1991; Cruise O'Brien 1996; Diouf 1996). Through mural painting and urban cleanup operations, Dakar's youth publicly called into question the discourses and practices of the postcolonial project. The roads themselves—neglected, crumbling, insalubrious—were indexed as evidence of national leaders' broken promises and state impotence, and they were reclaimed as platforms and canvases on which youth expressed their demands and alternative visions of nation. With time, however, state officials came to perceive these seemingly oppositional activities as critical to the everyday workings of the city, and they worked to recruit and absorb *Set/Setal* actors into their official programs for participatory governance (Fredericks 2014; see also Cruise O'Brien 1996). As Fredericks's study of municipal waste makes clear, these youth volunteers received meager daily wages and were offered no protections or benefits, even though they "became the backbone of the municipality's waste management system and remain the sector's labor force today" (2014, 537). In this way, the *Set/Setal* movement was both a reaction against economic liberalization and state withdrawal and a means to further these very same agendas. In this instance, moments of resistance "from below" become indistinguishable from authoritative visions imposed "from above."

Austerity programs, dwindling opportunity, and widespread discontent also helped generate new visions of economic possibility and new modes of urban participation and belonging. It was within this context of deepening economic and political predicament that transnational migration emerged as a critical means of buttressing household budgets and securing urban futures. Transnational migration was by no means a new economic or social strategy in this bustling city, of course; Senegalese had been migrating to other African countries, the Middle East, and Europe for over a century by the this time. They did so through the citizenship privileges afforded by France to educated urban elites during and after colonialism but also to work as laborers in factories and fields, to study at universities, to work in commerce networks, and through religious networks oriented toward engagement with Islamic centers of learning and worship in the Middle East and North Africa.[11] In the 1980s and 1990s, Senegal's globally mobile citizenry began seeking passage to newer destinations like the United States, Spain, and Italy (Riccio 2005; Stoller 2002; Tandian 2008),[12] lured by more accommodating immigration and travel regulations, new job opportunities and expanding migrant networks in these countries, and the increased value of foreign currency after the 1994 currency devaluation.

Thus, by the early 1990s, the transnational migrant had eclipsed the salaried man as a central figure of secular, postcolonial success (Bredeloup 2008; Riccio 2005), one whose acts of self-sacrifice—rather than expectations of a guaranteed state salary—propped up both household and nation in an era of economic calamity. Migration was considered a masculine endeavor at this time, one that typically separated men from their wives and families. Migrants increasingly stepped in where the structurally adjusted state had bowed out, providing for the everyday needs of individuals, households, and communities that were deeply impacted by the removal of social safety nets, the trimming of state budgets and staffs, and the devaluation of the nation's currency. Their earnings helped provide for everyday expenditures like school fees, health clinic visits, and rite of passage celebrations, and they also financed broader community initiatives like the building of wells and mosques (Buggenhagen 2002; Kane 2002). In Dakar more particularly, migrants and their families also invested heavily in small businesses (Diatta and Mbow 1999) and in the construction of concrete houses, apartment complexes, and stately villas for occupation or for rent (Buggenhagen 2001; Melly 2010; Tall 1994). While economic uncertainty of the 1970s–1990s brought state-run construction projects to a halt, infrastructural development and housing construction continued through the work of transnational migrants and their families and associates.

These urban actors, capital flows, and projects transformed the temporal and spatial dynamics of the city in several important ways. In contrast to the regular and predictable rhythm of the salary, migrants sent remittances in fits and starts when money was available. These unpredictable flows structured daily interactions and spending practices, including clothing

---

11. For more on transnational migratory histories, see Babou 2002; Buggenhagen 2001; Diouf 2000; Diop 2004; and Manchuelle 1997.

12. The drastic devaluation of Senegal's currency in 1994 meant that foreign currencies sent home by migrants were suddenly exchanged for double their former value, imbuing these monies with an almost magical quality and further solidifying the role that migrants would play in Senegal's postadjustment economy.

purchases, health clinic visits, and the quantity and quality of daily meals. Migrant-financed houses typically rose slowly and developed in spurts—a new layer of bricks here, a new roof there. In turn, these quite visible spending practices made absent migrants spectacularly present in the city as arbiters of national futures, fueling the dreams and desires of a generation of hopeful migrants. With time, migrants' hyperpublic purchases and projects helped shape popular conceptions of the diaspora as a place of unbridled economic possibility (Fouquet 2008) and of Senegal as a "culture [or nation] of migration" (Willems 2008, 278), one whose past and present alike have been shaped not by bountiful natural resources, as has been the case in some African countries, but instead by the industriousness and dedication of its globally dispersed population. In song, film, and public and government discourse, the hardworking migrant was celebrated for his practical knowledge, his humble beginnings, and his ability to manage or get by (*se débrouiller*) in a harsh economic climate. And by the dawn of the millennium, migrants were increasingly wooed and idealized by government policy, a topic I discuss in detail in the chapters that follow.

Like the salaried man before him, the self-sacrificing transnational migrant was imagined as a gendered figure. Though Senegalese women and families did migrate at this time—and, by the beginning of the millennium, in increasing numbers—transnational migration was nonetheless typically imagined as a solitary, masculine activity. This was reflected in common tactics migrants used to get abroad. Many migrants, often called *modou-modou*, were members of extensive transnational trade networks and were able to migrate through their affiliation with the Murid Way, a Sufi brotherhood whose role in global commerce is particularly well documented (Diouf 2000). In other instances, male kin living in the diaspora would help family members finance and apply for visas, or they would send their own passports for relatives left behind in Senegal to use. The coveted role of the hardworking migrant is thus frequently described by Senegalese and by scholars as deeply gendered, inherited or passed through networks of "brothers," both familial and spiritual (Ebin 1992)—even though women *do* in fact participate in these circuits in critical ways.[13] Academic and institutional analyses of the past two decades have tended to affirm this assumption: The nation was imagined as contingent on the exploits of (assumedly male) migrants who work in solidarity for a greater good, echoing assumptions

13. For more on women's participation in global migration networks, see Buggenhagen 2011, 2012; Kane 2002; and Ba 2008.

about the salaried man of earlier decades.[14] Seen from this perspective, by the 1990s, productive presence in places like Dakar was increasingly imagined as achieved through periods of absence abroad, and the spaces and privileges of the city itself often seemed most available to those who had left (Melly 2010, 2011). Both the nation and its capital city were reaffirmed in both subtle and dramatic ways as spaces and communities constructed through gendered movements, decisions, and investments.

At this juncture, various conflicting and overlapping shifts come into view: new claims to political and economic authority, new strategies of governance, new visions of urban presence and possibility, and new projects and identities that drew on and supplanted older urban forms. Most notable among these changes was the growing importance of migration to both national and household agendas. Migrants' itineraries and contributions were made necessary and visible by the liberalizing logics of structural adjustment, by languishing collective resources, by deep anxieties about social and economic "crisis," and by thriving religious institutions and new opportunities for work. But just as transnational mobility was cemented as an indispensable cultural value in Senegal, it also became an increasingly elusive and exclusive endeavor. It is this remarkable predicament that animates the remainder of this book.

The Age of Mobile Fixations: Building Urban Futures after Adjustment

At the dawn of 2006, Dakar, Senegal, seemed again on the brink of great metamorphosis. All over the city, the nation's grand potential was being asserted through the pouring of concrete and the launching of future-oriented urban schemes. Most prominent among these were *grands travaux de l'état* (large-scale public works projects overseen by the state and funded largely with foreign capital): the rehabilitation and extension of two different road systems, the national autoroute and the Route de la Corniche Ouest. Although Dakarois typically experienced and described these projects as indistinguishable parts of a singular effort to modernize and mobilize the city, they were in fact run by two different economic partnerships, each with a discrete purpose, distinct funding sources, a different team of experts, and unique timetables. Overseen by the Agence Nationale Chargée de la Promotion d'Investissement et des Grands Travaux (APIX), the Autoroute de

14. See, e.g., Diatta and Mbow 1999.

l'Avenir (Autoroute of the Future) project was a multiphase scheme that would include both a rehabilitated urban highway linking Dakar's northern and southern extremities and a high-speed toll portion connecting the peninsular capital to the rest of Dakar. Estimated to cost 200 billion FCFA (US$500 million), the project was financed through a public-private partnership between World Bank, which provided a loan to the Senegalese government; the African Development Bank; the French Agency for Development; the International Development Association (IDA); and an "unidentified" foreign group.[15] Just weeks after the autoroute project commenced, the Organisation de la Conférence Islamique (OCI), a global collectivity of fifty-six Islamic/Muslim majority states, initiated another road project. This second venture sought to refashion the aging Route de la Corniche Ouest into a showcase boulevard befitting the organization's Eleventh Islamic Summit, held in Dakar in March 2008. The effort also involved the construction of various upscale hotels, meeting venues, and restaurants along the reinvented Corniche in anticipation of this global conference.

Channeling the aura of Senghor and other postcolonial leaders, President Abdoulaye Wade claimed these projects to be integral components of his own authoritative vision for the city and the nation and as evidence that even his grandest dreams had the power to become reality (see De Jong and Foucher 2010).[16] Indeed, at first glance, this emergent landscape seemed to evoke the transformations of the postindependence era. But these projects and structures also expressed a break with modernist approaches to infrastructural development that emphasized planning, calculation, and "rationality" (see Scott 1998). Drawing inspiration instead from the seemingly meteoric rise of global cities like Dubai, the president and his allies sought to lure international attention and capital and to thus reposition Dakar as both "the most beautiful city in Africa" and as a global destination for foreign investment and leisure.[17] In contrast to the architectural

15. For more on autoroute financing, see http://web.worldbank.org/external/projects/main?projid=P087304&theSitePK=40941&piPK=51351134&pagePK=51351022&menuPK=51351215&Type=Financial.

16. Bachir Fofana, "Me Wade sur les Réalisations de ses Projets: 'Même quand je rêve, ça devient réalité,'" Le POPulaire, March 4, 2010. Despite the existence of a two-term limit that he himself had signed into law, Wade ran for a third presidential term in early 2012. The election drew international attention, as thousands of voters took to Dakar's streets decrying Wade's campaign. Wade lost in the second round of voting to his former protégée, Macky Sall.

17. While Abidjan was long considered the unofficial "capital" of Francophone West Africa, a series of political coups and uprisings led to a regional reorientation, one that has in large part favored Dakar. This shift solidified Wade's mission to turn Dakar into a regional center for finance and banking, tourism, and technology.

Figure 3. A pamphlet inserted into a local newspaper depicts a segment of the future autoroute

achievements that captivated Povey in the 1960s, these contemporary spaces and structures were not built to house national treasures or to display the talents and arts of a revitalized African spirit, one that was necessarily collective and firmly and explicitly rooted in a grand past. Instead, Dakar's twenty-first-century "renaissance" was focused on the construction of professedly globalized spaces of consumption and circulation that spoke little to postcolonial ideologies like *négritude* and instead appeared thoroughly detached from histories and shared struggles of the past decades. Though Wade claimed these projects as his own, most were made possible through partnerships that linked together national leadership, foreign capital and expertise, and loans and guidance from IOs, including World Bank. Targeting a new generation of global elites called "foreign direct investors," leaders hoped that a cosmopolitan elite might be lured to this African city—in some ways, *despite*, rather than because of, its Africanness—because it could offer the sort of generic comforts that they would expect to find at "home." The president's vision was thus fixed squarely on reinventing Dakar as a new kind of African capital city, one that was attractive to residents and foreigners alike because it claimed a strategic location, used space efficiently, and reiterated the steadfast dedication to foreign investment and economic "emergence" that the international community and voters had come to expect.[18] Through concrete overpasses and roundabouts—as well as through the spectacular billboards, passionate speeches, and public information

18. To get a better sense of the way this commitment to economic "emergence" is cast for both international and local audiences, see, e.g., Niane 2010.

campaigns that accompanied them—Wade and his allies projected an alluring if implausible vision of future possibility marked by wealth, abundance, and global connectivity.

But for many urban residents, these infrastructural projects and promises also brought into sharper view the urgency and inescapability of the present moment. While resurfaced roads and new highways linked together spaces of governance, global travel, and elite consumption—in turn defining a new political, economic, and social center—the majority of urban residents were left to contend with dilapidated roads unfit for passage, proliferating traffic bottlenecks and detours, ruptured sewage pipes, frequent power outages, and the seeming lack of state intervention and oversight in more "popular" quarters of the city. As new highways and shopping plazas were unveiled elsewhere in the city, Dakar's neglected side roads and spaces came into sharper view, splintering Wade's sweeping vision for the nation's future and centering attention on the uncertainty of the immediate present. Interestingly, Wade had ascended to the presidency six years earlier on a campaign that drew much of its strength from the capital city's streets and spaces. Grand caravans of supporters blaring music, vibrant banners, and campaign T-shirts helped Wade's party occupy urban spaces and rally votes in unprecedented ways (Foucher 2007). His rallying call of *sopi* (change) emboldened urban youth, who felt increasingly marginalized by the structural adjustment policies implemented during the previous administration (see Galvan 2001). But by 2006, public opinion had largely soured as unemployment and poverty persisted.[19] The city's streets, long platforms for political change, became for many urbanites signs of government detachment: in the shadow of rising future-focused complexes and highways, urbanites struggled to simply make ends meet and move through and beyond the increasingly congested city.

Marginalized by state-spun narratives of mobile futures, many urbanites—particularly the city's youth, who had been so crucial to Wade's election in 2000—clung ever more ardently to their hopes to migrate abroad. By the time I arrived in the capital city in the early days of 2006, more than three-quarters of urban households had at least one member working abroad (République du Sénégal Ministère de l'Économie et des Finances, Direction de la Prévision et de la Statistique 2004), and transnational migration was regarded as indispensable to the maintenance of the household and the nation. And yet, in many ways, these mobile aspirations were no

19. In 2006, World Bank documented notable economic decline in Senegal (see http://www .worldbank.org/en/country/senegal/overview).

less far-fetched than those project by the state. Since the start of the millennium, migration policies in receiving countries became more stringent, as conservative political movements based on claims of autochthony gathered momentum, anxieties over dwindling employment opportunities and over-burdened state welfare systems mounted, and "newer" migrants from other parts of the world, including postsocialist Europe, competed for limited visas. States also adopted more rigorous strategies to deter and discipline undocumented migrants, making once critical extralegal tactics increasingly likely to fail.[20] These shifts—which many of Dakar's residents described as abrupt and even violent ruptures in migration policy—were motivated both by heightened anxieties about "security" post-9/11, and more recently by a global economic downturn that diminished Europe's need for unskilled and semiskilled labor, particularly in migrant-staffed sectors like agriculture and housing construction. As movements were constricted, urbanites complained bitterly of being stuck in the city. But they continued to strategize, network, and pray, all with the hope that an opportunity to migrate might materialize. Some hopeful migrants turned to dangerous, extralegal means—like clandestine pirogue voyages—to get abroad. Even as fatalities mounted and public education campaigns warned of deadly risks, clandestine migration practices, economies, and imaginaries thrived and proliferated.

What I have been describing here is the crystallization of a new era in Dakar's contemporary history when mobility, construction, state authority, and meaningful urban presence are woven together in novel but familiar ways. In this era, both bureaucrats and ordinary urban residents are deeply engaged in a wide range of ambitious but generally ill-fated public projects, and poured concrete again emerges as a principal medium for communicating collective values and individual priorities. Rallying labor and capital from origins as diverse as North Korea, Libya, Saudi Arabia, France, Tunisia, and World Bank, President Wade used concrete to claim a public image for the Senegalese state after decades of retrenchment. High-speed roadways and centers for elite consumption echoed constructions of the colonial and early independence era, but they also spoke to new tactics of partnership and new expectations of unfettered capital flow that were thoroughly unique to the contemporary moment. Meanwhile, migrant-funded

---

20. European Union immigration controls were also tightened at this time, and in 2005, an EU border control organization called Frontex—which would later be responsible for policing West Africa's shores, detaining clandestine migrants, and organizing repatriations—was established.

construction schemes continued to transform the city's social and physical landscape, offering a powerful counterpoint to Wade's spectacular, state-centric declarations of urban rejuvenation and economic possibility. From the perspective of many urban residents, national futures were most clearly expressed not through government-managed, foreign-funded highway projects or commercial complexes but instead through the tangible, everyday efforts of Senegalese citizens living and working abroad. Despite their differences, however, these concrete visions shared a common focus: both affirmed and celebrated urban and global mobility as an indispensable mode of being and belonging in contemporary Dakar, even as it became an ever more elusive and exclusive endeavor.

It is this politically charged era that is the focus of this book. It is a historical moment that follows on the heels of structural adjustment but is not entirely distinct from this earlier period. Indeed, what I am proposing here is not a defined historical rupture or distinct "crisis" but rather the routinization and rationalization of the uncertainties and ill effects of this previous generation. As Gracia Clark (2005) has incisively argued, contemporary life and policy in most "adjusted" African countries is defined by a state of "permanent transition." Once seen as a series of temporary if acutely difficult technical interventions, austerity has instead become a permanent feature of the economic, political, and social landscape in places like Senegal. Moreover, the assumedly transitory hardships that accompanied these drastic measures—slimmed budgets, increasingly precarious and temporary employment opportunities, tardy or unpaid salaries and stipends, cuts to education and health, the growth of illicit economic activity, and even transnational migration itself—have been repackaged as signs of economic and social vitality (Clark 2005, 6; see also Melly 2013). Informal economic endeavors and survival strategies once dismissed as dysfunctional or as provisional responses are instead legitimized by governing institutions and absorbed into "formal" economic structures (see Elyachar 2005). In the process, conditions of chronic uncertainty are normalized (see Guyer 2007) and even celebrated as *productive* of economic opportunity, as I explore in the chapters that follow.

This sense of chronic uncertainty gives way to an unsettling mix of "fantasy futurism and enforced presentism," as Jane Guyer has described it (2007, 409). Once seemingly peculiar to the conditions of structural adjustment and military rule in places like Nigeria, she argues, this particular temporal sensibility is increasingly used to frame and justify policymaking around the world, in turn denying the near past and near future of moral, economic, or political investment or meaning. Gone, she insists, are past strategies "of planning and hoping, of tracing out mutual influences, of engaging in struggles for specific goals, in short, of the process of implicating oneself in the ongoing life of the social and material world that used to be encompassed under an expansively inclusive concept of 'reasoning'" (409). In their stead arise preoccupations with responding to the exigencies of immediate, everyday life and with offering long-term projections of growth and change.

Guyer's insight is remarkably useful for making sense of life and policy in contemporary Dakar, where urbanites cling to grand visions of mobile futures even as they cope with life in the inescapable present. Futuristic highways rise amidst infrastructural decay. Hopeful migrants plan clandestine itineraries that are snarled by intensified surveillance and repatriation efforts. Ambitious development projects are unraveled by the nagging realities of poverty, intense urbanization, and environmental unpredictability. It is this clash between futuristic claims and acute present realities that produces the *embouteillage*. In this charged social space, the relationships between construction, mobility, urban belonging, and authority are again redefined. The ethnographic chapters in this book pay keen attention to the *embouteillage* as a contemporary trope and metaphor, a particular temporal orientation, a mode of being in the city, and a space and site where citizen and state are reconstituted and reconnected in unexpected ways.

Generation in Crisis?

At the start of this chapter, I described a volatile encounter between students from the prestigious Université Cheikh Anta Diop and a squad of armed police officers called in to contain their protests. Angered by the state's apparent failure to provide for their physical and financial needs, a group of mostly male students had taken to the streets like generations of urbanites before them had done. They demanded that the government acknowledge and respond to their grievances, and, according to rumors, they asserted themselves as publicly present through their future-oriented claims to national leadership. The officers supposedly rebuked the students, reminding them that such positions of power and presence were reserved for those educated in the West. This alleged act of disavowal illustrates the precariousness of some urban residents' claims to space, presence, and effective action in contemporary Dakar, and it underscores the position migration occupies in the urban and national imaginary. When we place this encounter into historical context, however, we see that Dakarois' desires for and expectations of mobility are not particularly modern or new. Indeed, mobility has been articulated with practices and ideologies of secular governance, citizenship, and urban development and construction in Dakar since at least the colonial era. This dramatic altercation between disillusioned youth and state-deployed officers instead reflects enduring debates about what it means to govern, to belong, to succeed, and to move within and beyond the capital city.

This encounter also offers a glimpse of a cohort of young, urban men from diverse backgrounds who imagine their lives, city, and identities as mired by perpetual "crisis." This generation clings to great dreams of building, moving, and belonging even opportunities dwindle, and they speak wistfully of the perceived possibilities and privileges of a bygone postcolonial era. As I have tried to show, the "crisis" (*la crise*) about which they speak is by no means new but rather dates to environmental and economic turmoil of the 1970s and 1980s. Structural adjustment both aimed to ameliorate and helped exacerbate these conditions. Young people nonetheless experienced and described this moment as distinct and as newly urgent. By the time I arrived to conduct long-term research in Dakar, various routes to masculine adulthood and urban permanence—particularly bureaucratic work, university education, and transnational migration—had been eroded by economic austerity measures, internal political shifts, and narrowed international regulations. Full-time, salaried, dependable work opportunities had largely evaporated. The prestige and stability once afforded by bureaucratic work at various ranks had largely faded, and state employees of various ranks were typically as likely as their fellow urban residents to pin their personal hopes on migration abroad. The once coveted *diplôme* provided no certainty of work, universities were overcrowded, and a degree typically took many years to complete. Students could only invest themselves in their studies in contingent and partial ways as they attended to other urgent responsibilities, debts, and projects. At the same time, there were more qualified job candidates than ever, owing in large part to the withering of salaried work opportunities as well as a dramatic increase in the number of women who were completing advanced degrees, to the explosion in private professional schools granting degrees in the city, and to the now pervasive cultural assumption that education would enable future presence and success.

Seen from this perspective, the UCAD student protest can be read as a spectacularly masculine display of worth and belonging under conditions of enduring economic, social, and political crisis. It was likewise an effort to publicly reveal "the state" as itself mired in crisis—as unable to assert itself as relevant and meaningfully present, to provide for its citizens, and to assure social, economic, and political continuity. At the same time, this public skirmish does not configure citizen and state as opposed entities but instead underscores the ways in which they are in fact mutually constituted in moments of everyday encounter. The perceived "crisis" plaguing male urban identities is inextricable from that which afflicts the postcolonial, "adjusted" state. Authoritative visions imposed "from above" are complexly linked to and indistinguishable from moments of resistance "from below." And mobility is as much an institutionalized value as it is a profoundly individual and intimate one.

Finally, this charged encounter unraveled amidst and was inextricable from a complex urban landscape characterized by competing claims to presence, evaporating resources and opportunities, and fervent but ostensibly failing efforts to construct mobile futures. The seemingly ordinary and contained protest had quite visible ripple effects, profoundly altering debates, routines, and circulations throughout the city. This encounter, then, is as much about the frustrations and expectations of cab drivers, urban commuters, and a foreign female ethnographer as it is about disaffected youth and state employees. In the following chapters, I draw on research conducted with men and women of various backgrounds in Dakar in order to critically examine narratives and experiences of urban generation and routinized "crisis" and in contemporary Dakar.

TWO

Trafficking Visions

As Dakar's roads came alive each morning, a heavy veil of dust, fumes, and frustration settled on the city, where it lingered long past nightfall. Cars and buses inched slowly past detour signs, billboards, and roadside market stalls, along the bare earth, stripped of its tarred surface in preparation for monumental construction projects. In the distance, tangled veins of vehicles snaked for as far as the eye could see. As traffic came to an inevitable halt, other urban circulations gathered momentum. Narrow streams of vehicles splintered off in all possible directions, carving new paths that broke with imposed detour routes. Moving along surfaces not intended for driving, these motorists relentlessly contested and reconfigured road regulations and accepted practices. Meanwhile, other commuters descended from sweltering buses and vans, determined to resume their journeys on foot. They mingled with uniformed road crews directing traffic and with itinerant traders peddling mobile phone credit, daily newspapers, small bags of drinking water, or imported Chinese tea sets or shaving kits to stranded motorists. Cash and commodities quickly changed hands through open car windows before traders moved on. Through these same open windows, frazzled drivers exchanged insults and accusations with each other, sometimes sparking confrontations that spilled onto the streets themselves, and the occasional thief snatched purses and parcels left unguarded. Other commuters, settled in stalled vehicles, engaged in lively debates among themselves, eagerly circulating information, rumors, perspectives, and future plans. They moved fluidly from discussions of urban gridlock, electricity outages, and road detours to debates about government mismanagement of capital flows, international migration regulations, American economic policies, and tragic clandestine voyages. As they spoke, moved, and strategized, urbanites deliberately collapsed together different kinds and scales of mobility, rendering everyday urban circulations inextricable from movements, decisions, and profits made halfway around the world.

Moving through the vibrant and volatile spaces of the city's traffic bottlenecks, this chapter examines the changing contours of infrastructural authority and expertise, urban belonging, and ethnographic engagement in contemporary Dakar. In doing so, it raises critical questions about what it means to live, to plan, to build, and to govern amidst chronic uncertainty and narrowing possibilities. I focus in particular on the everyday movements and engagements of the city's taxi drivers, for whom questions about mobility were particularly urgent. In this way, I take my cue from Michel de Certeau (1984), whose oft-cited piece "Walking in the City" considers how urban residents make the city a habitable space through their everyday movements and narratives. Writing against what he calls "the pleasure of seeing the whole," Certeau wants instead to consider the minute and dizzying footsteps that bring the city into being. My interest here is not so much in decentering or appraising the "top-down" work of planners or architects—in my own research experience, it was always impossible to distinguish top-down planning from everyday life "from below" anyway. Rather, Certeau's work offers us insights into how to scholars might account for and theorize the "footsteps" that cluster around but never directly enter migratory flows. In this chapter, then, I accompany the city's cab drivers as they move through and engage with the city's landscape—as they drive, sit, wait, debate, assess, exchange, and carve alternative routes. Moving each day through *embouteillage*, I argue, Dakar's residents came to understand and articulate their place in the city and the world, and they worked to fashion habitable futures despite chronic uncertainty. At the same time, I also want to draw attention to *limits* of these engagements and narratives. I aim to highlight the ways in which the bottlenecked landscape itself shapes the conditions of life and possibility in the city in very powerful ways. Indeed, the city's traffic bottlenecks offered particular perspectives and opportunities, as we shall see, while foreclosing other ways of seeing and inhabiting the city.

What follows is not an ethnography "of" cab drivers. What I offer instead is an ethnography of the bottleneck itself as a constitutive site of urban politics and economies in contemporary Dakar. Through this act of re-centering, I shift attention away from road-centered visions for the city and nation and toward the reality of infrastructural impasse. When we focus on the bottleneck as a crucial site where visions of future selves and states are fashioned, cab drivers—and many other urban dwellers—come into view as central urban actors, purveyors of specialized knowledge, and participants in a vigorous debate about what it means to be mobile and why it matters. This chapter thus sets cab drivers' perspectives as normative rather than derivative, alternative, or contrary to official visions, raising questions about the shifting contours of authority, expertise, and belonging in this structurally adjusted city. Moreover, it elaborates the *embouteillage* not only as a charged urban space, event, and metaphor but also as a scholarly device that brings particular realities into ethnographic view.

The Traffic Bottleneck in Context

Established in the nineteenth century on a narrow peninsula, Dakar has always had little space for expansion. Decades of urbanization spurred by structural adjustment and ecological change, the constant traffic between Senegal's capital city and its rural hinterlands, the steady growth of private car ownership, and the drastic reduction of public works budgets (particularly in the 1980s and 1990s) have had a particularly profound impact on the city and its overburdened road networks. The resultant circulation problems are both chronic and acute, fueled by seasonal population shifts, weather conditions, and religious and secular holidays. Both the autoroute and Corniche projects thus were aimed at alleviating bottlenecks by expanding and enhancing infrastructural capacity. But at the same time, these projects temporarily exacerbated the city's traffic woes. Road lanes were closed, detours imposed, and surfaces uprooted. As a result, *embouteillages* rapidly proliferated throughout the city during the time of my research, either as a direct result of the narrowing or closure of roads or as a consequence of the traffic accidents, broken-down vehicles, and makeshift markets these obstructions generated. Put another way, *embouteillages* were both the impetus for the projects and their necessary result. This blurring of cause and effect generated among urban residents and bureaucrats alike a particular sense of historical inevitability and physical inescapability. The traffic bottleneck, it seemed, was a deeply entrenched fact of contemporary urban life, one that would surely persist despite recent infrastructural interventions.

Urbanites frequently compared and contrasted contemporary traffic jams with the urban gridlock of previous generations. For instance, *embouteillage* was a central experience during *magal*, the annual pilgrimage that Murid faithful make to the religious capital of Touba, located about two hundred kilometers from Dakar. The journey commemorates the return from exile of the Sufi order's founder, Amadou Bamba. Each year, adherents from around the world assemble in Dakar and board overcrowded cars, vans, and buses and make the slow trek to Senegal's interior; a trip that would otherwise take a few hours easily takes a day or more. The city's attention and resources—including water, electricity, and all roadworthy vehicles—were diverted to the holy city. Urbanites sometimes mentioned these voyages when we talked about bottlenecks, emphasizing that the experience of *magal* was just as much about the journey to Touba as it was about the events held in the holy city itself. In their descriptions of *magal*, friends and informants often highlighted the sense of collective purpose and belonging that emerged on traffic-clogged roads. They alternated between describing these road journeys as festive and spiritually rejuvenating experiences filled with anticipation on the one hand and as potentially dangerous voyages that demanded vigilance on the other.

These very specific narratives of traffic tie-ups and slowdowns as ambivalent but potentially transformative collective experiences helped give me a sense of the complex social and historical landscape of which contemporary *embouteillages* are a part. Urbanites tended to conceptualize traffic bottlenecks as places to avoid. The tenor of Dakarois' interactions and the rhythm of their schedules frequently revolved around identifying, anticipating, and averting problem zones. Daily trips and errands were strategically planned, when possible, to coincide with lulls in traffic. Friends and coworkers shared wisdom about areas of the city to avoid and the best times of day to travel. Commuters engaged each other with stories of time spent in traffic, flat tires, missed appointments, tense encounters with angry motorists, respiratory problems caused by the oppressive heat and exhaust fumes, and clothing soiled by accumulating dust. They shared advice about alternative routes, and they gossiped about the poor planning efforts of government leaders. Moreover, discussion of urban bottlenecks often conjured among urban residents a nostalgic longing for a simpler, less hectic, less materialistic life in one's natal (or one's family's natal) village. Friends returning from a visit to the countryside, for instance, would often describe their rural respite as restful, free of *embouteillage*. Reflecting on his experiences living at a remove from his family in a village in Guinea, one cab driver spoke at length about the slower pace of life at home, where there were no paved roads and no vehicles to cause traffic bottlenecks, and where one ate the sweetest mangoes, picked from the trees, without having to pay anyone anything. But even as they spoke of their frustration with bottlenecks, urbanites engaged with them in all sorts of productive ways. It is this tension that came to define my research and that fuels that analysis that follows.

Dubious Characters or Urban Experts?

As my research project began to take shape, I came to see Dakar's taxicab drivers as ideal informants for an ethnographic study of mobility, urban construction, and belonging. My enthusiasm, however, was often met with skepticism and words of caution from city residents themselves. Dakarois typically regard the *taksimann* as a shadowy character who must be handled with a hearty dose of skepticism.[1] He is considered coarse and unpolished, lacking in formal education or worldly experience, and a bit foolhardy and wily. Urban residents accuse the *taksimann* of flouting established rules and of engaging in dangerous behavior that jeopardizes the well-being of his passengers and other motorists. This characterization is vividly captured in "Taximan," a popular hip-hop song featuring Senegalese pop artists Viviane Ndour and Fou Malade. In the song, the urbane and articulate Viviane clashes with a crass and frivolous cab driver, played by Fou Malade. Despite the fact that he has left his license behind, the driver takes Viviane on a wildly meandering trip, all the while chattering incessantly in a Dakar brand of Wolof and complaining of traffic checkpoints and *embouteillages*. Though he claims to be "the best driver on earth or perhaps in the air," the driver's own narrative suggests otherwise—he claims, for instance, to have been expelled from Dakar after having hit a person, a horse, and a cow within the span of one minute. Though intended as a humorous exaggeration, this popular song nonetheless reflects and reaffirms general public conceptions of taxi drivers as marginal members of urban society—either newly arrived from the rural hinterland or raised in the city's peripheral *banlieues* (suburbs)—who lack sophistication, direction, and authentic stakes to the city. Most importantly, perhaps, taxi drivers are considered to be disrespectful of the city's roads, the regulations and norms that govern them, and the city as a space of order and cosmopolitan refinement. From the perspective of many urban residents, then, the *taksimann* had little worthwhile to contribute to a conversation about the city's and the nation's future and, by extension, to my ethnographic study. Indeed, this dubious urbanite posed a potential threat both to collective visions and to my own physical and moral well-being.

While expatriates echoed some of these assumptions about cab drivers' suspect allegiances and unsavory personas, they were typically more concerned

---

1. See, e.g., Mutongi 2006.

with what this particular group of urbanites might offer my ethnographic project. As one Canadian development worker put it, cab drivers could serve as an important means to an end—a path toward finding other informants, for learning my way through the city, or for getting to an important interview—but not as legitimate "ends" in and of themselves, particularly for a study on transnational migration and economic development. This development worker's concerns echoed those expressed by other urban residents, but they also aligned with development organization practices that tended to build programs around social groups deemed likeable, trustworthy, and easily tracked. Perceived as unreliable and excessively mobile, taxi drivers were both unlikely urban protagonists and unruly targets of development intervention.

Yet it was precisely this routine denial of cab drivers' productive presence—in discussions about planning futures, in conversations about ethnographic research, in the spaces and institutions of the city itself—that made these men such fascinating and well-positioned subjects for this study. For one, my *taksimann* informants claimed a wide range of affiliations, experiences, and backgrounds that mirrored the city's diversity. They often proclaimed these ethnic, religious, and national attachments in proud and public ways. For instance, drivers frequently adorned the interior spaces of their cabs with the images of important Sufi saints and leaders or, more rarely, Catholic rosary beads. Many also claimed to possess valuable expertise about the layered histories and interconnected spaces of the city. They touted their willingness to move beyond planned detours, to problem solve, and to put themselves and their cabs on the line to deliver their passengers more quickly. They also saw themselves as key participants in the circulation of political rumors, gossip, and tales, as possessing inside knowledge about brokered deals and shadowy liaisons. Moreover, the cab drivers I met were often outspoken in their political views and offered—often without prompting—keen assessments of elections, economic projects, clandestine migration, and international politics. Rebuking public images that cast them as dubious experts or inauthentic urbanites, then, they claimed both urban and ethnographic legitimacy through their everyday movements and narratives by professing their unique relationship to and situated knowledge about the city's networked roads and spaces.

To foreground the experiences and narratives of cab drivers is also to query the work of anthropological knowledge production more generally. Over the past several decades, scholars have critically examined field-making practices, drawing attention to the actors, movements, spaces, and engagements that tend to "slip out of the ethnographic frame" in conventional anthropological studies (Clifford 1997, 23; see also Gupta and Ferguson 1997). These interventions have helped shed light on the "means" of our research—the roads and vehicles that move us through and connect us with our field sites, the intermediaries that facilitate our itineraries, the cultural translators who explain the terrain, the journeys and commutes we make to field sites, the institutional practices that facilitate or impede research agendas, and the cash flows that forge connections—that have long lurked in the shadows of ethnographic accounts. Building on these methodological debates, I join a growing contingent of urban anthropologists in centering cab drivers as essential nodes in an elaborate and always shifting urban infrastructure.[2] By focusing on these marginalized actors, their blurred movements, and our taken-for-granted exchanges (of services, cash, knowledge, advice, and research data), I aim to draw attention to the profoundly unequal relations of power that shape all ethnographic encounters and itineraries.[3]

Making sense of cab drivers' movements, anxieties, and claims required an ethnographic approach that was both flexible and contingent. At the heart of this work was my use of mobile interviews, conducted as we navigated clogged roads and side streets. This approach gave me and my interlocutors a way to speak about the layered spaces and networks of the city, and it gave them an opportunity to demonstrate their experiences and ideas in concrete ways rather than talking about them in abstract or distanced ways. While some of the encounters I describe in this book were fleeting interactions with people I did not see again, other relationships were much more intimate and enduring, sometimes extending beyond my fieldwork years and into follow-up trips. My interactions and inquiries with these men sometimes spilled beyond the confines of the taxicab itself, onto roadsides and into markets, neighborhoods, homes, and a community mosque. I spent time, for instance, at a key post where the same group of cab drivers would wait for clients each day. My *taksimann* informants frequently relished the opportunity to share their perspectives and to introduce me to an expanded network of urbanites—traders and salespeople, families with loved ones

2. Notar 2012a, 2012b; Hansen 2006; Lawuyi 1988; and Stoller 1982 are particularly notable here. See also Featherstone, Thrift, and Urry 2005; and Czeglédy 2004.

3. Talal Asad's (1973) seminal writings on the deeply unequal relations of power that both enable and shape ethnographic encounters remains indispensable here. Joanne Passaro (1997) has written more specifically on the challenges and assumptions that undergird urban ethnography, focusing more specifically on the ways particular kinds of field sites, informants, and modes of being in "the field" are deemed acceptable and privileged over others, thus disabling certain lines of inquiry from the start.

abroad, neighborhood leaders, unemployed or underemployed men looking for work, even an imam.

My relationships with cab drivers and the social worlds they shared with
me were, without question, deeply inflected by gendered, classed, and racial-
ized hierarchies, assumptions, and practices. Elite women do drive and own
cars in Dakar, and women seemed as likely as their male counterparts to ride
as passengers in others' vehicles or to use public transportation—including
buses, *cars rapides* (brightly colored minibuses), taxis, and *clandos* (affordable, communal taxis that operate outside of legal regulations)—on a daily
or weekly basis. But almost without exception, cab drivers and other public
transportation operators were men. Taxi drivers frequently described the
city's roads as dangerous spaces characterized by inept drivers, irresponsible
car rapide operators, constant distractions, crumbling infrastructures, and
increasing violence—and thus as spaces altogether unfit for women drivers.[4] They spoke frequently and usually quite lovingly of wives, girlfriends,
mothers, and daughters, or of their plans or desires to eventually marry, but
during the course of my research in Dakar, only one driver introduced me to
his wife. Instead, the social spheres through which these men moved each
day—and to which they eagerly gave me access—were predominantly masculine. It was through this gendered lens, then, that drivers came to view and
understand their relationship with me as a foreigner and a researcher, as a
young woman in need of (male) guidance as I made my way along unfamiliar roads in a city and a culture that was not necessarily my "home."

My encounters and discussions with the city's taxi drivers were also
heavily mediated by our differing racial, national, and class positions. Because it is significantly more expensive than other means of urban transport,
a cab ride is typically a privilege afforded only by the city's wealthier residents or foreign visitors. For many cab drivers, my economic privilege and
my obvious foreignness marked me as a member of a transnational elite who
moved at whim and without restriction both within the city and far beyond.
This status was reinforced when they learned I was an American. My status as
a mobile elite, in turn, had a deep impact on the relationships I forged with
cab drivers and on the narratives and perspectives they shared. It positioned
me, for instance, as a possible ally in cab drivers' own efforts to get abroad.[5]
Like many urban men, taxi drivers quite frequently described themselves as

4. This dovetails in interesting ways with urban men's assertions about the pirogue (dugout
canoe) as a masculine space, as I discuss in chapter 5.
5. These experiences resonate in powerful ways with those described by Chu (2010) in her
ethnography of migratory pursuits in Fuzhou, China.

potential migrants. They turned to me, then, for advice about visa requirements, for instance, or for help in acquiring particular kinds of valuable *papiers* (papers)—such as a "letter of invitation"—which they imagined would help support their eventual applications for a visa.[6] Other drivers proposed I bring them along to the United States to work as a chauffeur or in various other capacities.

It was precisely these sorts of transactions and asymmetries that urban skeptics worried would compromise my research agenda. On the contrary, my encounters with these intermediaries brought into sharper view important questions about expertise, futurity, and belonging in this "city under construction." Taxi drivers' experiences and claims reflected their daily, intimate engagements not only with a young, white, female American anthropologist but also with a city under construction, a mobile and privileged clientele, an increasingly exclusionary urban economy, and constantly shifting ideas about belonging, success, and participation. The analysis that follows explores the shifting urban, social, and economic terrain upon which cab drivers must work to relentlessly position themselves. Rather than imagining their claims, narratives, and engagements as marginal, informal, or inauthentic, I centralize cab drivers' everyday efforts to make sense of a rapidly changing city and to assert themselves as present in meaningful ways.

Gendered Anxieties and Urban Impermanence

As large-scale infrastructure projects were gathering momentum in Dakar in the spring of 2006, so too was a much more modest road-centered initiative. The program—called Sister Taxi—provided loans to qualifying women for the purchase of a taxi from the brand-new fleet the program had acquired.[7] Sponsored by the Senegalese government (through the Ministry of Family, Feminine Organizations, Infancy, and Childhood) and by Auto Espace, a prominent car dealership in the city, the Sister Taxi program meshed well with broader moves in Dakar and elsewhere to empower women through

---

6. This collective quest for documents of support was shaped in part on French visa application procedures, which focus on an applicant's "dossier" and less on an interview process. Letters of invitation and other documents, American embassy officials assured me, would be of little interest in United States visa application processes. Nonetheless, talk of acquiring necessary papers was pervasive in the city.

7. Despite my best efforts, I was not able to interview or even drive with one of the famed "taxi sisters." This speaks both to the public's remarkable fascination during the time of my research with these brand new cabs and their unconventional drivers but also to the tiny size of this program.

microcredit opportunities aimed at entrepreneurship and financial independence. The government and media also touted the project as a bold and necessary step toward "cleaning up" the image of Dakar's transportation system and as persuasive evidence that a new kind of city and economy were emerging. Although the program was quite small—there were only *ten* "taxi sisters" in the city during the time of my research—it received a good deal of public attention. The cabs, which could be reserved in advance by phone, were especially popular among upwardly mobile Senegalese women and expatriate businessmen, who preferred to travel with the sisters because of their ostensibly refined mannerisms and clean cabs. While a few cab drivers shrugged off the women and described the Sister Taxi program as a fad that would inevitably fade from public view, many other drivers saw the project as a direct and hostile affront to their established livelihoods. Several male drivers explicitly accused this small cadre of women of encroaching upon their territory or of receiving preferential treatment from the government.

It quickly became clear that the uproar this small project had generated among the city's male cab drivers far surpassed its actual potential impact on their lives and incomes. The Sister Taxi controversy instead reflected much broader and deeper anxieties among cab drivers about the precariousness of their presence in the city—anxieties that are at the heart of this ethnography. Unlike the taxi sisters, the vast majority of the city's male taxi drivers did not own their own vehicles and held little hope of ever doing so.[8] Instead, drivers paid the owners (*borom-yi* in Wolof, *proprietaires* in French) of the cab about 150,000 FCFA (roughly US$300) on a monthly basis and took home about 40–50,000 FCFA (US$80–$100). Most drivers shared access to a cab with another driver who either owned the cab himself or who also paid an owner a rental fee. Taxi owners were wealthier than the drivers; some owned small businesses in the city, for instance, or were living and working in the diaspora. Indeed, cab ownership was seen as a sound and relatively safe investment during the time of my research: the services of cab drivers were always in demand, an owner's fee was nonnegotiable and regularly collected, and there was no need to hire an extensive staff or to recruit dependable managers.[9] There was little risk for the *borom*, cab drivers often emphasized

8. During the time of my research, a law was passed in Senegal that prohibited the import of vehicles that were five years old or older. Most urban residents, of course, could not afford to purchase a relatively new vehicle. But this law also drove up the price of older vehicles already on Dakar's roads, further excluding cab drivers from ownership opportunities.

9. This benefit was particularly appealing to Senegalese living abroad, who often regarded the need to supervise staff as an obstacle to productive investment in Dakar. Instead, diasporic cab owners relied on wives or brothers to collect monthly rents from taxi drivers, and if pay-

in interviews and conversations, as it was the *taksimann* who shouldered most of the responsibilities for the cab. They negotiated rates directly with passengers depending on factors like distance of the proposed trip, time of day, traffic conditions, weather, and the cost of fuel. Drivers were expected to pay for their own fuel, so it is they who absorbed price shocks, not the owners, whose rates were set independently of global oil market trends. Drivers were also usually required to pay for (or, less frequently, to contribute to the cost of) repairs to the vehicle, so the condition of the cab was primarily their personal responsibility. Many of my *taksimann* interlocutors described a sort hand-to-mouth existence, one subject to the whims of global oil prices, greedy cab owners, and daily traffic conditions. Cab drivers thus saw the Sister Taxi program as offering an indisputable advantage—the hope of eventually owning one's own cab—to women, and they typically placed blame squarely on the government, which they saw as indifferent to their collective plight.

Formal credit opportunities for the purchase of taxicabs were not limited to women, however. During the time of my research, programs resembling the Sister Taxi initiative but offering credit to male taxi drivers also began to surface in Dakar. These programs were likewise seen as helping to modernize the city's aging transportation infrastructure and were typically managed or sanctioned by the state, sometimes in conjunction with foreign governments.[10] Though enormously appealing to those with whom I worked, these formal channels of credit and the plush new cabs they afforded were available only to a very small minority of the city's cab drivers, as most drivers found they could not qualify for credit or could not commit to the large monthly payments involved. Yet these exclusive programs did not incite the same sort of ire among cab drivers that the Sister Taxi project did. This was owed, in part, to imaginaries of the city's roads as masculine spaces and of the profession as an exclusively male endeavor, as I described above. In their reflections on the Sister Taxi program and its consequences, a number of male drivers were careful to emphasize that the road was no place for women and that the project was thus sure to fail.[11]

---

ments were not made or other conditions are not met, it was relatively easy find new drivers to fill vacated spots. Urban residents thus often recognized the taxicab as material evidence of an altogether different sort of mobility, that of transnational migration.

10. One such program, for instance, was supported by the government of Saudi Arabia in anticipation of the Organization of the Islamic Conference (OCI) meetings in Dakar in 2008.

11. These assertions about the road as a masculine domain of urban life echo in quite revealing ways those made in chapter 5 about the pirogue as a male space.

But male drivers' opposition to the program also stemmed from much broader anxieties about diminishing opportunities, gendered expectations, and shifting patterns of belonging in this city under construction. While about half of the cab drivers with whom I worked and traveled were born in Dakar or one of the *banlieues* on the city's periphery, the rest were migrants from rural Senegal or the neighboring countries of Guinea, Guinea Bissau, Côte d'Ivoire, Gambia, Mali, Sierra Leone, and Liberia. Their reasons for migrating were as varied as their backgrounds: While some came to escape violence, social instability, discrimination, or unemployment in their country or region of origin, others sought adventure or new opportunities. Some came to join family already living in the city, while others saw Dakar as a transit point on a longer itinerary. Many of these men left families behind in their natal villages, while others had managed to bring family to settle in the city. What both native and newly arrived cab drivers shared in common, however, was a complex set of obligations and expectations that kept them firmly tied to the city and the profession as well as to their families and communities, both near and far, who depended on their earnings. Fulfilling families' needs and desires brought men social visibility and respect, but few were able to do so without struggle. Married drivers described the challenges of providing for one or multiple wives and their children. Regardless of marital status, drivers were often expected to help support other family members who had no other dependable source of income. As one driver put it, "As soon as you make a little money, and you walk through the door of your family's home, your money is gone. You always need to worry about your brothers and your mothers, even if you don't have any children." Unwed drivers faced the additional obstacle of not being able to afford bridewealth payments or to otherwise position themselves as worthy suitors through gifting or conspicuous consumption practices, for instance.[12] These men frequently bemoaned women's rising expectations for material goods, and they worried they could not compete with wealthier diasporic Senegalese for the attention and commitment of local women and would thus remain unwed indefinitely. Whether married or unmarried, newcomers to the city or lifelong residents, Dakar's male taxi drivers emphasized that they were profoundly dependent on the opportunities afforded by city life.

And yet, these men described living in a state of increasing precariousness, more uncertain than ever about their ability to remain long-term in a

12. For a more nuanced and historically situated discussion of these marriage exchanges, see Buggenhagen 2012.

city they experienced as expensive, hostile, and exclusive. During the time of my research, the cost for everyday necessities like rice, fish, cooking oil, and fuel skyrocketed. Rental prices soared as well, sending many cab drivers deeper into the urban periphery in search of affordable housing options. At the very same time that life was becoming more expensive and obligations more weighty, traffic on Dakar's roads was screeching to a halt as infrastructural projects gathered momentum. Though urbanites continued to rely on taxicabs for transportation, trips took much longer, which left cab drivers able to accommodate fewer clients each day. Many drivers demanded higher fares as a result, but these modest price increases could not make up for the significant financial losses they suffered. Drivers worried aloud that the city's *embouteillages* would eat away at their take-home pay, which was already stretched so thin. The city's worsening traffic jams fueled heated debates and pointed accusations of government neglect and favoritism. Many drivers argued that President Wade was building the roads for investors and that he had not considered the impact of the ambitious projects on the lives of everyday residents—especially those who relied on the roads to eke out a living.

As daily itineraries, movements, and incomes became more strained, my *taksimann* informants described their continued presence in the city as uncertain. Some drivers spoke of needing to take small loans from friends to pay the owners of their cabs, for instance. Other men anticipated having to send their families, who had accompanied them to the capital, back to their natal villages, where housing, food, and educational expenses were much less significant. Several young men worried that they would be forced to live indefinitely with their parents, unable to establish their own households and families without sufficient resources. It was within this context of increasing urban precariousness that the Sister Taxi initiative surfaced. Drivers' resentment toward the program and its pioneering female drivers thus reflected complexly layered anxieties, obligations, and realities. From the perspective of many male cab drivers, the Sister Taxi program represented a threat, both symbolic and real, to men's ability to provide for their families, build futures, and assert belonging in culturally legible ways, at the very moment when viable economic, social, and street routes were becoming overburdened, narrowed, and impassible. This program was read as symptomatic of much broader, more troubling shifts underway in Dakar: increasing urban congestion, the government's disinvestment in many citizens' lives, shrinking opportunities and closed routes, and a gendered "crisis" that threatened male modes of being and belonging—even if these women posed, in fact, very little threat.

Transnational Selves in Suspension

Despite their seemingly territorial claims both to the city's roads and to the profession, the vast majority of taxi drivers I met emphasized that driving a cab was a temporary occupation that did not define a driver's sense of self or his aspirations for the future.[13] Particularly during the time of my research, the job did not promise a dependable salary or social prestige, as I have made clear above. Instead, for most men, driving a cab was a means to an end; it was a hopeful stepping-stone to more appealing opportunities in other sectors of the city or far beyond. Driving a cab thus a kind of aspirational transnationalism, one that linked middle-class identities, global mobilities, and urban futures.[14] My *taksimann* informants frequently introduced themselves as *entrepreneurs*, using the French word, and they spoke enthusiastically of their efforts to save money to attend one of the city's private professional or business schools, for example, or to start a small business like a *cybercafé*. But the largest proportion of these men—young and old, newcomers and natives—expressed a committed desire to eventually migrate abroad. Many rural newcomers, in fact, had been lured to Dakar and the profession with the explicit goal of migrating to Europe or the United States. In their minds, driving a cab held the promise of personal connections and financial resources that might facilitate these hopeful futures. Cab drivers' urban imaginaries, itineraries, and projects thus were inherently transnational ones. This conceptualization of Dakar as a strategic stopover on a longer transnational journey—rather than as a final destination in and of itself—reflects a critical shift in the ways this capital city is experienced and theorized by its residents. As urban opportunities have dwindled (particularly after structural adjustment) and residents' global horizons have expanded, longtime residents and newcomers alike increasingly look to transnational migration as a means to provide for families, settle debts, accumulate wealth and prestige, and realize masculine adulthood.

However, like many urban residents, taxi drivers were unlikely transnational migrants. The very same factors that shaped their desires to migrate abroad in the first place—namely their experiences of urban impermanence and economic uncertainty—excluded them from legal migratory networks. Few cab drivers possessed the elite connections, economic resources, tech-

---

13. I knew of only three drivers out of close to a hundred who had become cab drivers because their fathers had driven a cab.

14. For more on middle-class aspirations in "emergent" countries, see Liechty 2003 and Jeffrey 2010.

nical skills, or specialized training that would have made them attractive candidates for European or American visas or work permits. For instance, in previous decades, many Senegalese were able to successfully migrate to the United States after acquiring (and then overstaying) short-term tourist visas. In order to be a competitive candidate for this sort of visa, an applicant was required to furnish evidence that he had established a life in Senegal to which he would necessarily return. "Proof" of one's intention to return was evidenced in things like bank account records, deeds to land, or home ownership. Few cab drivers could provide documentation of this sort. As one *taksimann* put it, "If I already had a house, why would I need to migrate?" From this perspective, urban precariousness impelled cab drivers and many other Dakarois to consider the possibilities offered by transnational migration, but their tenuous claims to the city also excluded them as potential migrants.

By the time I arrived to conduct long-term research in Dakar in 2006, urbanites hoping to migrate faced additional obstacles and increasingly slim odds. Various Western countries had begun to crack down on illicit migratory practices (such as the overstaying of tourist visas and clandestine entry tactics) and to more carefully consider and monitor legal entry practices and policies, particularly in the wake of global economic recession, mounting concerns about security (especially post-9/11), and the growing popularity of conservative political movements focused on autochthonous conceptualizations of citizenship (see chapter 1 for a more detailed discussion). Not only were the borders and entry policies of various receiving countries tightened, but a European Union organization called Frontex began to intensively patrol the shores of West Africa in an effort to deter clandestine migration. These myriad shifts reflected the growing popularity of "selective migration" policies—which emphasized the receiving country's right to "choose" immigrants who possess certain desirable qualifications— particularly in France (where it was called *immigration choisie*) and the United States. Such policies and ideologies excluded the vast majority of Dakarois from legal migration and generated fervent debate among urban residents about the increasingly fraught relationship between transnational mobility and urban belonging.

This point is well illustrated by an encounter I had in May 2006. In an effort to make a little extra cash on what promised to be a difficult day traffic-wise, Ibrahim, my cab driver that morning, picked up me and three men who were likewise headed to Plateau. As he navigated a cab filled with strangers through thickening traffic, Ibrahim tuned into a radio program in Wolof that was discussing the *immigration choisie* debate in France. The once-quiet cab quickly became the site of lively debate as we discussed the impact of selective migration policies on Senegalese society. This long and complex discussion tied together dozens of seemingly unconnected issues—from structural racism in France to unemployment among educated youth to the lack of a "culture of investment" in Senegal, from the housing construction frenzy in Dakar to the very immediate problems posed by the road projects themselves. Woven into this discussion were the very personal perspectives and urban experiences of the five participants themselves. Ibrahim, for instance, explained that he had been driving a cab for thirty-two years, working hard to save money so that he could migrate. Finally, as the cab neared Plateau, Ibrahim observed aloud, "Migration from Senegal is like these road projects." Governments shut down routes without any coordination or planning and without concern for the projects' impacts, he explained, and people are left scrambling, forced to make their way alone. This chance encounter, generated by the conditions of urban *embouteillage*, gives us a glimpse of the ways transnational selves are forged and hindered on Dakar's roads. It underscores, too, the ways in which urbanites experienced selective migration policies as inextricable from other processes of narrowing and exclusion.

This traffic in meanings did not escape the notice of governing institutions and authorities. A top official at the American embassy was remarkably explicit about this during an interview in the spring of 2006. In her discussion of the seeming rise in clandestine migration practices at that time, she explained her personal strategy for making immigration policies clear to the general public:

> If I want to know how well our messages about visa processes are being absorbed by Senegalese, I gauge the street. If the messages that are being circulated while people sit stuck in traffic, chatting on *cars rapides*, or in markets—if these conversations reflect our policies, then we're on the right track. People are getting the message: not everyone can migrate. As a country, as a people, we Americans have decided that we will not use migration as a strategy for developing places like Africa. We have channeled resources for development through institutions like the USAID. We don't want people to waste their time and money waiting for visas they'll never get.

This embassy official insisted that making sense of transnational migration as a practice and priority required navigating Dakar's traffic clogged roads and conversing with other residents en route. It was here, amidst conditions of seeming impasse and frustrated movements, that transnational visions were contested, crafted, and publicly circulated. The official's statement also gives us a glimpse into the ideology and practice of selective migration—which decouples development from certain migratory flows, restricts access to legal migratory channels, and separates out and supports a privileged mobile elite.

Cab drivers and other urban residents often interpreted this relentless narrowing of migratory routes as a deeply personal assault on their ways of being in, moving beyond, and imagining the city. As we sat stuck in traffic on a particularly hot day in the summer of 2006, Sidy negotiated with an ambulant trader selling small national flags on plastic pedestals. He eagerly selected an American flag from the bundle, positioned it proudly on the dashboard of the cab, and handed the vendor 500 FCFA (about US$1), which was no small sum of money for a cab driver to pay. When I pressed him on his selection, Sidy explained, "Senegal is a good country, for those with money. I should have left Senegal years ago. I should have taken a pirogue like the others who left. I should have been a clandestine migrant and gone to Spain. But now it is too late. Now, I have no choice. But what other way is there but migration? I can't buy a cab, and I can't find another job. Instead, I must drive this cab—someone else's cab." Sidy explained that he was working in Dakar to support his wife and children, who lived in a small village about two hours from the city, and he worried constantly about getting by in the city while making ends meet in his natal village.

In contrast to Sidy, Alpha was a Dakar native with no children or extended family to support. He was in his mid- to late thirties and had not married, a fact he lamented. When I explained my research interests in migration, Alpha became animated and began to recount a decade's worth of unraveled hopes and plans to migrate—to Canada, to Europe, to the United States. He said that he had a friend living in New York who had encouraged him to apply for a tourist visa ten years earlier, but he had put it off because the application fee was more than he could afford without a loan from a family member or friend. He knew plenty of people who had been successful ten or twenty years ago in migrating abroad on short-term visas, he assured me. But now, a decade later, "these routes abroad have been closed," Alpha explained. "And now," he added bitterly, "I'm just sitting [*toog*] in the city, sitting in this *embouteillage*."

Despite their different backgrounds and circumstances, both Sidy and Alpha described being stuck in Dakar, unable to migrate abroad. They explicitly linked their failed transnational itineraries to their everyday, embodied experiences of living, driving, working, sitting, saving money, and strategizing in the increasingly congested and restricted capital city. What

Sidy, Alpha, and many men like them described were transnational selves caught in *embouteillage*. This assertion meshes well with the observations of Michael Lambert, writing about rural-urban migration a decade prior to my own research: "I am confident that most Senegalese would concur that frustration is the most common Senegalese experience of transnationalism. People are funneled from the rural hinterland to Dakar where they find themselves at a bottleneck—not having found what they were in search of, yet unable to move forward to more promising destinations" (2002, xxi). Both newcomers to the city and lifelong residents expressed deep concerns that mobility—a defining value and transformative mode of being in contemporary Senegal—was, increasingly, not a possibility for them. For these anxious urbanites, the traffic *embouteillage* offered both an opportunity for reflection on their everyday predicaments and a vibrant cultural framework for making sense of their precarious place in a rapidly changing city. It provided a meaningful way to describe their stalled projects of self-making and to link their personal circumstances to broader, more abstract processes of rapid urbanization, chronic economic uncertainty, urban inequality, narrowing migration policies, and infrastructural rehabilitation and breakdown.

By no means were these experiences and narratives of *embouteillage*—of being unable to move within and beyond the city, migrate, come of age, accumulate wealth, or fulfill expectations and commitments—shared by all of Dakar's residents. This was made quite clear, for instance, on the city's congested roads. All urban commuters had to deal with traffic jams and barricaded roads. In fact, my colleagues at APIX even described the city's *embouteillages* as a sort of democratizing force in contemporary Dakar, as a public phenomenon that impacted and united city dwellers of all backgrounds, including APIX staff members themselves (see Melly 2013). Few of my *taksimann* informants would have shared this perspective. While wealthier residents could often afford their own cars, the city's poorer residents typically made their commutes in road-weary, overcrowded vehicles that were poorly ventilated and held dubious safety records. Because buses moved along fixed routes, drivers could not invent new paths to dodge traffic jams like drivers with their own automobiles could. Although cab drivers had more flexibility to define their own routes than other public transport drivers did, they nonetheless felt similarly trapped in their vehicles each day as traffic jams and detours proliferated. Many of them drove aging, unreliable vehicles with rusted holes, tattered upholstery, broken windows, and missing or malfunctioning parts. As these taxis made their way across uneven surfaces or sat stalled in traffic, they were much more prone to breakdowns or flat tires than newer, privately owned vehicles. Cab drivers also frequently pointed out the impact that traffic congestion had on their bodies. A number of drivers complained of respiratory problems from breathing in exhaust all day, and they insisted to me that these physical ills were not shared by the city's elite, who spent less time on the road and whose air-conditioned cars helped filter the air they breathed. Others complained that the city's worsening *embouteillages* left them poorly nourished, since they had less time to eat and less money to spend on substantive meals.

My *taksimann* interlocutors also frequently emphasized that some well-positioned urbanites were able to move through and beyond bottlenecks and barricades better than others. In one memorable instance, a resourceful taxi driver named Musa pulled up to a guard stationed at a blockade erected along Dakar's Corniche highway project. Traffic along this segment of the road had been entirely restricted to residents who lived in the grand villas along this stretch of road and to those working at or visiting the embassies nestled in the elite coastal neighborhood. Everyone else was redirected along narrow back roads. Hoping to bypass this detour, Musa approached the guard and invented a lively tale about how I was a Portuguese diplomat on my way to an urgent meeting regarding clandestine migration policies at the embassy. We were given immediate permission to pass, and Musa and I sped away, amused by the guard's gullibility. As we drove along this deserted stretch of highway under construction, Musa remarked that this was the way life in the city worked: certain people still managed to get things done, he said, especially if they were foreigners or could afford to pay bribes.

This playful experiment gives us a glimpse of the remarkably uneven social terrain upon which *embouteillages* materialized. Dakar's traffic bottlenecks made publicly visible and tangible the intensifying inequalities that characterized the city under construction. They gave urbanites a means to perceive, theorize, and debate the complex and historically unstable relationship between mobility, urban space, elite status, and the global. Taxi drivers' deepening anxieties—that they were unable to move within and beyond the city, migrate, come of age, accumulate wealth, or fulfill expectations and commitments—existed in marked tension with other Dakarois' experiences in and claims on the city. Indeed, as Musa reminds us, some people—particularly those who can claim transnational privilege, who have financial resources, or who are cunning and resourceful, as he was—do manage to get through *embouteillages*. The next section takes this observation farther by considering the ways in which urban residents used the bottleneck to challenge these inequalities, fashion mobile selves, and claim urban presence, redefining authority and legitimacy in the process. Seen from this perspective, the *embouteillage* was not just evidence of lives put on hold; it also offered valuable opportunities for generating mobile futures.

Urban Life in the Meantime

Early in 2007, I met Baba, an unmarried *taksimann* who lived in his parents' home in the Ouakam neighborhood of the city, and we became easy and immediate friends. We were approximately the same age, we both cast ourselves as devoted urbanites, and we shared a passion for politically charged Senegalese hip-hop. When he learned of my ethnographic research on urban life and transnational migration, Baba worked to position himself as an urban expert, a political activist, and an indispensable interlocutor. He provided me with his cell phone number and called and messaged me frequently to check on my progress. He volunteered himself for interviews, helped me "map" the city and its spaces by cab, and introduced me to people who might help my research. Baba took every available opportunity to voice his disapproval of President Wade and dismiss his grand infrastructural projects as lacking in substance and vision. Like many of his fellow cab drivers, he griped about the projects' impacts on his ability to move through the city and make a living, and he frequently bemoaned the lack of more exciting, secure, and lucrative job opportunities. He was relatively well educated—he had completed *lycée* (French-style secondary school)—and saw his work as a *taksimann* as a poor fit for his skills and aspirations. Instead, Baba described himself as an entrepreneur, and he daydreamed about small investment projects he would start that would snowball into large-scale development efforts. He also chronicled his unsuccessful efforts to migrate abroad: his flight to the Canary Islands several years ago, where his hopes to find a way to Spain were quickly dashed, and his annual efforts to "try the American visa lottery," which likewise has always ended in failure.[15]

However, Baba's fiery rhetoric was complicated and unsettled by his own daily movements through and engagement with the city. It quickly became clear that driving a cab was not just a means for Baba to make an income or something he was "stuck" doing because there were no other viable opportunities; it also enabled him to circulate continuously through the city, to insert himself into potentially useful networks, and to engage in various kinds of worthwhile transactions. For instance, Baba was an active member of one of the city's many *tontines*, or informal rotating credit organizations,

15. For a sustained discussion of visa lottery practices in West Africa (more specifically in Togo), see Piot 2010.

most of which are run by women. Despite his meager income, he faithfully traveled each week to a busy intersection in the Fass neighborhood of Dakar, where he left his contribution of 1,500 FCFA (roughly US$3) with a small group of women who sold mangoes and other seasonal fruit to motorists. This was the only way he was able to effectively save money, Baba explained, and he hoped to use the earnings he accrued from this system to eventually migrate. Meanwhile, he worked hard to forge relationships with clients that might lead to future opportunities—he regularly served a diplomat and his family, took tourists on day trips to Lac Rose (a tourist area about forty miles north of the city), and, of course, befriended an American anthropologist. Though these relationships could not directly aid Baba in his efforts to migrate abroad, they nonetheless enabled him to fashion himself as *potentially* transnational, as always on the verge of moving, connecting, becoming, and belonging in the city and beyond.

My travels and conversations with urbanites like Baba underscore the fact that the *embouteillage*—both as a contemporary condition of being and as a material space—was not simply characterized by tedious waiting, passive detachment, disconnection and exclusion, or despair. Though urbanites bemoaned and feared the city's rapidly proliferating traffic bottlenecks, they also sought out the opportunities such circumstances provided. Indeed, *embouteillages* emerged as a critical means of generating short-term possibilities and concrete strategies in an urban climate where such temporalities and opportunities had otherwise seemingly evaporated. They enabled urban residents like Baba to insert themselves into vibrant economies, to foster productive relationships and engage in dialogue, to fashion future-focused selves, and to articulate claims—however partial and hesitant—on the city. During the time of my research, for instance, many cab drivers had begun to package their abilities, experience, and expertise as evidence of their status as entrepreneurs, and bottlenecks provided unique opportunities to cultivate these kinds of identities. Baba's participation in a rotating credit scheme—one that, ironically, was run from within a roadside market—is just one example. Several other cab drivers circulated business cards, typically printed on lightweight cardstock and bearing the driver's name, his cell phone number, and information about his "services," which often included things that exceeded typical cab routes, like tourist outings and courier trips. Other men stored basic English-language manuals on their dashboards, which they claimed to study during traffic slowdowns so that they might better serve tourists—and, as an added bonus, so that they might better position themselves as qualified migrants. Drivers turned time spent waiting—for traffic to move, for the economy to pick up, for a chance to marry and start a family—into opportunities to shape themselves as eagerly, potentially, and almost mobile.

The city's taxi drivers were not the only ones to take advantage of and insert themselves into *embouteillages* for personal or collective gain. Vibrant makeshift markets mushroomed and dissolved alongside bottlenecked roads.[16] Itinerant traders, mostly men but some women, wove through traffic peddling an assortment of local and imported goods: cell phone credit, secondhand clothing, alarm clocks, small plastic bags filled with water. These traders were typically migrants from rural Senegal, and many of them had come to the city determined to migrate to the United States or Europe, often through the transnational networks established by the Murid religious order. Successful trading might help these adherents climb the institutional ladder and eventually migrate abroad. But in an era when all kinds of migratory movements were more intensely restricted, many of these hopeful migrants instead found themselves caught in Dakar, eking out a living on the city's streets, uncertain of how long they would be able to remain. Although crime is relatively rare in Dakar in comparison to many other large African cities, brazen thieves on foot were sometimes drawn to *embouteillages*, too, and rumors circulated on a daily basis about purses or packages being stolen through open cab windows. These (assumedly) male figures searched for physical gaps through which to quickly pass, and they were said to profit enormously from others' immobility. Other urbanites made the most of temporal pauses on the city's streets to develop their interior selves through prayer. Drivers often kept prayer beads tucked into the fabric of their *boubous*; when traffic would thicken and grind to a halt, drivers would recite prayers. One Friday during afternoon prayer, worsening traffic brought the bus on which I was traveling to a standstill. With little choice but to wait for things to improve, the driver and several passengers abandoned the bus, and, prayer mats in hand, joined other worshippers performing ablutions amidst stalled vehicles. It was in these constricted and charged moments and spaces that the city came alive as people used the break in urban flows and routines to reclaim street surfaces, forge vibrant connections with each other, or immerse themselves in market transactions.

Embouteillages also forced open unexpected paths forward. When bottlenecks formed, streams of vehicles splintered off in all possible directions,

16. Interestingly, President Wade sought—and quickly failed—to wipe out informal markets entirely in November 2007, just months after my departure. Wade argued that street trading was *causing* traffic jams (rather than feeding on them) and that this was deterring investors, as these floating markets had made the city a notorious site for bottlenecks.

carving precarious new routes that broke with imposed detours. Moving along surfaces not intended for driving, these motorists relentlessly contested and reconfigured road regulations and accepted driving practices. Paths once considered dangerous, selfish, or unquestionably illegal were recast by many (though certainly not all) commuters as necessary detours, as temporarily justifiable given that official detours routes allowed for little movement. State officials frequently turned a blind eye toward these movements, accepting them as temporary resolutions to problems that could not have been otherwise solved (see also Lave 1988; Verran 2001). With time, then, some of these well-trodden paths became small but critical capillaries that kept the city alive. Taxi drivers were among the most eager and willing participants in these route-making practices. While Dakar's commuters often dismissed cab drivers as reckless, irresponsible, or oblivious, several of my *taksimann* informants countered that, in an age of proliferating bottlenecks, they were uniquely positioned to transport residents quickly and efficiently to their destinations, as they knew the city and its obscure side streets better than any other motorist and because they were willing to experiment and take risks. These cab drivers thus used *embouteillages* and their clever responses to them as evidence of their urban expertise. Moreover, they often linked their route-making practices to broader discussions about permissible movements, as my encounter with Musa made clear above. As they broke with established routes and pushed on through the city, taxi drivers and other urban travelers came to understand the limits of state intervention, planning, and authority in this era of chronic uncertainty, and they conceptualized their own contingent, deeply embodied responses to bottlenecks as critical to keeping the city in motion.

National and international leaders similarly approached *embouteillages* not just as moments of breakdown (of official messages, of traffic, of state authority) to be averted but also as opportunities to promote their programs and disseminate their visions of a mobile Dakar. Stuck in traffic, motorists and passengers confronted extraordinary state-sanctioned messages about the power of mobility. APIX's communication team worked to erect towering billboards at sites where bottlenecks tended to form, reminding traffic-weary drivers that these conditions of impasse and hardship were fleeting and would eventually lead to great futures. Larger-than-life images of smiling, bright-eyed children were paired with a simple message: "My future is today!" (*Mon avenir, c'est aujourd'hui!*) The OCI, too, promoted their mission in high-traffic areas, constructing a truly remarkable billboard featuring vivid images of tourist- and business-scapes and state-of-the-art roads. One such sign, situated at the end of the Corniche just before one entered the downtown area, enthusiastically proclaimed, "Senegal, En Route to the Top" (*Senegal: En Route Vers le Sommet*), obscuring the view of the ocean behind it. These state-sanctioned messages mingled with other conceptualizations of a mobile Dakar. Billboards cropped up in these same spaces, advertising money transfer services, flight deals to Jeddah and Lisbon, and cell phone promotional offers. Within the space of the traffic *embouteillage*, urbanites came to understand urban and transnational mobility as inextricably linked and as critical means for fashioning futures.

Although these hyperpublic road projects and the resulting traffic jams generated extensive criticism and controversy among urban residents, Wade was nonetheless reelected in 2007 on a campaign that explicitly indexed these incomplete projects and their unrealized potential. This message circulated on billboards, television promotions, and leaflets that featured the incumbent's portrait alongside images of roundabouts and grand highway structures. Members of the president's reelection team handed campaign materials through car and bus windows while residents sat stuck in traffic. Political graffiti sought to make the stakes clear to motorists and passengers. And makeshift caravans strapped with speakers and decorated with images of Wade and his opponents' images transformed Dakar's bottlenecks into a charged political arena. Though there were other important issues on the table during this election—staggering unemployment rates, the skyrocketing cost of staples like rice and gasoline, and the "crisis" of clandestine migration among them—Wade nonetheless worked to reorient the electorate's attention toward the unfinished public works campaigns, adopting the campaign slogan "Together, Let's Continue to Build Senegal" (*Ensemble, Continuons à Bâtir le Sénégal*). The president's claim for a second term in office, therefore, hinged not only on the ambitious scope and aims of these urban renewal projects but on the fact that they remained *unaccomplished*, their dramatic potential to spur urban and global flows unrealized. Wade and his staff framed the city's bottlenecks not as a liability or as an indication of his administration's failure but—quite to the contrary—as the most important reason to reelect him and as a sign of what was to come if they did.

Moving through the city under construction with urbanites like Baba, I came to recognize the *embouteillage* as an ethnographic glimpse into urban life in the *meantime*, as a space and moment where residents worked to bridge the realities of a stalled and oppressive present with distant expectations of mobile futures. At the same time that urban residents decried *embouteillages* as visible signs of lives held in suspension, they inserted themselves deeply into these spaces—sometimes willingly and strategically, sometimes much less so. Within these volatile moments and spaces, a new Dakar emerged,

Figure 4. A billboard in support of Wade's 2007 reelection campaign proclaims, "Together, Let's Continue to Build Senegal."

as urban residents recuperated mobile visions, recharted legitimate urban routes, engaged in future-focused transactions, and opened up possibilities for effective belonging.

Bottlenecked Citizenship

My focus in the previous chapter was on describing an emergent era in Senegal's history, the cohort of urban men who come of age in this era, and the future-focused projects in which these urbanites are deeply engaged. In this contemporary moment, mobility is defined as an indispensable mode of being and belonging in Dakar even as it proves to be an increasingly elusive and exclusive collective value. Building on these insights, this chapter has focused on taxi drivers and their urban journeys as a means to centralize the urban *embouteillage*—both as a generative social space and as a condition of being in the city—as the defining feature of this emergent historical era.

In many ways, Dakar's taxi drivers were the embodiment of this era of *embouteillage*. Their daily routines, social worlds, and aspirations had been profoundly shaped by decades of unrelenting austerity measures. They were typically familiar with and sometimes quite persuaded by the vocabularies and logics of liberalization, casting themselves as entrepreneurs, for instance, or debating the benefits of ongoing privatization efforts. Most of these men nonetheless lived in a state of economic precariousness, always uncertain about their ability to reach social adulthood, to fulfill commitments and repay debts, and to remain long term in a city they perceived to be increasingly expensive and exclusionary. Cab drivers' anxieties intensified as large-scale construction projects strained urban flows and threatened their incomes and their sense of well-being. These projects, they insisted, focused on catering to and caring for a globally mobile elite from which they were excluded. At the same time that they described lives held in suspension, many of the city's taxi drivers nonetheless expressed grand dreams of migrating abroad and building houses, families, and reputations for themselves, even as migratory routes upon which they relied were relentlessly narrowed. As they moved through the city's congested spaces, taxi drivers forcefully wrote themselves into the city's future, fashioning themselves as always on the cusp of becoming transnational and inserting themselves into spaces, transactions, and relationships that might help them realize these not-yet identities. They also situated themselves as critical nodes in an emergent urban infrastructure, as indispensable experts who played a key role in generating knowledge, connections, and legitimacy in the city under construction.

In these times of rapid change and inexorable stasis, the traffic *embouteillage* offered cab drivers and other urban residents a vocabulary for conceptualizing and debating urban exclusion, authority, and expertise as well as a social space in which to push against and redefine the contours of belonging and governance. The bottleneck indexed deep concerns about the suspension of lives and itineraries, but it also offered unexpected strategies and occasions for recuperating the meantime—for elaborating networks, hatching plans, revising legitimate practices, and claiming identities that helped bridge the inescapable present with far-off, mobile futures. For urbanites, the *embouteillage* was at once a profoundly local formation and a thoroughly global condition.

Inspired by these journeys and encounters, I began to grasp the *embouteillage* as an ethnographic commitment and as a culturally meaningful lens through which to make sense of the complexities of belonging and governance in contemporary Dakar. This move enabled me to bring into the same frame various paradoxes that characterized urban life. In the *embouteillage*, mobility and immobility, exclusion and belonging, present impossibilities and future potentialities came into view not as opposed urban orientations but as deeply and complexly related ways of being and belonging in the city. With this in mind, I began to conceptualize citizenship itself as bottlenecked. Seen from this perspective, urban belonging in Dakar emerges as an effect of urban and global infrastructures that are constantly narrowed, overwhelmed, rerouted, repaired, opened, and blocked. Urban belonging is always volatile, comprised of multiple temporalities. And though it appears as highly exclusionary in the present tense, it holds, too, the radical promise of future belonging and presence. Building on these insights, the chapters that follow continue to develop the concept of *embouteillage* as a framework for understanding the paradoxes of urban life, governance, and belonging in places like Dakar.

THREE

Inhabiting Inside-Out Houses

"I want to take you to see the house I was born in." It was this seemingly straightforward invitation that had brought me to Dakar's SICAP Liberté III neighborhood one afternoon in June 2007. My kind host, Atouma, was a thirtysomething native of the city who worked selling tires in a small shop owned by a Senegalese man living in Europe. Atouma and I had been introduced a few days earlier by a cab driver with whom we were both acquainted. Like many young men I met, he explained that he hoped to migrate abroad someday, and he was eager to take part in my research. As he led me to his family's home that afternoon, Atouma introduced me to various residents of the close-knit neighborhood—older women with sons and daughters living abroad, youth looking for ways to pass the time, village elders who had known Atouma's family for decades. Atouma's father, I learned as we walked, was a former police officer, and his family had acquired a simple one-story house in the neighborhood through an affordable housing program in the late 1950s. While many of the rather modest houses in the neighborhood were constructed during this initial building phase, several homes on each street were newer vertical constructions, which residents explained were made possible by remittance *transferts* sent by Senegalese migrants living abroad.

I was somewhat bewildered when we finally reached Atouma's family home, an uninhabitable five-story structure that dwarfed the older houses surrounding it. It was easy to see why he was proud to show me the ambitiously designed structure. Its elegant proportions, sinewy staircases, and unobstructed views of the tidy neighborhood were indeed impressive. What I found curious, however, was Atouma's initial profession that he had been "born" in this house, when the structure's raw walls and uneven cement floors betrayed its newness. There was no original foundation upon which

Figure 5. Houses under construction. Often funded by Senegalese living in
the diaspora, these ambitious structures are typically built
slowly, brick by brick, as money becomes available.

the family was building; the entire lot had been razed and the walls rebuilt
from scratch. It was evident that some time had passed since construction
had begun, as sand and debris had accumulated in the structure's interior
spaces and some of the supporting walls had gradually begun to erode from
exposure to the elements. When I asked Atouma when the house was likely
to be complete and ready for occupation, he seemed bemused by my question and shrugged, insisting that it was something that his family had never
explicitly discussed. His five brothers—who lived and worked in Europe,
the United States, and Gabon—were financing the project, he explained.
All five men had wives and children to support, and several were struggling
to keep up with their many commitments and expenses. While their family
home slowly materialized, Atouma and several other relatives lived with his
mother's sister a short walk away.

The unfinished structures and spaces I am describing here are neither
remarkable nor unusual but are instead *defining* features of Dakar's contemporary landscape. All across the city, large houses (*kër-yi*) in various stages
of construction stand as witnesses to and evidence of transnational movements of labor and capital. Frequently funded by diasporic Senegalese, these

ubiquitous structures lead many Dakarois to assume that everyone must be migrating. The urban houses migrants and their families design are undeniably inspired by time spent abroad: Mediterranean tiled roofs, "American kitchens,"[1] Parisian balconies, and Western-style bathtubs point to the origins of the capital used to build these homes. At the same time, these houses nearly always integrate a more African-style family gathering space, one that is either enclosed or open-air, as well as other definitively African exterior aesthetics (see Pellow 2003). Some transnational migrants buy lots that have not yet been developed or raze existing constructions to start from scratch, while others extend vertically on already existing properties, building what are called *étages*. Savings accounts and home loans are not very popular or accessible economic strategies for the majority of those who build.[2] Instead, fistfuls of cash sent via Western Union or passed by hand though transnational networks of migrants, merchants, and families are put directly into purchasing bricks, mortar, and window shutters. While some houses seem to near completion within just a year or two, many others linger for several years or even a decade, slowly eroding as families and hired contractors wait for money from abroad. Some constructions boast newly laid bricks or fresh paint, while others are obscured by overgrown vegetation and are overwhelmed by debris. These nascent houses are, in some ways, *turned inside out*: their insides are neither private nor contained, but rather spill into public spaces and onto city streets.[3] They are prone not only to the scorching sun and driving summer rains but also to intense social scrutiny, rumor, political debate, and vandalism. These structures have profound impacts not on hidden domestic relations or households, but on imaginations and experiences of the city as a shared and contested space.

At first glance, Dakar's inside-out houses seem to offer a powerful counterpoint to the large-scale infrastructural schemes I described in the previous chapter. Indeed, the cultural values and expectations that these houses express and generate—particularly those pertaining to home, continuity,

1. A *cuisine américaine* is an enclosed cooking space complete with a stove and oven, a refrigerator, a sink, and, oftentimes, enclosed cabinets.

2. Interest rates for home loans can easily reach or exceed 15 percent, two to three times available rates in the United States. For an excellent discussion of formal and informal savings and credit institutions in Senegal, see Kane 2002.

3. Gabriele Vom Bruck (1997) similarly described the houses she studied in Yemen as "inside-out," though I had not come across this article prior to my own usage of the term (Melly 2010). Bruck's piece is particularly attentive to the ways that private and public are blurred within the spaces of the house. I make a similar argument, but I also seek to turn "inside-out" assumptions about the house, migration, and belonging in much broader ways, as I demonstrate in this chapter.

and family—are sometimes remarkably incongruent with those that the state and its allies in governance seek to cultivate through road construction and renovation. At the same time, however, inside-out houses and state-sponsored infrastructural projects transformed the city's landscape in ways that were quite complementary. These projects collectively affirmed construction and global mobility as important means of being, belonging, and governing in contemporary Dakar even as they are themselves mired in *embouteillage*—caught between the deep uncertainties of the present moment and fantastic expectations of mobile futures. Though they appeared at first glance to be stalled, empty, or eroded, these housing structures made visible and possible vibrant urban economies, unforeseen social and political opportunities, and new patterns of settlement and claims to belonging. By centralizing the city's "bottlenecked" houses as normative and productive features of the urban landscape, I seek to turn conventional anthropological understandings of migration and belonging inside out so as to capture the complexities and paradoxes of inhabiting contemporary Dakar.

The Migrant-Built House in Historical Context

The contemporary concrete house in Dakar has a complex history, one that speaks to the shifting relationship between the postcolonial state and its urban residents. During colonialism, so-called African quarters were spatially segregated from the "European" sections of the city, including Plateau, the administrative and financial center of Dakar inhabited by French colonial officials, their families, and other elites. The architecture of contemporary Plateau, which still houses the city's elite,[4] is testament to its colonial heritage; the grand villas with *étages* (additional stories or floors) and administrative buildings built by the French still remain in various states of preservation and decay. The Africans, in contrast, lived on the city's margins, just close enough to be able to supply labor to the European district, in homes dismissed by the colonial state as impermanent and insalubrious (Ndione and Soumaré 1983; see also Betts 1971).

In the late 1950s, just prior to independence, rapid urbanization and fears of outbreaks of disease in these African districts prompted colonial government officials to institute programs aimed at relocation and "sanitation" (see Betts 1971). OHLM (Office des Habitations à Loyer Modéré) and

---

4. Plateau residents today are largely expatriates, wealthy Lebanese business owners and doctors, and elite Senegalese who can afford the high rents and tend to live in more nuclear family-type arrangements.

SICAP (Société Immobilière du Cap-Vert) thus emerged. These public housing initiatives aimed at providing affordable housing to selected Dakarois with moderate incomes, particularly to state functionaries and their families. It was through one of these late colonial–era initiatives that Atouma's father first acquired their family home. After independence, SICAP and OHLM gained momentum, and their modernizing missions expanded. Urban and national leaders were particularly interested in experimenting with styles of community-making that broke with the French grid system, drawing in particular on Scandinavian notions of the modern suburb (Bugnicourt 1983). These homes were relatively modest and small, with little room for extended family or visitors from the village, reflecting socialist ideals and Western notions of family. The land on which these dwellings were built was not private but was owned by the state.

While some residents received assistance from the state in making permanent homes in the city, however, scores of people who were settled in sections targeted for development were uprooted and relocated to peripheral areas, both on peninsular Dakar (as was the case in Grand Yoff, for instance) and on "mainland" Senegal (such as in Pikine), to make room for new construction.[5] These urban and peri-urban spaces have very unique and complex histories of settlement and land use that cannot be explicated in great detail here. What is of central importance to our purposes here is the intimate involvement of the postcolonial state in the production of the concrete urban "house" as a particular urban form and a claim of access to urban space and a privilege that was available to some and not others. Those who were resettled were forced to continue to live in impermanent situations where there was no guarantee that they would not be removed by the state again (Tall 1994). "Irregular" settlements quickly expanded. Residents in these unauthorized zones had no access to urban infrastructural benefits, such as potable water and electricity, and their participation in markets and urban exchanges was made more difficult by their peripheral situation (Ndione and Soumaré 1983; see also Simone 2004a). These policies and movements thus index a particular relationship between the postcolonial state and elite citizens, one that combined reconfigured colonial institutions with socialist notions of state intervention and that produced particular patterns of unequal access, ownership, and social permanence.

5. In contemporary Dakar, resettlement programs continue, especially as a means to facilitate the construction of the Autoroute de l'Avenir, a project I discussed in greater detail in chapters 1 and 2.

At the same time, pockets of privately owned land existed in Dakar from the time of colonialism. In the 1970s, some Lebu inhabitants and others who had acquired land through sale or favors began to sell their holdings,[6] encouraging intense real estate speculation and creating "a class of private real estate promoters" (Ndione and Soumaré 1983,113). This situation of land speculation was exacerbated by experiments like the Improved Parcels of Land project. In 1971–1972, the state partnered with World Bank to create Parcelles Assainies[7] (often simply called "Parcelles"), a new approach to affordable housing that offered land ownership at the margins of the city to lower-income urban residents (Tall 1994). World Bank and other governing bodies promoted private land ownership as a crucial component of a stable democracy and a liberalized economy founded on individual responsibility and enterprise. Some of Parcelles' residents, in turn, sold their land, contributing to the speculation already underway in places like Yoff and Grand Yoff and further expanding the emergent distinction between contingent practices of dwelling and much more permanent claims to ownership.

By the 1980s, as structural adjustment policies gathered momentum, there emerged a more intense and deliberate move to privatize and "regularize" land in Dakar. While rural lands continued to be administered through village authorities, the Ministry for Urbanism was charged with controlling the sale and purchase of *terrains* (plots of land) within the city.[8] SICAP became a "privatized" real estate company, though the state was considered a major stakeholder. Habitation à Loyer Modéré, or HLM (as the actual housing sections are called), SICAP, and Parcelles Assainies came to simply refer to particular geographic sections of the city, and the complex state–citizen relationships that they once described were obscured with time. These gradual shifts coincided with intense urbanization, as structural adjustment policies removed subsidies and other government support for agricultural production, prompting rural dwellers from across the region to seek employment opportunities in cities like Dakar. What resulted was a burgeoning urban population with few job prospects, inadequate economic resources, limited access to critical infrastructures, and dwindling options for affordable housing.

6. The Lebu are acknowledged as the original inhabitants of Yoff and Dakar more generally. They are an ethnic group considered to be closely related to the Wolof, the linguistically and politically dominant ethnic group in contemporary Senegal.

7. "Improved Parcels of Land" is the translation offered by Bop (1983). In fact, the French verb *assainir* also means "to clean up," or "to disinfect."

8. Land can, in some instances, still be obtained by going through *chefs* of the neighborhood, who then deal with the Ministry of Urbanism.

It is into this growing gap that transnational migrants—like Atouma's brothers—have inserted themselves over the past several decades, providing for the urgent material needs of the families and communities they leave behind and transforming Dakar's physical and social landscape in the process. Parcelles Assainies, for instance, has evolved over the past decade and a half from a low-income housing experiment into a densely populated neighborhood that, in the words of one of my interlocutors, "would not exist without the diaspora." The intense population growth in this section and others has been fueled in large part by the settlement of transnational migrants' families from other parts of Dakar and from rural areas, but also by the more affordable housing options these constructions provide to newcomers, many of whom come to the city with the hopes of earning money and migrating abroad.[9] Across the city, diasporic Senegalese build houses for themselves and their families, but they also finance villas and complexes to rent for a profit. They run import-export businesses that bring luxury materials like Italian marble and European hardwoods into Senegalese markets. They own construction companies, home furnishing outlets, and equipment rental companies. These varied investments speak to transnational migrants' deep attachments to family, community, and "home," and they underscore the relative vitality of the housing construction sector and its perceived status as a "safe" investment amidst economic uncertainty. But these investments also index a critical shift in the relationship between state and citizen in Dakar. Urban residents with whom I spoke often perceived migrant-built houses as evidence that the state had turned its back on the majority of its population, leaving individuals and families to fend for themselves. State resources and energies, they argued, were funneled instead into the high-speed highways, grand monuments, and spaces of elite consumption that I examine in chapter 1.

In contrast, government officials often decried migrant-built urban villas as exceedingly lavish, wasteful, and even selfish. Bureaucrats insisted during interviews that these projects diverted money from "productive" and "lasting" development initiatives. APIX administrators worked to find ways to

9. Writing in the mid-1990s, Tall (1994) argued that constructing houses in this neighborhood offered migrants a degree of prestige, but my own research a decade later suggested that the neighborhood's status has begun to fade as the area has become more populated. Instead, my interlocutors often explained that Parcelles offered more affordable land than in other parts of Dakar and yet was still in close proximity to economic opportunities. In nicer sections of Yoff today, land is sold at about 120,000 FCFA (roughly US$240) per square meter, while land in Parcelles averages 20,000–25,000 FCFA (roughly US$40–$50) per square meter. Ten years ago in this same area of Yoff, land was priced at about 20,000 FCFA per square meter; the cost of land is roughly *six times* what it was a decade ago.

"rechannel" migrant-earned capital away from the housing sector and into investment projects like those I discuss in the following chapter. In a 2007 address, President Wade went so far as to blame the country's clandestine migration "crisis" on the social pressure—exerted, in particular, he claimed, by *mothers*—to "construct a beautiful house" (quoted in Bouilly 2008, 16). At the same time, however, many of these same officials acknowledged that transnational migrants fill gaps in housing that the structurally adjusted state is simply unable to address. Moreover, these construction projects have spurred a paradoxical ideological and economic *reinvestment* of the Senegalese state in the Dakar's housing sector. During the time of my research, for instance, the ministry that oversees urban housing construction (Ministère du Patrimoine Bâti, de l'Habitat, et de la Construction) partnered with four other state offices, dozens of private sector companies and banks, and five different Spain-based Senegalese migrant associations to run a series of international housing fairs (Salon de l'Habitat du Sénégal) to encourage the Senegalese diaspora in Spain to invest in houses in Dakar. One employee of the ministry stressed to me that these kinds of housing construction projects offered the state an opportunity to serve as an intermediary between citizens and the private sector, which he saw as a key element to economic growth. Through this reconfigured role, then, the state has the potential to achieve public visibility and reassert its relevance as a critical urban actor.

When put into historical context, the migrant-built house emerges, then, as a conspicuous and contested sign of the fraught relationship between state and citizen in contemporary Dakar. It is a historically and culturally meaningful statement of one's desire and capacity to provide for households and communities, to stake claim to and shape city spaces and resources, and to articulate visions of the future. By building a house, the transnational migrant positions himself as a crucial urban agent whose productive absence sustains and transforms the faltering capital city. There is much more to the story of the migrant-built house, however. As the introduction to this chapter makes clear, many of the houses that transnational migrants and their families build remain unfinished for long periods of time, slowly eroding as they rise. How do we make sense of these very particular material and ideological realities? And how do these complex aesthetics come to shape urban livelihoods and expectations?

The Aesthetics of the Inside-Out House

Unfinished, unruly, and often uninhabited, the inside-out house appears at first glance a rather uncomplicated failure of both form and function. Indeed, a good deal of the scholarly literature on the house would suggest just that. For most who write on the topic, the house is primarily a dwelling—an assemblage of spaces, structures, practices, and beliefs aimed at sheltering and nurturing those living within its walls. Inspired by and departing from Lévi-Strauss's (1982, 1987) and Bourdieu's (1970) considerations of the house as a dynamic, lived structure and space, there have emerged dozens of articles and edited volumes.[10] What these diverse works generally share in common is a committed focus on the interior spaces and intimate relations that come to shape and define the house. Even in their focus on growth, change, lived practice, and blurred boundaries, contemporary scholarship on the house tends to focus too rigidly on realized dwellings and household practice. Howell, for instance, suggests that the house is an appealing analytic concept precisely because it *resists deconstruction*, thus enabling the ethnographer to "avoid the pitfalls of definitions, and, hence, engage in more meaningful comparative research" (2003, 32). In a particularly noteworthy volume, Miller (2001) attends to the materiality of houses and to their power as cultural forces, but his attention is focused quite intently on lives lived "behind closed doors" of these houses. Heidegger (1971) further argues that dwelling is made possible by building, and that building necessarily has dwelling as its end goal. These perspectives have little to offer an analysis of Dakar's houses in process. Are these emergent constructions thus without meaning or specificity, since so many are unoccupied? Is it only through dwelling that the house becomes socially significant? What happens when the "house" is not an easy category or contained dwelling, but rather a blurring of present circumstances and future possibilities?

Scholars of transnational migration have shown particular interest in houses as material and ideological structures. Migrants frequently build at "home" in their natal villages as a means to resume historical and personal connections, but they do so in ways that also call attention to their

10. Lévi-Strauss famously developed the term "house societies" (1982). He theorized the house as an analytic poised to reinvigorate discussions of social structure and relatedness, which he saw as too frequently "haunted by the idea of descent" (1987, 165). McKinnon notes a productive tension in Lévi-Strauss's formulations of the house, which is at once characterized by "permanence, hardness, and immobility" even as it is a "living, moving, growing body" (2000, 163)—a tension one likewise notes in the housing landscapes of Dakar. Bourdieu's (1970) study of Kabyle houses is likewise a careful and detailed study of house spaces and structures among this Berber group. He argues that it is through daily practice of men and women that the meanings of the house come into being. These theorists' work has served as the point of departure for a generation of scholars, many of whom break with structuralist modes of theorizing the house. These include Waterson (1990), Keane (1995), Carsten and Hugh-Jones (1995), Fehérváry (2011), Robben (1989).

transnational privilege and experiences, particularly through architectural design and imported materials (Thomas 1998; Van Der Geest 1998). In other instances, they build homes in emergent areas and unfamiliar cities, thus profoundly reshaping and asserting their attachments with "home" while creating new places and forms of belonging (Buggenhagen 2001; Pellow 2003; Leinaweaver 2009). Echoing many of the assumptions described above, this rich literature tends to conceptualize houses as dwellings—as places that contain domestic relations and engender households. In this formulation, the house's (assumedly habitable) interior spaces and relations become the natural starting point for an examination of transnational migration. These works carefully analyze the motivations and desires of migrant builders and their families while paying far less attention to the ways that nonmigrant publics engage with these structures and practices. These accounts are less attentive to the public life of these artifacts, and as a result sometimes gloss over the ways in which these houses transform and are transformed by nonmigrant livelihoods, spaces, and expectations on a much broader scale. In doing so, the literature on the migrant-built house tends to reaffirm that migrants and their families are the central actors in these transnational processes and that it is their identities and claims to "home" that are most threatened by mobility.

The houses that are the focus of this chapter, in contrast, were not stable objects, concepts, or facts.[11] They were instead *defined* by their material and ideological instability; they were caught up in a relentless cycle of construction and deconstruction. Dakar's inside-out houses were produced by *embouteillage*: They came into being when builders' future-focused plans were relentlessly unraveled by the urgencies of everyday obligations and debts, volatile economic conditions in Senegal and abroad, a lack of credit opportunities, the rising cost of land and construction,[12] and the ambitiousness

---

11. Telle (2007) similarly argues that Sasak houses are unpredictable and unruly. However, in contrast to my own study, she focuses on the ways that those dwelling within the house negotiate and live within this volatile space.

12. There are various factors influencing the skyrocketing cost of land in Dakar, including Wade's ambitious and cosmopolitan infrastructure projects, ongoing urbanization and population growth, more thorough land privatization efforts, and ongoing political instability throughout West Africa, which has led to an influx of people and capital from throughout the region. The 2002 coup d'état in Côte d'Ivoire had particularly acute effects on Dakar. Violence and instability forced many Ivoiriens to flee to Senegal and also encouraged the rerouting of huge sums of capital from Abidjan to Dakar. Because the purchase of land is open to anyone, regardless of residency status or nationality, many wealthier Ivoiriens thus have invested in real estate in Dakar, further contributing to problems of land speculation and inflated rents. More-

of their expectations and designs—indeed, by the very same factors that frequently impel transnational migrants to leave and to build in the first place. In this sense, the city's inside-out houses bear a striking resemblance to the pirated videos that have occupied Brian Larkin's (2008) attention. In Nigeria, Larkin argues, economic uncertainty, techniques of replication, and the realities of technological breakdown produced videos with distorted images and poor quality sounds. Like Dakar's inside-out houses, these de-graded images were not anomalies but instead were unremarkable features of Nigeria's media landscape. It was thus not in spite of the material state of these films but *through* them that "modernity" came to be concretized, understood, and lived for Nigerians. It was not so much the content of the film—which is of little interest to Larkin in this particular piece—but rather the *form itself* that gave shape to African conceptions of the modern. These films did not offer a secondhand, damaged, or failed vision of some fully formed, ostensibly Western modernity—for those who consumed and cir-culated these films, this *was* modernity.

Likewise, in Dakar, urbanites often acknowledged that building efforts and material structures were shaped and constrained by conditions of chronic urban and global uncertainty, but they nonetheless did not tend to cast these projects and structures as failures of an ideal form—whether that form be a finished house, a modern city life, or a neoliberal "investment."[13] In fact, as my encounter with Atouma helps illustrate, my stubborn focus on the "completed" house seemed wildly out of sync with residents' own experiences and concerns. Urbanites instead emphasized the importance of building (*tabax*) itself as a potent and enduring means of engagement with the city, its spaces, and its possibilities. Whereas dwelling in the city referenced a day-to-day relationship with an assumedly already-built (or at least habitable) structure, building involved ongoing collaboration with a constellation of actors, materials, expectations, designs, streams of capital, expert knowledges, and physical spaces. More specifically, from the perspec-

over, many NGOs and IOs have relocated from Abidjan to Dakar over the past decade. This has brought more expatriate workers to the city and has also undoubtedly spurred price increases and real estate speculation.

13. My findings here both echo and diverge from those offered by Buggenhagen, who writes of Senegal's unfinished houses as a sign of "the projected prosperity of a globalizing economy and to the subsequent foreclosure of an array of intended social projects. The unfinished villas and the incomplete neighborhoods they form are iconic of the incomplete and often failed processes of social production that exist in a dialectical relation to global economic processes" (2001, 378).

tive of most urbanites, to build in Dakar testified to a family's productive and enduring relationship with the diaspora. Urban residents would frequently point to unfinished *étages*, for instance, as seemingly indisputable evidence of continued transnational ties. It was thus through building that the abstractions and invisibilities of transnational migration were made present, tangible, and measurable to those who did not migrate abroad and that transnational migration was produced as a transformative way of being urban. In contrast to much of the literature on the topic, I contend that transnational migrants and their families were not the only or central actors in house-making; in fact, they sometimes had little control over the process and the structures it produced. Their products, moreover, were not always "dwellings" in the strict sense of the word. Instead, the inside-out houses were hyperpublic territories inhabited not by individuals or families but by the *city itself*. These structures thus indexed the insufficiency of dwelling itself as a mode of being; by engaging in continual construction projects, urban residents make important future-focused claims on the city.

The ubiquity and unruliness of the inside-out house cemented, in turn, a very particular cultural aesthetic in Dakar. Building was a temporally complex process that defied linear narratives of progress and development (Ferguson 1999). It was not defined in opposition to decay, reversal, or dispersion but rather incorporated these processes.[14] In Dakar, these temporal complexities brought about a very particular, culturally situated urban artifact, then, one that was materially unstable, always on the verge of becoming, shifting, collapsing, mutating, and unraveling. Yet although this urban aesthetic was shaped by conditions of chronic uncertainty, it was certainly not reducible to them. Even residents who lived in seemingly "completed" houses spoke of their construction efforts as ongoing. Indeed, as several key interviews in this chapter suggest, urbanites seemed to take great pleasure in the unruliness of construction sites—in staircases that led nowhere, in raw walls left exposed to the elements, in plans too grand to be realized in the present tense—and focused little on the aspects of functionality I had assumed to be most important. The sections that follow consider the ways in which this inside-out aesthetic shapes much broader ideas about urban life, mobility, and possibility.

14. Nielsen similarly argues from the perspective of Mozambique that "house-builders living on the fringes of Maputo 'make a life' (*kusama utomi*) by building cement houses which might never fully be realized" (2011, 416). These houses enable "reversible times" that help urbanites find social stability amidst uncertainty.

Generating Families and Fortunes

A couple of months before I met Atouma, I toured a sprawling construction site in an elite section of the city called Ngor. Ousmane, the builder of the home, was a middle-aged man of Lebu descent who had worked as a laborer in France for over a decade and had recently moved back to Dakar to begin his own housing constructing company. He had laid the foundation for his own family villa nearly three years before our conversation, he explained, and continued to add to the structure as money and labor became available. As with Atouma's family home, however, it was evident that no new work had taken place for quite some time. The highlight of the tour was a grand sculptural staircase that reached toward the blue sky above us. When I asked Ousmane where this staircase would lead, he became wildly excited. The new *étage*, he explained, would be built for his future second wife and for the children they would have; perhaps he would even build enough bedrooms to take a third wife. Although he only had one wife at present, he assured me that the elaborate plans he had for the second floor of his villa would make this future family a certainty.[15]

As this narrative suggests, building in Dakar is a complexly gendered act, one that solidifies and shapes relations between men and women. While women have historically been less likely to migrate and build, this is quickly changing (Babou 2002; Ba 2008), particularly among divorced or widowed women who seek independence or to make a place for themselves in the capital city (Buggenhagen 2012). The two women I met who were engaged directly in building projects were both divorcées, and both were seen as powerful but rather controversial figures in their neighborhoods. These women remained exceptional, at least in the eyes of the public, and they were generally seen as engaged in masculine domains of urban life. Indeed, in popular discourse, houses are generally considered to be objects built by men for women and families. Migrants living abroad send capital for construction projects in Dakar to brothers or business associates in the city, and these men are responsible for decision-making and site visits in the absence

---

15. As I noted in chapter 1, polygyny is common in Senegal. Men customarily offer a bride-price arrangement to the woman and her family. Houses are a particularly desired form of this arrangement. In addition, husbands and wives most often retain separate finances. Men are responsible for providing a living arrangement, either through the construction of a house or the payment of rent. While some wives maintain separate residences, others share a single compound or villa.

of the migrant. Male teams of laborers carry out the project, typically under male leadership. The finished home, on the other hand, is considered to be the female domain, as are the patterns of accumulation, domestic budgeting, and dwelling that take place within these enclosed spaces (see Buggenhagen 2001). Villas frequently bear names like "Kër Astou" (The House of Astou),[16] signaling the profoundly gendered nature of the spaces the builders produce. While these homes can and do generate credit for women's trading activities and conspicuous consumption practices, the prestige created by building (*tabax*) itself is often only indirectly available to women in Dakar.

Moreover, as Ousmane's and Atouma's narratives of home construction demonstrate in strikingly different ways, the inside-out house was thought to bring about family. Both men insisted on the house itself as the origin point in their family narratives. Indeed, many Dakarois lamented that they could not marry for the first time or with additional wives because they were unable to build a house.[17] To become head of household (*borom kër-gi*), a man must not only marry but also establish a home apart from his father (Buggenhagen 2001, 382). Seydou, a thirtysomething-year-old taxi driver, told me about how he had paid 500,000 FCFA (US$1,000) to board a pirogue headed to the Canary Islands, desperate to find work in Europe. His attempt failed, but he insisted that he would try again. He tried to explain to me why he had risked so much to go abroad:

> Women today demand millions of CFA [thousands of dollars] and a house before they will consider marriage. They say it's hard abroad. But no matter how hard it is, *immigrés*[18] are still able to manage. If you work abroad, you can have a house [*gagner une maison*]. You can build. *Immigrés* don't have to rent.

Seydou's assertion typifies the assumption among many urban men that marriage is increasingly reserved for those who are able to migrate and, as

---

16. Astou is a common female name in Senegal.

17. As I discussed in chapter 2, Senegalese have typically sought to marry young, but the economic pressures involved with marriage payments, everyday household expenses, debts, ceremonies, and having children, especially in Dakar, have meant that many urban men remain single well into adulthood. This is increasingly the case for women, too, who delay marriage to pursue education or career opportunities or who bemoan the lack of marriageable candidates.

18. My informants sometimes used the term *immigré*—or immigrant—to refer both to those who migrated *from* Senegal and those who migrated *to* Senegal. In collapsing immigration and emigration together, these urbanites effectively drew attention to mobility *itself* as a critical means of being, de-emphasizing the importance of the direction of one's movements.

an implicit corollary, build a house. Bocar, a Toucouleur man native to Dakar who had a wife and three children, echoed Seydou's sentiments. Bocar had only left Senegal twice, both times as a hopeful clandestine migrant. Though he had close friends who had died trying to reach Europe, he was eager to try again nonetheless. "How can I think of staying? There are no jobs, and everything costs so much. Life in Senegal is expensive. And renting is not living . . . It is not good for my family to live like this." Bocar was certain that the welfare and security of his family was being threatened by their need to rent. Although he was native to Dakar, he still saw his presence in the city as contingent and precarious, and he actively sought avenues abroad so that he could make deeper roots in the city.

In contrast to Bocar and Seydou, Ousmane set his sights on and channeled his resources toward an anticipated, if improbable, future. These temporalities were not available to the majority of Dakar's residents, who found it increasingly difficult to make ends meet on a day-to-day basis. The taxi drivers I interviewed and worked with daily were among the most vocal about this. None of those with whom I spoke owned or were building a home in Dakar; most lived day to day, struggling to make ends meet, to provide for large households with few working members, and to repay debts. Those who were married rented tiny apartments for their families or lived alone in the city while their wife or wives and children remained in the village. Many of these men, however, were unmarried and lived with their parents (if they were from Dakar) or rented a small room on the city's periphery that they often shared with other single men. For the vast majority of urbanites, life in the city was focused squarely on channeling resources and attention toward urgent everyday expenses.

Building a home also signals an important break with "remittance" practices and an interest in "investment" on the part of the diaspora.[19] Remittances are imagined, in most cases, to provide basic necessities and sustain a household on a day-to-day basis. In Senegal, a migrant often sends sums of money, perhaps monthly, to his wife, mother, or even his sister to take care of the family's daily needs for food, rent, schooling, and clothing. On the contrary, my research showed, a migrant who seeks to construct a house in the capital city of Dakar often relies on the help of his brother, his friend, or a business associate or contractor who receives the money and puts it to use. Thus, money sent for housing construction is separated from money sent for the household and signals participation in entrepreneurial activity.

---

19. Many people in fact would use the French term *investissement* to refer to houses.

The distinction between investment and remittance is also to some degree a geographical one. In contrast to "the village," where life is imagined to be arduous and luxuries are few, Dakar is often experienced as a space of relative excess and indulgence. While a house in the village is seen as a necessity, constructions in Dakar are described as ostentatious and costly. One builds in a village for the benefit of one's family or because one was born there; in Dakar, people are not always constructing for their families, nor are they necessarily native to Dakar.[20] Migrants and families who choose to build in the capital city are particularly interested in the potential for economic belonging and profit that such projects provide.

These conceptions of investment and future possibility are illustrated well by the experiences of Mansour, a middle-aged man from a village in southern Senegal who had worked for two years in Saudi Arabia and now owned a home furnishings store in Yoff. He chatted with me at length about his investments: his shop, called *Confort Mondial* (World Comfort), which sold imported living room sets and bedroom furniture and catered specifically to transnational migrants constructing in Dakar; and the two houses he had built, one in a neighborhood of SICAP, another in a section called Ouest Foire. Neither was finished—Mansour described in great detail the additions, changes, and finishing touches he planned—but both were habitable. Surprisingly, however, when I asked which of these emergent houses he and his family lived in, he responded that they lived in neither. He rented the houses out to other families for a profit, and he and his family rented a much more modest apartment in another section of the city. He said that they would likely move into one of these houses in the future, once he had exploited them as rental properties. Mansour's curious revelation again unhinges the practices of building and dwelling, drawing our attention instead to the temporal deferment migrant-built houses both reflect and produce.

Claims to have been "born" in houses not yet suitable for living, open-ended plans for building, aging walls without roofs, families contingent on future *étages*—these narratives and artifacts offer a glimpse not of abandoned projects or goals left unaccomplished, but of what *could be*; they foreground latent possibilities and future articulations while obscuring present impossibilities. How do these structures come to life in urban Dakar, then, and how do nonmigrants interact with and live amongst these imposing

20. This may account for some of the discrepancies I found between building practices in Dakar and the construction practices that Buggenhagen (2004) describes in Senegal's holy city of Touba.

signs of urban belonging? If building is a public action that opens up possibilities, reconfigures temporalities, refashions the city space, and enables urban belonging, where does this leave those who cannot build?

Belonging Turned Inside Out

Beneath the surface of Atouma's bubbling pride in his family's emergent home there lurked deep concerns about his personal future. As we chatted in the cool interior of his mother's sister's home later that afternoon, Atouma lamented that he was the only son who had not married, the only son who had not migrated, and the only son who was not constructing a house. Though he "feared the seas" and did not want to board a pirogue for a risky clandestine voyage, he also was emphatic that he could not stay in Dakar for much longer. He currently worked selling tires in the city's Medina section, in a small shop owned by a Senegalese man who spent the majority of the year living in Europe, and he felt unfulfilled and uncertain. He spoke regretfully about his meager economic resources and his inability to marry, adding wistfully, "How much longer can I live in the house that my brothers are building?"

Atouma's anxieties surfaced in a very particular context, one in which claims to the city and its resources have become increasingly contentious. In contemporary Dakar, chronic economic and social uncertainty exists alongside hyperpublic celebration of global mobility, elite consumption, and foreign investment. The city, long a crossroads for the global transit of capital, goods, people, and knowledge, has itself become bottlenecked, as various kinds of flows are constrained, rerouted, or halted in the wake of global and local political and economic shifts. Urbanites like Atouma find themselves "stuck," unable to move on as anticipated. They describe and inhabit a city that is both increasingly expensive and exclusionary. In this charged context, debates about the contours of urban belonging have flourished. Africanist scholars have noted a pronounced preoccupation with origins, particularly in expanding urban centers, and have suggested that in the kinds of volatile and profoundly "globalized" circumstances I am describing here, conceptions of rights are increasingly founded on claims to autochthony (Nyamnjoh 2006; Geschiere 1997; see also Comaroff and Comaroff 2001). This has likewise been the case in Dakar, as I discuss briefly in the introduction. But these contests over origins and newness exist in remarkable tension with quite contradictory assumptions that one must in fact *migrate abroad* to be fully present in contemporary Dakar. Indeed, surrounded by rising homes and the incessant sounds of construction, the urbanites with whom I worked and lived were more inclined to frame urban membership in terms

of their future prospects than in terms of histories of occupation, ownership, or ethnic belonging.

Atouma was relatively privileged, compared to many urbanites I met,
and his family's deep ties both to the city and the diaspora should have
assured his long-term residence in the capital city. Yet he expressed deep
concerns about his future prospects, namely about his own ability to build.
Atouma's pleading question—*How much longer can I live in the house that
my brothers are building?*—was echoed by countless other urban men during
the course of my years in Dakar. These pervasive anxieties about migration,
building, and belonging are inextricably linked to conceptualizations of effective male presence in a structurally adjusted Dakar, as I have described in
previous chapters. In centralizing these narratives and claims, our scholarly
assumptions about the relationship between transnational migration and
belonging are turned inside out: in an era when transnational mobility and
investment are celebrated, in a city assumed to be built and sustained by the
diaspora, it is perhaps the nonmigrant whose future presence in the city is
most precarious. From this perspective, the city's unfinished houses are not
simply straightforward statements about absent migrants' enduring connections with "home" and their professed desires to eventually return. These
volatile and ubiquitous structures and spaces help produce the transnational
migrant as singularly present. When we turn the migrant-belonging para-
digm inside out, then, what is revealed is a much more complexly layered
patterning of belonging and access that is contingent, above all, on one's relationship to and involvement in transnational migration processes.

Despite their perceived exclusion from urban belonging according to
these standards, however, city residents like Atouma play an integral role in
the production and policing of this form of belonging. Who was building,
how quickly, and with what money and materials was a popular topic of
discussion during the time of my fieldwork. City residents noted a direct
correlation between the rate at which one built and the type and viscosity of
the flow. If a project was nearing completion unusually quickly, neighbors
might whisper about the migrant's activities in Europe. Was he involved in
selling drugs or some other illicit activity? A close friend, who had recently
returned from Europe to live in the house he had built, often made reference to these emergent houses to demonstrate his point that many migrants
were involved in illicit activities abroad. "Even if they are eating only rice in
Paris," he once said, "there is no way that they could build such a grand villa
so quickly." At the same time, if the construction of a house took an inordinate amount of time, the builder was susceptible to scathing critique of his
spending habits abroad. Accusations of squandering (*gaspillage*) of money

on women, alcohol, or personal consumption were likely if a house sat for many years without a new layer of bricks. While many residents wanted to migrate for the explicit purpose of building a house, they nonetheless blamed these houses for the risks taken by hopeful migrants.

At the same time that nonmigrants described themselves as excluded from urban (and thus diasporic) belonging, they also continually carved out a space for future presence. Men with family members abroad insisted that they would join their brothers or friends in Europe and would build a house for their families. Others vowed they would find clandestine paths abroad. Many women, too, spoke of seeking educational opportunities or employment abroad, as a couple of their female friends had done. Others described their preference for finding husbands who worked abroad, as they gained economic credit and social prestige through their husbands' projects and expenditures. Regardless of their financial circumstances or contingent presence in the city, my male and female interlocutors often imagined a different future, one that would give them access to spaces and resources not available at present. In doing so, they cast urban belonging as a process, an ongoing, shifting, and complex relationship to transnational mobilities of labor and capital.

New Urbanities and Precarious Possibilities

The proliferation of the city's inside-out houses also opened up much more concrete opportunities for urban belonging. In 2007, I lived in a seaside neighborhood in Yoff that was being steadily transformed by ambitious housing construction projects. The particular area in which I rented is located just across from the international airport and was home to mostly well-to-do transnational families (many of whom have lived or still do live abroad), expatriates, government ministers, and prosperous Senegalese merchant families. Yoff more generally was not as densely populated as other sections of the city, though construction was intense and, in many cases, rapid. Transnational migrants were lured to build in the area because it was less congested, boasted spectacular ocean views, and offered both privacy and prestige. Some of the neighborhood's finished houses remained vacant most of the year; the Senegalese who invested in building them, the majority of whom were transnational migrants,[21] typically preferred to rent to

---

21. A real estate agency representative who managed properties in Yoff surmised that 85–95 percent of the people looking to rent out houses or apartments in Senegal had made the capital for the project abroad. She said that their agency typically arranges rent payments with a family member or business associate in Senegal.

Figure 6. Clothes are hung to dry along the walls of an unfinished house. Urban residents see these clothes as a sign that squatters, typically from rural Senegal, are occupying the property.

expatriates and often sought upward of 1,000,000 FCFA (US$2,000) per month in rent. But the quarter's ambitious construction projects have also enabled new patterns of residence and new claims to urban presence. Newcomers hailing from Senegal's agricultural hinterlands, devastated by prolonged economic crisis and ecological ruin, found work laboring at construction sites, transporting materials in the city, or working as security guards for finished villas. Many of these men lived in makeshift homes in the shadow of the houses they construct, sometimes without electricity or running water; others found apartments on the city's fringes. The city's inside-out houses also required and enabled an otherwise socially invisible staff of rural workers, many of whom were given a small payment (or were able to squat for free) in exchange for their work building, guarding, or tending to otherwise vacant properties. Many of these villagers were Serer, an ethnic group concentrated in rural areas in west-central Senegal and in the Sine-Saloum delta region, and most were poor, even by Senegalese standards. In the small corner of Yoff where I lived, Serer was spoken with remarkable regularity, a rather astonishing fact considering that interactions in Dakar's public spaces tend to take place almost exclusively in Wolof or French. These new urbanites sometimes brought their families to live with them. Their wives frequently took advantage of their position in the city and supplemented the family's income by finding small jobs. These men and women inserted themselves into vibrant urban economies and networks with the hope of developing deeper roots in the city that would enable them to stay after the construction projects have ended.

Youssoupha was one of these new urbanites. He was a middle-aged Serer man from the Sine-Saloum region of Senegal who had come to work as a *gardien* in Yoff. Prior to his recent move to Dakar, Youssoupha had never left the rural region in which he was born, and his new city life was still confined to a small corner of Dakar. He was responsible for looking after a sprawling property that was rented to expatriates by a Senegalese woman living in Paris. He lived in the garage of the villa, slept on a small second-hand sofa, and cooked rice on a portable gas stove. He made the equivalent of US$100 each month, an enticing sum for a *villageois* who had arrived with very little, but an amount that proved quite inadequate in the city. As the property's only *gardien*, Youssoupha was expected to remain on site around the clock, seven days a week, and he rarely strayed more than a few blocks from his home. This, however, did not prevent him from establishing an impressive social network that spanned the neighborhood. A self-described "entrepreneur," Youssoupha found innovative ways to supplement his small salary by running errands, bartering and selling his possessions, and "meeting the right people," as he often described it. He engaged in relations of debt that, in turn, produced particular kinds of future-focused social possibilities (Roitman 2003). In the seven months that I knew him, he quickly learned conversational French, a strategic move that, he explained, would offer him other opportunities. His professed goal was to find work as a chauffeur for a wealthy embassy worker or expatriate businessman in the neighborhood. He was certain that, after he gained the respect and trust of his foreign employer, he would be invited to work in Europe or the United States. Soon after, he repeatedly explained, he would begin to build two houses: one in Fatick for his ailing mother, and one in Dakar like the one in which he worked.

Ramatoulaye, also a Serer *villageoise*, was one of Youssoupha's many acquaintances in our seaside neighborhood. She was likewise new to the city and in search of work. She and her three young children had settled on a small parcel of land that had been cleared to accommodate a half-built house. This construction project, settled on a prime piece of real estate, was in its infancy, and its roofless walls provided little protection for its caretakers. Instead, the foursome lived in a makeshift house made of discarded wood propped against the larger concrete structure. In the shadow of many elite residences, some of which had swimming pools, backup generators, and security gates, Ramatoulaye and her children went about their days without electricity, running water, or privacy. The family's intimate moments were lived in public: apart from sleeping, they spent little time in the cramped house itself. Instead, bathing, cooking, arguing, crying, praying—these became spectacles consumed by neighbors, day laborers, and passersby. Unlike Youssoupha, Ramatoulaye had no formal monthly salary on which to depend. Instead, she made ends meet by cooking, washing laundry, or doing odd jobs in the neighborhood. She earned small amounts of cash or bartered her services in return for goods that she needed—for used clothing or for vegetables, for instance. In the spring of 2007, a crew of men arrived to dig up the road in front of her house so that new underground sewage and water lines could be installed. During this period of construction, Ramatoulaye's house quickly became a hub of activity and a central node in a thriving local economy. Laborers, many of whom were themselves Serer, would often spend their breaks here, while Ramatoulaye prepared plates of rice and sauce, stewed on a portable gas stove, or *chere,* a Serer dish made of pounded millet.

This brief ethnographic consideration illuminates new spatial mappings that do not neatly mirror colonial approaches to spatial separation. In this small corner of Yoff, a historic fishing village, center and periphery are folded into each other. The relative wealth garnered through transnational migration fortifies elite neighborhoods and produces dramatic new exclusions and conceptions of urban belonging and effective presence that are detached from patterns of residence. At the same time, however, the dramatic instability of housing construction and its material forms offered new opportunities for urban dwelling, however precarious. In these new urban geographies, Youssoupha and Ramatoulaye found themselves to be both invisible and hypervisible. These newcomers and others like them inserted themselves into vital networks and claimed prime real estate, but their presence was always partial, contingent, and temporary. Shifts in housing construction or remittance flows, for instance, could threaten their continued stay in the city. In contrast, as Youssoupha and others explained, building a house could assure long-term presence in the city, and so these new urbanites fixed their attention on the future, always envisioning their current circumstances as temporary, as a means to a much more fantastic end. When I returned to Yoff in 2010 after a two-and-a-half-year absence, neither Ramatoulaye and her children nor Youssoupha were anywhere to be found. After chatting with other *gardiens* in the neighborhood, it was still unclear whether they had returned to the village or had moved onto other opportunities elsewhere in Dakar. Their unexplained absence underscores the volatility of urbanites' engagements not only with the inside-out houses that are transforming the city's landscape, but also with the city and the future much more generally.

A City Unsettled

Dakar's inside-out houses are neither exceptional nor aberrant. In so-called sending communities throughout the world, transnational migrants and their families engage in construction practices that shape the contours of communities and stake claim to home. The ethnographic details presented here underscore the need to unhinge "home" and "house," to consider the role that building, rather than just dwelling, plays in the construction of belonging as a process, as always on the horizon. Inside-out houses are the material evidence of *embouteillage*, produced by the collision of ambitious future visions and chronic everyday uncertainty. The aesthetics of these long-lingering projects—where insides and outsides are not well defined, where walls seem to fall as they climb—produce very particular ideas about how the transnational migration and "home" are articulated. Seen through this lens, Dakar appears for many urbanites to be a city of exclusion, where only those absent can truly belong through housing construction. The act of dwelling, in other words, is seen as insufficient grounds for making claims on the city, and so urban residents turn their attention toward and repeatedly emphasize their desires to *build*. These not-yet houses also demonstrate that belonging is a process that is both rooted in present circumstances and future possibilities, for at the same time that nonmigrants see themselves as excluded from full belonging in Dakar, they constantly foreground their future hopes to migrate and to build. And yet, new forms of belonging and new possibilities for urban engagement and enrichment also flourish in these bottlenecked spaces.

Dakar's inside-out houses and the broader economic and social landscape of which they are a part challenge scholars to reconsider the link between transnational migration and localized belonging.[22] These complex

22. Bernal (2014) offers an excellent consideration of the complex relationship between migration, nation, and citizenship in an era of transnational migration.

structures illuminate critical paradoxes about urban life and beg us to ask: in what ways are urban permanence and effective participation in places like contemporary Dakar increasingly contingent on leaving the city under construction? And what kind of city might these bottlenecks and dislocations produce? The next chapter moves into the city's bureaucratic offices to again consider these questions.

FOUR

The Adjusted State in the Meantime

In February of 2006, just as urban renewal projects were gathering momentum across the city, I made my way to the downtown headquarters of APIX, Senegal's national agency for the promotion of large-scale investment and public works projects. APIX was widely known to urban residents during the time of my research, largely because of the very visible role the quasi-state agency played in the construction of the Autoroute de l'Avenir. I had come, however, seeking information about a much more obscure project housed at the agency, one called the Entrepreneurial Diaspora program. During what was supposed to be a brief meeting, a senior official named El Hadji described to me APIX's efforts to design and install a financial infrastructure that would link Senegal to its vast diaspora through formalized channels of migrant-earned capital. He explained that the initiative would provide "diasporic entrepreneurs"—Senegalese living abroad who would invest at "home"—with a clear and feasible path toward securing a business license, with a legible "map" of institutions and their specific functions, and with access to the technical and financial expertise required to establish durable and profitable investment projects. Heartened by my interest in the program, El Hadji quickly offered me an internship (*stage*) with the agency. Getting the Entrepreneurial Diaspora initiative up and running had been on APIX's agenda for the better part of a decade, my new colleague explained as I signed the necessary paperwork, but momentum had grown behind the project in recent months. With luck, he enthusiastically declared, I would be there to witness the program's public debut.

APIX's Entrepreneurial Diaspora program, I soon learned, was one of several "migrant-investor" initiatives taking shape across the city.[1] These programs were frequently devised, governed, and sanctioned through collaborations between the migrants themselves and the Senegalese state, IOs, NGOs, foreign governments, and private sector offices throughout Dakar. APIX representatives were involved to varying degrees with at least four such initiatives during my tenure there. What these diverse governing projects shared in common was a commitment to rechanneling migrant-earned capital—which typically travels informal and seemingly opaque extrastate routes—onto formal, legible routes and into economically "productive" ventures. In this way, migrant-investor programs would enable the state and its governing allies to better quantify, monitor, and direct this dense global traffic of financial resources. Program architects insisted that the migrant-investor schemes they envisioned would stand in stark contrast to migrants' housing construction projects, which they dismissed as unnecessarily lavish and economically wasteful.[2] While a migrant building a house was preoccupied with the short-term, consumption-focused needs of his family, officials explained, a truly *invested* migrant was motivated both by individualistic desires for personal profit and by altruistic nationalist sentiments. In an era of heightened clandestine migration concerns and chronic economic uncertainty, various program architects explained to me, migrant-investor programs had the potential to generate broad and enduring economic change. Migrants' investments would not only create jobs and generate capital that would be reinvested, they would also make an important statement to foreign investors that "natives" had confidence in Senegal's economy. Just as importantly, these programs would pave the way for a new generation of national leaders—migrant-investors—who were equipped with the capital, expertise, and enterprising spirit necessary to lead Senegal's liberalized economy. Migrant-investors would be partners in—rather than targets of—development. In short, these programs would tap into and make publicly visible Senegal's "greatest natural resource"—its mobile citizens.

1. The migrant-investor phenomenon I am describing here is by no means unique to Senegal. Rather, this study contributes to an already rich and diverse scholarship that considers migrant remittance practices around the world. A number of scholars have noted in particular a dramatic shift over the past decade in how migrants and their earnings are classified, appealed to, and governed by states (Barro 2008; Bernal 2014; Coutin 2007; Hernandez and Coutin 2006; Leichtman 2002; Mohan 2006; Weekley 2004), IOs (DeHart 2010), and private interests (Weekley 2004).

2. For more about the state's active and explicit role in the migrant-built housing market, see Barro 2008.

Despite officials' soaring rhetoric and insistent contrasts, however, the migrant-investor programs I describe here remained largely unfinished, without enrolled investors, for long periods of time. Much like the migrant-built houses that officials so vehemently rejected as unproductive and contrary to the state's liberalizing mission, these institutionalized programs were bottlenecked: they publicly valorized, institutionalized, and codified mobility as a redeeming national value that could sustain the Senegalese state in an era of ongoing structural change and economic uncertainty. But at the same time, these programs made spectacularly visible the *limits* of these ideologies and approaches in an era when migratory flows of all sorts were more tightly regulated, as I discuss in chapter 1. These ambitious, future-focused programs were unraveled by two important realities. For one, Senegal's citizens abroad simply did not have the capacity to "invest" in the ways these programs required. The migrant-investor was, in fact, more myth than reality. Administrators acknowledged this fact but nonetheless pushed forward with their efforts to design migrant-investor programs. In doing so, however, program architects faced a second sobering reality: the very act of formalizing informal financial infrastructures rendered these routes ineffective and unattractive to the typical remitting migrant. Migrant-investor programs, I quickly realized, were both critical and impossible modes of governing Senegal after structural adjustment.

Centered squarely within APIX's offices, this chapter chronicles the relentless making and unmaking of two migrant-investor programs with which the agency was involved—APIX's own Entrepreneurial Diaspora program and a second scheme (the "Italian plan," as my APIX colleagues had dubbed it) managed by the Italian embassy and the International Organization for Migration (IOM), an intergovernmental organization that played a particularly visible role in managing the region's clandestine migration "crisis." The ethnographic story that unfolds in this chapter is as much about the migrant-investor concept itself—its origins, its promises, and its perils—as it is about the transformation of the adjusted state more generally. At first glance, it is easy to cast these programs as empty spectacle or ritualistic excess, as a collection of signs without meaning or substance, or as evidence of a structurally adjusted state wildly out of touch with both its citizens and its own capacities (see, for instance, Apter 2005; Comaroff and Comaroff 2001; Piot 2010). In fact, during the early days of my internship, migrant-investor schemes—indeed, the institution of APIX more broadly—appeared as little more than "arbitrary symbolic acts" (Mbembe and Roitman 1995, 337) intended to conjure meaningful state presence in an age of withered resources, unfulfilled promises, and growing popular restlessness. Seen from this perspective, institutionalized migrant-investor schemes are both symptoms of and responses to the longstanding "crisis" of state legitimacy in Africa.

But the more time I spent at APIX, the clearer it became that these scholarly frameworks did not quite capture the complexity of bureaucratic projects and practice in structurally adjusted Senegal. As Brenda Chalfin (2010) has pointed out in her work on state sovereignty and the customs service in Ghana, contemporary research on the shifting contours of citizenship and governance devotes remarkably scant attention to the experiences, beliefs, and practices of state agents themselves. And yet, she argues, "if the conventional locus of state authority is indeed disappearing, how this happens and is experienced needs to be considered rather than assumed" (43). Taking Chalfin's admonition seriously, I offer here an ethnography situated within state offices, amongst state actors, rather than one that focuses exclusively on the state as diffusely and discursively produced and enacted. I focus specifically on the networks, narratives, expectations, and mundane activities of one cohort of state workers who are invested in building migrant-investor programs. I pay close attention to how these officials understand and configure "the state" as mired in uncertainty, strained by decades of structural adjustment reforms, but also as poised on the brink of reinvention and forward momentum. In doing so, I probe the apparent "crisis" of state legitimacy and authority in Africa and elsewhere and offer alternative ways of conceptualizing this moment and its varied effects.

When analyzed from this particular vantage point, migrant-investor programs come into view as much more complex assemblages of expertise, anticipation, and experimentation than many theories of the contemporary African state might allow. Caught between the imperatives and realities of economic liberalization, APIX staff members found themselves constructing programs that would not likely be completed, engaging in collaborations that would surely dissolve, and articulating future possibilities in which they ardently believed but which they also deeply doubted. Decades of adjustment and liberalization, in other words, had produced a state forever in suspension, wedded to the goals of mobilizing capital and liberalizing governance even as these goals proved elusive. What I am describing here is not a state of limbo or passive waiting, but rather of frenzied activity and ongoing construction that forged new alliances and produced novel articulations of citizenship and possibility. APIX staff sometimes used the term *embouteillage* to refer to specific instances of build-up and strained passage. In the analysis that follows, I also employ *embouteillage* not as another descriptor to tether to "state"—one that could supplant notions of Africa's "failed," "weak," or "shadow" states—but as a particular lens for analyzing and making sense of the simultaneous impotence and omnipresence, retrenchment and extension, momentum and stasis, of the structurally adjusted state. This approach also brings into view the ways in which state workers are themselves caught up in the *embouteillages* they seek to dissolve, and it enables attention to the anxieties that state agents shared with those they governed.

Mobility, *Embouteillage*, and the Adjusted State

In the late 1970s, World Bank and its partners identified Senegal, a so-called stable democracy with a "weak" economy, as a crucial site for experimentation with structural adjustment reforms. Until this point, most of Senegal's industries were nationalized, its markets were considered "closed" to foreign investment and were tightly regulated by a centralized bureaucracy, and the government offered social services and employment as a means to secure political patronage. In order to combat stagnant growth, made worse by rapid ecological degradation and worldwide economic recession, the bank offered the Senegalese government a series of loans with strings attached—most notably that the state cede some of the power it claimed (over budgets, markets, the currency, and its citizens) to the international economic community. These loan conditions precipitated the sale of state assets, the privatization of publicly held lands, the removal of social safety nets and agricultural subsidies, and the dismantling or downsizing of state offices themselves—all in the name of a new brand of liberalism, one sold, implemented, and governed on a global scale by World Bank and its sister organization, the International Monetary Fund. National priorities shifted to accommodate the logics of market fundamentalism, at least on paper, and the thoroughly global vocabularies of foreign direct investment, deregulation, and decentralization infused bureaucratic life. What resulted, in many ways, was a pared-down state—one whose credibility as an institution was eroded, one beholden to a slightly different set of foreign interests than it had been in previous decades, and one with dwindling leverage in the lives of its citizens. Into the presumed "gap" left by the adjusted state has risen a network of alternative institutions, including World Bank and other IOs, as well as NGOs, corporations and foreign investment firms, and various extralegal networks, all of which play increasingly crucial roles throughout the "developing" world in the provisioning of services and the recognition of rights formerly granted by the state (Ferguson

2006; Piot 2010). At the very same time, however, this erosion of state authority and presence has been accompanied by a paradoxical expansion and rede-
ployment of "the state" in other guises, an extraordinary reconceptualization
of what the state can do and for whom (Hibou 2004).

APIX is a vivid example of these simultaneous shifts in governance—of
the concomitant strengthening of non–state governing networks and the
reinvention and extension of the "state" as a relevant contemporary actor.
Formed in 2000, APIX was developed with the help of World Bank, which
provided the Senegalese government with blueprints of successful programs
already in use elsewhere.[3] Yet the agency is often celebrated as an achieve-
ment of the state itself; indeed, staff members' origin narratives describe the
organization as the cornerstone of President Abdoulaye Wade's neoliberal
economic agenda upon his landmark election to office, one that indexed
the triumph of open-market ideologies and that helped pave the way for
the emergence of the investor as a key actor in Senegal's hopeful economic
"emergence."[4] As a "parallel bureaucracy" (Dahou and Foucher 2009, 22),
APIX exists outside Senegal's ministry system, and its director general and her
staff answer directly to the president.[5] It is dedicated to facilitating economic
regulatory reforms, promoting private sector investment, and overseeing
large-scale national infrastructure projects, and it does so in close conjunction with World Bank. This politically charged "collaboration" between a
remarkably powerful IO that claims a purportedly apolitical agenda on the
one hand and an economically dependent postcolonial nation on the other
has produced a starkly different sort of state institution, one whose singular

---

3. The agency is currently a member of World Bank Group's Multinational Investment Guarantee Agency (MIGA). MIGA member organizations across the world, currently totaling over
four hundred (not all of which are affiliated with states), are given access to expertise and resources aimed at creating, maintaining, and promoting a business-friendly environment in any
context. A quick glance at a handful of websites managed by other MIGA members reveals the
profound similarity in approach and form shared by member organizations—from the "one-
stop-shop" concept to the designation and promotion of "priority sectors." What is particularly
interesting is that this close relationship between World Bank and APIX was rarely discussed and
never celebrated in the agency's presentations.

4. Though a similar organization dedicated to investment promotion existed under the leadership of Abdou Diouf, origin narratives that circulated within APIX's offices unambiguously
emphasized Wade's role in expanding, retooling, and repackaging the agency, thus marking
him as a liberal reformer whose policies and ideologies contrasted sharply with those of his
"socialist" predecessor.

5. Senegal's system of governance is modeled on that of France, with a popularly elected
president who, in turn, chooses a prime minister to serve as head of government. In consultation
with the president, the prime minister appoints a council of ministers to lead more specialized
posts. The number of ministries in operation varies, as new ministries are instituted and others
are folded together or dissolved.

aim is to "sell" Senegal as a potential site of neoliberal investment.[6] This new vision of the state replaces bureaucratic methods of structuring time and space (see Weber [1946] 2009) with more fluid, networked, "postbureau-cratic" modes of engagement. Indeed, APIX was envisioned as an antidote to the kind of "red tape" bureaucratic state practice that Gupta (2012) describes. Most importantly, perhaps, this "adjusted" state is no longer beholden to the needs or expectations of its citizenry in any direct way; it is neither a provider of resources and services nor a manager of diverse national interests. Instead, APIX's prime purpose is to "accompany the investor" as he moves through an unfamiliar and often precarious economic and political terrain, all with the hope that invested capital and expertise will eventually generate broader economic and social change. In this way, this new state office is made visible and present through its very purposeful and strategic *absence*. Indeed, APIX is a quasi-state office that helps keep "the state"—cast as meddling, paternalis-tic, and opaque—out of the way of investment.

The layout and design of APIX's downtown headquarters are a powerful testament to this new vision of state presence and purpose. Most Senegalese ministries are housed in aging independence-era structures that are dimly lit, poorly ventilated, and sparsely furnished. People from various economic and social backgrounds pass through these offices each day as they file peti-tions or seek documents. APIX, in contrast, is situated on a quiet, tree-lined street a short walk from the presidential palace. The colonial-style building boasts a pristine white façade, well-manicured grounds, and an entranceway dressed in marble and staffed by uniformed guards. A team of chauffeurs lingers in the doorway, waiting for orders to shuttle an employee to a meet-ing or to pick up a client at the airport. Foreign dignitaries, potential inves-tors, and NGO representatives register at the guard station; those without appointments are typically turned away. Approved visitors then make their way into the air-conditioned interior, past life-sized posters promoting Sen-egal as an ideal investment destination. Many guests linger in the lobby as they wait for their appointments, sinking into imported upholstered chairs while they sip Nescafé and peruse glossy brochures about Senegal's agricul-tural or tourism sectors. Others head elsewhere: through heavy doors and into the main services area, called the "One Stop Shop" (Le Guichet Unique), where a young and largely female staff caters to the needs of potential and current investors; or to an adjoining building that houses the agency's docu-mentation center, stocked with promotional and legal materials, masters'

---

6. For more a more thorough explanation of this shift in governance, see Harvey 1989.

Figure 7. A view of the entrance to APIX's downtown headquarters

theses, statistical records, and a photocopy machine. Distinguished visitors are typically escorted up a sweeping staircase to conference rooms and well-appointed administrators' offices. Here, modern technology and open layouts are intended to promote teamwork among senior staff members and to enable collaboration with representatives from other public and private sector offices throughout the city. These grand headquarters, then, celebrate cosmopolitan mobility, Western-style collaboration, and consumption as integral to Senegal's emergent future. Moreover, they seek to identify and appeal to a quite different constituency than the typical postcolonial office. By catering to a global elite, APIX makes a bold statement about the level of attention and care an investor—not the country's citizenry as a whole—can expect from the Senegalese government.

APIX also offers a glimpse of a new generation of state *fonctionnaires*. Ministry bureaucrats are often described as having acquired their positions through nepotism, as passive or lazy, as prone to corruption and bribery, and as spending too little time working and too much time socializing. In contrast, APIX administrators cast themselves as perpetually in motion, as navigating through other offices in the city, heading to meetings and workshops, and attending international conferences or investment fairs. To be *en mission*—on a business trip—is an important marker of status within APIX, one that signals a worker's degree of involvement in the essential tasks of mobilizing capital, expertise, and attention. The more time one spends *en mission*, the more senior one's position is typically considered. Moreover, the vast majority of APIX's administrators have been educated abroad or have lived there for significant amounts of time. On numerous occasions, top-level employees introduced themselves to me or to visitors as "part of the diaspora," or as "American" or "Canadian," depending on where they had lived while abroad. I initially found this style of self-presentation quite curious, as most of these employees seemed rather firmly emplaced in Dakar, where they had built homes or were raising families. What soon became clear, however, was the social respect and visibility that staff members achieved through their present-tense claims of engagement with the diaspora. Through their narratives and performances of mobile pasts and continued connection, APIX administrators positioned themselves as ideal citizens. They also explicitly distanced themselves from other state functionaries, who were assumed to be "stuck" in the city and to lack the cosmopolitan sensibilities and global experience necessary to guide the Senegalese state in the twenty-first century.

For APIX staff members, the most important feature that distinguished the organization from the conventional Senegalese state ministry was that, at APIX, "things move" (*ça bouge*). Within the agency's headquarters, one rarely heard investment spoken of as something that was "created"; instead, staff members usually explained that the necessary capital simply did not exist or could not be generated within Africa and that it instead had to be redirected from elsewhere. APIX's mission was tightly focused on mobilizing (*mobiliser*) or channeling (*canaliser*) investment, generating and sustaining momentum, and fostering durable connections that extended beyond the African continent. Staff members also sought to mobilize expertise, institutional protocols, legal codes, and entrepreneurial values, all described as imported from abroad. This emphatic commitment to mobility infused daily routines, meeting agendas, presentations to investors, promotional materials and newsletters, and staff members' own conceptions of self and work. With this goal of mobility in mind, the agency was constantly constructing, revising, and publishing flow charts aimed at mapping routes through state offices and clarifying the bureaucratic steps investors must take to implement their projects. Staff members worried not just about implementation of projects but also about retention of investors, and they frequently discussed strategies to convince investors not to "let money sleep" (*laisser dormir l'argent*) but instead to constantly reinvest it and keep it moving. This sense of momentum and constant motion was what distinguished "real" investment activity, many claimed, from practices like the construction of houses for family or for rent.

The agency's ambitious autoroute project, which I discussed in chapter 2, was perhaps the most tangible and visible manifestation of this mobility-focused mission. Launched in 2006, the large-scale construction effort was the product of a "public-private partnership" financed largely through the private investment of foreign companies and a loan provided to the Senegalese government by World Bank; it was overseen by APIX on behalf of the Senegalese government. The new structure was intended to ease congestion within the growing peninsular city, to better link it to peri-urban and rural areas, and, by extension, to attract potential investors to the capital city with its promises of efficiency and modernity. This project and many others like it reaffirmed the centrality of Dakar to contemporary projects of nation-making, despite constant calls for neoliberal "decentralization" (see, for instance, Foley 2009). Perhaps most importantly, the autoroute venture signaled a convergence of various "flows"—of traffic, capital, resources, expertise—and made tangible the agency's commitment to "mobility" as a means to transform the nation and its capital city. It was within the spaces of the emergent autoroute that APIX emerged as a publicly recognizable state entity for most residents. Here, one encountered towering billboards erected by APIX, proclaiming *"Mon Futur, C'est Aujourd'hui!"* ("My Future Is Today!") and a small army of jumpsuit-clad staff members, hired to facilitate movement in the city and to serve as the "face" of APIX on the traffic-clogged roads. In APIX's headquarters, too, a glass-encased replica of APIX's autoroute project, complete with miniature trees and a few vehicles, featured prominently during tours and presentations to groups of investors and foreign dignitaries. APIX staff members insisted that Senegal's hopes for attracting large-scale investment hinged on the success of this infrastructural project, as it would help link Dakar's airport and harbor to the rest of the country as well as to other countries. "Investors would think twice about investing in a country where things don't move. You can't welcome Philip Morris [the tobacco giant] at the airport if the car you send to greet him can't get through the *embouteillages*," one APIX staff member pointed out. From this employee's perspective, one shared by many of his colleagues, urban mobility was the globally recognizable value upon which investment—and thus Senegal's economic future—would necessarily be built.

Bottlenecks were not confined to the city's streets. From the perspective of many APIX team members, the typical postcolonial state office was ineffectively organized, which prompted bureaucratic tie-ups when it came to processing paperwork, enacting legislation, or creating substantive change. APIX staff often used the term *embouteillage* to refer specifically to these lags in bureaucratic office life. In fact, the agency's tenacious commitment to anticipating and alleviating bottlenecks was thought to further distinguish their agency from other arms of the state and helped to sharpen their mobility-focused rhetoric. Daily agendas at APIX revolved to a notable degree around finding ways to simplify tax codes, streamline dossier review

Figure 8. A billboard erected by APIX reads, "Public Works of the State. Amina's future is being built today. Yours is, too. My future is today!"

processes, and facilitate communication and circulation between state offices. APIX's "One Stop Shop" allowed potential investors to deposit paperwork, ask questions, and research tax and import regulations without having to make appointments at multiple ministry offices. Senegal's customs office (Direction Générale des Douanes) maintained a post within APIX, where a customs official was on hand for much of the week to meet with investors and help APIX staff sort through dossiers more quickly. For APIX employees, to combat bureaucratic bottlenecks was to resist "politics" (la politique) and to centralize the seemingly apolitical pursuit of economic development, regulatory change, and, most importantly, unfettered mobility. As one staff member put it, "APIX is different [from other state offices] because we don't have politics. In a developing country like Senegal, the state should focus solely on building the economy. But most of the ministries are too concerned with politics to get things done." From this perspective, politics—internal struggles for power, acts of patronage, self-interested posturing—limits mobility, inhibits change, and marks the bottleneck as the most prevalent feature of the postcolonial state. APIX, in contrast, offered a new vision of what the Senegalese state could be: a state freed from the burden of politics and also of "development" in its older guises, reborn as an impartial but dedicated facilitator of global connections, collaborative discussions, and capital flows.

Despite all of this talk about mobility and institutional change, however, everyday life was just as mired in *embouteillages* at APIX as it was in conventional ministry offices. Institutional and ideological change was slow and investors were comparatively few. As World Bank put it, "Senegal aspires to be a high-middle-income country by the next decade but has been stuck in a low-growth equilibrium since 2006. Senegal has not shared the rapid growth experienced by many other sub-Saharan African countries over the last decade. Compared with the average growth rate of 6% for the rest of sub-Saharan Africa, growth in Senegal averaged only 4% between 2000 and 2010, and only 3.3% in the period since 2006" (World Bank 2003, i). Indeed, Senegal's share of the world GDP has been stagnant since 1980 (International Monetary Fund 2012)—this, of course, despite decades of economic restructuring and austerity. While 2006, the year I arrived at APIX, boasted improved foreign direct investment (FDI) rates from previous years (UNCTAD 2010), growth according to this measure has been stagnant since then. As of 2009, FDI inflows in Senegal were on par with those of countries like Liberia and Chad—two African countries associated with violence, corruption, and unrest.

These grim rates and flat projections were experienced intensely within the offices and meeting rooms of APIX. Even with a soon-to-be expanded and improved highway system, a "modernized" investment code that provided attractive incentives, and institutionalized structures aimed at streamlining procedures, APIX officials reluctantly acknowledged that both "cultural" and "political" obstacles to investment persisted. Administrators complained about dozens of different sorts of stoppages and slowdowns that made luring foreign direct investment difficult: general hiring practices based on nepotism rather than merit, office routines in place within other state offices that slowed down APIX's own practices, pervasive reliance on payoffs and bribes and intermediaries at all levels of government, unreliable flows of electricity that made generators indispensable, and workers who disappeared for long lunch breaks. From the perspective of many APIX employees, these challenges produced an unpredictable investment climate, one that was likely to intimidate foreign investors in particular. Moreover, with so many developing countries "opened up" by pro-market reforms over the past decade, it was sometimes difficult to make a case that foreign businessmen should build an enterprise in Senegal instead of heading to more "promising," established, or familiar destinations like South Africa, Mauritius, Ethiopia, or beyond. How does one "sell" Senegal—a relatively small country with few lucrative natural resources, whose modest national economy was built historically on peanuts—to an audience of profit-minded investors with no obvious attachment to the country?

APIX staff members thus found themselves stuck, caught between grand expectations for the future and the realities of the present moment. These quasi-state workers were obliged to promote foreign investment and believed ardently in the project of liberalization, and yet they also recognized the limits of their approach and anticipated the failure of their appeals. APIX was a place where "things move"—and yet where many projects and efforts seemed snarled. This pervasive sense of predicament reflected a deep uncertainty that had pervaded the city in this era after structural adjustment: though liberalization was supposed to have paved the way for economic change, state workers like those at APIX still found themselves applying the same principles with less than remarkable results decades after adjustment had begun. Mobilizing flows—of capital, expertise, and information—was an organizing mantra, and yet it was the bureaucratic bottleneck that seemed to structure everyday life and policy.

From Remitting Migrant to Risk-Taking Entrepreneur

It was within this space of predicament that crafting an Entrepreneurial Diaspora program came to occupy a central position on APIX's agenda. At its heart, APIX's hopeful program was geared toward transforming remitting migrants—whose economic transfers had propped up Senegalese households in the aftermath of structural adjustment reforms for decades—into risk-taking entrepreneurs whose desire for profit could generate national economic change. APIX staff members' goals were threefold: to locate a potential pool of investors whose (presumed) economic resources had never fully been acknowledged or accessed by the state, to formalize economic practices already taking place informally and in turn bolster investment rates, and to draw attention to "native" confidence as a means to persuade foreign actors to consider Senegal as an investment destination. Imagined to straddle both foreigner and national categories, to be equally adept at navigating global and local economic and political terrains, and to be motivated both by patriotism and desire for profit, APIX's "diasporic entrepreneur" emerged as a perfect embodiment of the institution's commitment to mobility and as an ideally positioned actor who could help steer Senegal along its uncertain path toward economic emergence.[7]

APIX was not alone in its ambitions to mold a new cadre of investors, as the introduction to this chapter makes clear. Indeed, by 2006, the figure of the migrant-investor had achieved an almost spectral presence in governing offices in Dakar. At the time of my research, there were at least half a dozen programs in various stages of construction, renovation, and operation in the city, all designed to appeal to this sought-after figure of development. These efforts tended to be collaborative in nature, linking together public offices, NGOs and IOs, and the private sector. While some programs, including APIX's emergent Entrepreneurial Diaspora initiative, were not particularly well known to city residents, others were made visible by Senegal's expansive multilingual media, through Internet message boards, and through newspaper and billboard advertisements promoting special banking and transfer services and loans to start new businesses. What these programs shared in common was the assumption that the migrant was in a privileged position—both socially and economically—and could act as an arbiter of economic development in an era when few other tactics seemed to work. The migrant-investor formulation was regarded as the most of-the-moment approach to economic development in an age of unrelenting austerity and rapid global change.

These proliferating migrant-investor programs were not new but instead reflected a rich local history of remittance-driven development activity. Even as they cast their plans as fresh and novel, program architects spoke of finding momentum and inspiration for their own efforts in established religious and secular practices of pooling migrant resources in Senegal. These "traditional" activities were typically more community-centered and anonymous than contemporary investor-focused configurations, and they aimed, first and foremost, to provide for the segments of Senegalese society whose needs were not being met by the structurally adjusted state. Among the most visible and extensively researched of these collective practices are the redistribution efforts of the Murid Way, whose transnational trade networks have been extensively addressed in the academic literature on Senegal, Islam, and globalization.[8] Regardless of whether they were themselves members of the

7. Senegalese migrants are, for example, represented by a ministry—the Ministère de Sénégalais de l'Extérieur—that emphasizes their exteriority, and yet APIX initiatives to encourage their investment were subsumed under the larger umbrella of "internal" investment promotion.

8. Murid faithful living and working around the world are mobilized through discourses of religious obligation and send remittances to shayks, who then use monies to provide for the communities migrants leave behind. The Murid capital city of Touba (also spelled Tuba), which

Murid fold, many APIX employees were dazzled by the incredible scope and success of these religious networks. In interviews and daily conversations, they would often cite Touba's remarkable transformation from agricultural hinterland into global religious metropolis as a model for their own secular development initiatives. If religious leaders had the power to galvanize this sort of spiritually focused mission, one employee considered aloud, couldn't the state likewise mobilize its diasporic citizens in support of a secular development movement? Perhaps, he suggested, existent Murid remittance practices might even provide readymade networks whose "investors" could be lured toward national development projects.

Contemporary migrant-investor formulations also echoed another historical tradition of organized remittance practice, that of codevelopment. Formed in the 1980s to enable "partnerships" between African migrants and communities and the French government, codevelopment programs were founded on the assumptions that people, rather than states, should be the main arbiters of development, that development should be decentralized and should focus on creating infrastructure and opportunity in rural areas, that migration can enable a spirit of mutual collaboration that benefits both sending and receiving countries, and that the moment of partnership indexes a thoroughly consensual relationship between the global north and south (see, for instance, Naïr 1997).[9] Typically, the French government would match collective contributions made by migrants through codevelopment initiatives, and Senegalese government officials would in turn coordinate projects using this money, now regarded on paper as an anonymous "gift" sent by the French government on behalf of nameless migrants. This codevelopment model has generated scores of contemporary programs

---

maintains its independence from the Senegalese state and is administered by Murid religious authorities, has been constructed almost entirely through the dutiful contributions of its globally dispersed adherents. Compelled by ideologies that recognize hard work as a form of prayer, Murids in diaspora help to finance the building of roads, health clinics, and social welfare initiatives in a region where "the state" is conspicuously absent (see, for instance, Buggenhagen 2012; Diouf and Rendall 2000; Foley and Babou 2011). In their analysis of the construction of a Murid hospital in Touba, Foley and Babou (2011) provide an excellent discussion of the complex relationship between Murid-led development efforts and the Senegalese state.

9. Since at least the 1980s, diasporic Senegalese have participated in various migrant clubs or "hometown" associations, usually organized on the basis of ethnic, national, or regional similarities, that use pooled resources to construct wells, health clinics, schools, and other community development initiatives in rural Senegal. By the 1990s, as ecological and economic conditions in sending communities worsened and as bilateral aid practices fell out of fashion in the West, the success of these small and relatively informal migrant collectives spurred institutionalized strategies for African development that came to be known in France as "co-development" (see Grillo and Riccio 2004).

that link various European receiving countries (particularly France, Spain, and Italy) with Senegalese (and indeed other African) villages and towns; monies have been used to build wells and schools, fund healthcare initiatives, or fund women's small-scale enterprises, for instance. These models were available and familiar to APIX employees as they considered the directions their own program could take. Representatives working on behalf of codevelopment programs frequently intermingled with APIX associates at meetings, panels, and other development-oriented events, and they shared ideas about implementing programs and creating sustainable economic change.

However, the migrant-investor configuration also represented a significant departure from traditional household- and community-centered interventions toward increasingly formalized programs that cultivated the values of national-level development, individual responsibility, and economic risk taking. According to El Hadji, a senior APIX official with whom I closely worked during my internship, both religious and codevelopment approaches were well-meaning but flawed interventions that did not do enough to appeal to the migrant as an autonomous individual, a rational actor, and a profit seeker. These models, he insisted, were therefore not sustainable in the long term and were instead "destined to remain development projects"—an unambiguous disparagement in the purportedly postdevelopment era—that needed constant intercession on the part of governing actors. In contrast, El Hadji insisted, APIX sought to craft an independently functioning "investment device" (*une mécanisme d'investissement*) that attracted participants quite simply because it offered lucrative ways of doing business and building wealth. This sort of migrant-investor program would generate continual reinvestment and perpetual motion. It would coopt proven strategies already in use and retool them for the benefit of the state. And it would bring visibility to the migrant, no longer an anonymous member of a collective but reborn instead as a risk-taking entrepreneur who sought individual success and economic profit but was also able to sustain economic loss.

El Hadji's comments also point to broader shifts in the ways that migration and remittance activity are conceptualized: practices once considered informal, transitional, or contrary to national development have become legitimate, formal, and even heroic modes for individual economic empowerment and large-scale transformation. Over the past decade, "local" or "cultural" responses to the instability generated by budget cuts and currency devaluations during and after structural adjustment have been repackaged as purposeful "global" policies adopted by states, IOs, NGOs, and the private sector (Elyachar 2002). Within this context, it is the migrant—whose absence abroad once stood as a reminder of the *failures* of the postcolonial state to provide opportunities for its people—who has become the darling of economic development initiatives worldwide, many of which are put into place through "collaborative" efforts that link public and private sectors (Coutin 2007; DeHart 2010). In other words, the invested migrant surfaced in state offices and institutional reports as an ideally situated global actor whose ability to make do for decades without reliance on the state, quite ironically, served as a model for state policy after structural adjustment. This global reconceptualization of the role of the migrant is clearly reflected in a decade's worth of World Bank and UN reports and addresses that celebrate the transformative potential of transnational migration and remittance activity (Isotalo 2010). African migrants' resources in particular have been described as "under-utilized" (Norberg and Cheru 2009) and as "not yet reaching their full development potential," particularly for women and the poor (International Fund for Agricultural Development 2009, 2). Through these public pronouncements, displacement and mobility are repackaged as neutral global values that generate local change, and the social and economic volatility that such movements produce is couched as economically productive "risk taking" on the part of individual migrants. Faceless migrants marginalized by decades of neoliberal reforms are thus reconfigured as exemplary contributors to a new world order, one in which mobility and modernity are inextricably and lucratively linked (Chu 2010). And the depleted coffers of the adjusted state are renewed by the very people that adjustment had driven away.

Myths of the Migrant-Investor and the State "Left Behind"

After spending a few weeks exploring APIX's institutional landscape, I set to the task of learning more about the budding Entrepreneurial Diaspora initiative. I was able to locate some very preliminary documents on the project, including reports filed by various APIX representatives after trips to Spain, as well as a small collection of materials describing similar projects launched in other developing countries with high rates of emigration. APIX officials had also established a website that offered a few bulleted points on the importance of such an initiative, but it offered no outline of what the program would do or how it would work.[10] It quickly became clear, however,

---

10. At the time this chapter was written, this link could no longer be located on APIX's website.

that the Entrepreneurial Diaspora program was not yet much of a *program* at all. My early inquiries at APIX were thus guided by what had seemed at the time to be a simple question: for whom would the Entrepreneurial Diaspora program be designed? What kind of migrant-investor did the agency and other offices like it hope to meet? Answering these questions quickly proved a daunting task. Part of the challenge was that the contours of the Senegalese diaspora itself were so uncertain. During a meeting at the Ministère de Sénégalais de l'Extérieur, Senegal's ministry for the diaspora, a senior official explained that his office had no firm statistics on emigration to offer. While the ministry projected that two million Senegalese lived abroad, he was certain this was probably an underestimation. These official figures, he explained, reflected the number of Senegalese who had either registered at embassies in their host countries or who had filled out immigration cards upon arrival at the airport; many undocumented migrants do neither.[11] The ministry had ambitious plans for conducting a census of households throughout Senegal, but the project was stalled: the relatively small ministry staff had neither the resources nor the expertise to carry out such a large-scale effort at this time.

APIX staff members typically blamed bureaucratic inefficiencies and the failure of the conventional state for the "missing" emigration numbers, even as they acknowledged the challenges of the collection task.[12] But they also

---

11. More conservative estimates of the size of Senegal's diaspora put it at 460,000 people (Ratha and Xu 2008). Within the same office of the Ministère de Sénégalais de l'Extérieur, one official estimated the population at two million, another at three million. The reported economic contributions of these migrants vary, too: World Bank, for instance, estimates that remittances total US$874 million (Ratha and Xu 2008); the International Fund for Agricultural Development, a specialized agency of the United Nations, suggests US$660 million (International Fund for Agricultural Development 2009); and a report issued in December 2007 by the Senegalese Ministry of Finance claims US$1.1 billion (see Mohamed Gueye, "Transferts d'Argent: Les Emigrés Envoient Environs 9.9 Milliards au Pays," *Le Quotidien.* December 28, 2007).

12. There are various constraints and circumstances that account for these disparities and contradictions in published estimates. The quantification of the Senegalese diasporic population is an enormous task, one that is made more difficult by shrinking government budgets and small staffs in liberalized Senegal. Government staff at the Ministry for Senegalese of the Exterior were still trying to figure out how to coordinate a large-scale census of this incredibly dispersed population; Senegalese live throughout Europe, North America, the Middle East, Asia, Africa, and Latin America. The task was particularly challenging given that so many diasporic Senegalese live abroad under "irregular" circumstances; many who are *sans papiers* work hard to remain legally invisible, as I discuss later in this chapter. The vagueness of the category of "diasporic Senegalese" also likely contributes to the contradictory numbers that I have shown here. Would those Senegalese born abroad count, for instance, even if they did not have formal Senegalese citizenship? And how would the state count those traders who did not necessarily have residency abroad but instead lived more globally itinerant lives, typically spending part of the year in Senegal?

seemed to find my insistence on locating emigration facts and figures quite curious and even counterproductive. APIX employees were quite accustomed to managing ambiguity; indeed, while uncertainty hampered office practice in some ways, it also enabled it. In this case, that the Senegalese diaspora was in many ways unknowable helped produce it as an untapped resource worthy of state exploration and attention. Moreover, APIX administrators were reluctant to bound this population in any meaningful way. For instance, when I pressed staff members at APIX about the sort of migrant they imagined luring, they typically offered one of several similarly vague responses: "There really is no typical diasporic entrepreneur." "We are open to anyone." "We meet all sorts of investors here at APIX." At collaborative meetings, too, participants did not dedicate much time to defining a target population or hypothesizing about what kind of migrant might be interested. Instead, administrators focused on casting as wide of a net as possible.

Yet program administrators in all sectors of the city shared several tacit assumptions about the migrant-investor as an individual and as a development actor, assumptions that in turn have deep impacts on institutional conceptions of participation and presence. The presumed gender of the migrant-investor became clear, for instance, during an interview with Khady, an APIX staff member charged with overseeing "internal" investment projects. Young, bright, and remarkably poised, Khady was the only investment promotion staff member I met who had been educated at Dakar's Université Cheikh Anta Diop and who had never lived abroad. Nonetheless, in the absence of a more formalized Entrepreneurial Diaspora program, investments made by Senegalese migrants abroad fell under her purview. Khady helped run a few investment fairs for migrants living abroad, and she typically spent a good deal of the summer appealing to *venants* (return migrants) who had come to spend time with family in Senegal. When I asked her to describe the migrants she met through these initiatives, she explained:

> There really is no "typical" investor from the diaspora. This is why we hold targeted events in various countries [to meet many kinds of people]. He could be educated or not educated; a successful banker or a street merchant; married with wives in Senegal or with a spouse in Europe. Some of these investors are individuals, others are already partnered with French businessmen, for instance. Some have experience, while others do not.

While this conception of the migrant-investor was indeed very open, incorporating migrants of various income levels and educational backgrounds, it was nonetheless implicitly constrained by gender. Khady readily acknowledged this assumption when I asked if the migrant-investor was likely to be a man, explaining, "I suppose so, though we really are open to anyone. But perhaps the program would appeal more to men." Her assertion echoed much broader assumptions about the category of the migrant-investor. Administrators would often emphasize that their initiatives would be "open to anyone," but when pressed, they also acknowledged that it was more likely that the investors they were seeking would be men. As I explained in chapter 1, while women increasingly *do* migrate from Senegal, migration is nonetheless generally conceptualized in Senegalese society as a primarily masculine domain. Moreover, with few exceptions, investment was considered to be—and, in many cases truly was—a sphere dominated by men. In fact, there was an unspoken assumption among those at APIX and elsewhere that Senegalese women living abroad would not be as interested in "investment" as their male counterparts because they were likely to use their earnings to provide for the needs of family members or other short-term household projects. Women were imagined as important small-scale entrepreneurs or market vendors but rarely as large-scale investors. It is interesting to note, too, that women occupied a significant number of positions within APIX. The director general was in fact a woman, one who was regarded at the time to be among President Wade's closest political allies and, according to rumor, a possible candidate for prime minister on various occasions. Women also held the majority of posts in the "One Stop Shop," and there were several women in upper management positions. It was women, then, who frequently met with, guided, and wooed this largely male cadre of investors. By signaling migration and investment—two assumedly masculine activities—as key strategies for participating in contemporary Senegal, staff members helped to craft implicitly gendered iterations of citizenship and belonging. By extension, the state took on a tacitly feminine guise, as its staff, which included a notable number of women, played the roles of host and guide to both national and foreign investors.

These gendered conceptions of state and citizen were further reinforced by another shared assumption about the ideal migrant-investor and his role in economic development. At some level, all migrant-investor programs were premised on the assumption that the national body was "losing" its most valuable resource and its most dependable source of future wealth and vitality through migration. APIX employees, for instance, made frequent reference to the popular adage that Senegal's wealth lies in the resourcefulness, hard work, and resilience of its people and not in the richness of its soils or in vast resource reserves. Rechanneling remittances through formalized investment programs, then, enabled the state to recover the losses incurred by migration. Of particular concern at APIX and in other offices was the impact of "brain drain" (*la fuite des cerveaux*), the luring of Senegal's top tier of professionals to more lucrative careers abroad. This educated population represented not only the gravest loss for the state, particularly in an era of ongoing austerity measures, but also its most visible potential, as educated migrants were imagined to occupy a more privileged position and to possess wealth and expertise so desperately needed by the debt-laden state.

This discourse of loss was pervasive within offices that housed migrant-investor–type programs. One program administrator I interviewed in 2006 likened migrant-investor programs to a voluntary "tax" (*un impôt*) levied on the diaspora as a means to recapture the development potential, both economic and social, that is "lost" with migration. During a meeting at the Italian embassy, an event I describe in greater detail below, one participant suggested that the state needed to be "repaid" (*rembourser*) for its investments in migrants' schooling or health. This underlying desire to cultivate and capitalize on migrants' sense of duty and obligation infused interviews and planning sessions, even as program architects insisted on profit-focused investment models that were purified of emotional attachments and that appealed to migrants as rational economic actors. Even those administrators who were reluctant to frame migrant-investor programs through the vocabularies of obligation nonetheless acknowledged that no migrant would be lured to invest in Senegal on economic principles alone. By harnessing the vocabularies of loss, debt, and "voluntary" repayment, public- and private-sector actors borrowed existing cultural assumptions about migrants' enduring obligations to the families, households, and communities that supported them before their voyage and extended and retooled them to talk about the relationship between migrants and the state. These discourses are undeniably gendered, fixed squarely on the assumption that migrants (generally assumed to be male) are particularly responsible for the care of the wives (often plural), children, and mothers (who sometimes help finance their voyages) that they leave behind.

It was the state's presumed neglect of its citizens that helped produce transnational migration as a crucial household-level economic strategy in the first place. Yet state agencies like APIX, in partnership with other public and private enterprises, worked to recast the Senegalese state as *itself* "left behind" by these migrants, as struggling to cope in an era of global change, and as reliant on the generosity of its citizens abroad. Program architects often dismissed particular household-level expenditures—like the construction of large family homes, as I discussed in chapter 3—as unproductive or even selfish use of capital that might otherwise be used for legitimate and economically "productive" projects that would in turn benefit the larger society. While APIX employees and others acknowledged housing construction as a powerful assertion of presence on the part of absent migrants, they hoped to draw attention to "investment" strategies as a means of achieving social visibility while dutifully acknowledging one's debts and obligations to the national community. Migrant-investor programs emerged, then, as a thoroughly gendered expression of state-citizen relations that enabled both state and citizen to build a new sense of presence and purpose.

Yet these borrowed discourses of loss, obligation, and repayment had their limits. Program planners were well aware that the migrants they sought to woo were already entangled in more intimate and urgent relationships of debt and duty. In fact, despite their optimistic rhetoric of "redirecting" and "rechanneling" capital, administrators frequently confided in interviews that it was not simply a matter of rerouting remittances from households into state projects and coffers. APIX administrators described particularly keen challenges in crafting an Entrepreneurial Diaspora program. Because APIX was charged with overseeing "large-scale" investment that exceeded ordinary remittance levels, its own cadre of migrant-investors would need access to a rather remarkable financial "excess" (*un surplus*) that could be transformed into large-scale investment in projects like telemarketing centers, factories, or agribusiness schemes. As Hamed, one of the most senior staff members at APIX, put it during an interview:

> The numbers [characterizing diasporic investment potential] are misleading. One cannot just expect migrants, whose earnings often singlehandedly supported households of ten or twenty people, to redirect money into investments. These migrants must think about the day-to-day and must act in the moment.

In contrast, the sort of investor that APIX was seeking could "think about the future" and had disposable income. This administrator's appraisal highlights the drastically different temporalities that remitting and investing migrants inhabit. While the investor's economic "excess" enables a future-oriented perspective, most migrants are forced to focus squarely on repaying debts accrued in the past and on urgent present-day expenses and thus have little ability to plan for the future in any purposeful way. Limited incomes must be stretched to provide for large households and communities, accumulating savings is difficult, debts and obligations are heavy, and "excess" remains a mirage. During the time of my research, this institutional appeal to a migrant's sense of national, moral obligation remained largely a rhetorical move. After all, it was the Senegalese state's intensified focus on accommodating investors at the expense of providing for its citizens, I suggest, that had helped dissolve any sort of financial "excess" citizens could perhaps once claim. As Hamed's honest assessment of the situation makes quite clear, officials acknowledged the limits of their aspirations and strategies, and they expressed a deep ambivalence about the programs they hoped to construct. As I have explained, many of APIX's staff members had themselves spent time living abroad and had personal experiences dealing with the entanglements of social debt and familial expectation. They lived in neighborhoods constructed with remittance money sent by Senegalese living abroad, and they knew very well the everyday negotiations that took place between migrants and the kin and communities they left behind. So at the same time that these employees worked to produce migrants as ideal investors—at least in the abstract—and cast the state as worthy of its diasporic citizens' financial attention, program architects were also quite sensitive to the plight of Senegalese households, to the obligations that migrants and their families juggled, and to the impossibility of APIX's program expectations and strategies. The institutional discourses of obligation, debt, and excess were remarkably productive in that they generated discussions and planning sessions, propped up hopes, and forged connections between public and private sector offices, but they also created a condition of institutional immobility, as employees anticipated the limitations of the program and thus hesitated to put plans into motion. While the Entrepreneurial Diaspora program was imagined to overcome *embouteillage*—to offer APIX a means of advancing its liberalization agenda when few other approaches had proven successful—it in fact produced new moments of institutional impasse. Indeed, as late as 2010, the initiative had no enrolled investors, and the category of "diasporic entrepreneur" remained as open and amorphous as it appeared in the early days of my internship.

That is not to say that there was no investment on the part of the diaspora, or that Senegalese living abroad did not consider themselves to be risk-taking, future-focused entrepreneurs. Quite to the contrary, as other chapters of this book make clear, transnational migrants, both male and female, were heavily invested in imagining and building Dakar and Senegal more generally. Discourses of entrepreneurialism, the productivity of risk, and national obligation infused everyday discussions about migration and urban life. Moreover, capital from the diaspora fuels both small- and large-scale ventures, bolstering in particular the city's real estate, construction, import-export, and transportation industries. I had several friends and informants who returned from the diaspora to launch particular projects or businesses in Dakar, and I had heard of several Senegalese living abroad who had used APIX's services to partner with others on various investment projects. Nonetheless, the Entrepreneurial Diaspora program remained in a state of *embouteillage*, trapped in many ways by its own ambitions. Indeed, from my vantage point within APIX's grand headquarters, it quickly became clear that the migrant-investor—armed with excess capital, led by desires for profit and nationalist goodwill, freed from familial and community obligation—was more a figure of bureaucratic myth than an actually existing, identifiable actor.

The Mirage of Formal Routes and the Limits of Collaboration

Migrant-investor programs in Dakar were also haunted by another reality: the act of formalizing preexisting financial infrastructures that operated outside of state control rendered these routes ineffective, cumbersome, and unattractive to the typical remitting migrant. Formalizing capital flows, in other words, was both the neoliberal solution and problem. This became particularly clear one morning in July 2006 during a meeting of public and private sector officials convened by the Italian embassy and the IOM's Migration for Development in Africa (MIDA) office in Dakar.[13] Gathered around the conference table were representatives from various sectors of economic governance: from state ministries, and NGOs, and IOs; from large bank branches; and from smaller development-oriented consulting firms. El Hadji and I served as APIX's representatives. Nearly everyone in the room was well acquainted; most had worked together on similar collaborative projects in the past, and many had met or interviewed with me in my capacity as an intern at APIX. Damiano, a representative from the Italian embassy, and Mariama, his Senegalese counterpart from MIDA, were working to develop a program that would offer Senegalese migrants legally residing in Italy a singular, formalized route for accessing credit, requesting technical assistance, assembling necessary paperwork, and initiating and sustaining their investment project. Over the course of several months, Damiano had visited public- and private-sector offices throughout the city, introducing himself, describing his plans, and gathering information about the city's in-

13. On its website, IOM is described as "the leading inter-governmental organization in the field of migration" that works primarily through its partnership with other governing organizations. Its professed mission is to "mobilize competencies acquired by African nationals abroad for the benefit of Africa's development" (http://www.iom.int/jahia/Jahia/mida-africa/). IOM played a particularly visible public role during the clandestine migration crisis of 2006 and 2007.

vestment landscape. This July meeting, then, was aimed at bringing together representatives from these diverse offices and unveiling the embassy's hopeful migrant-investor project.

After calling the meeting to order and offering a few well-worn statements about the profound economic potential of Senegal's diaspora, Damiano and Mariama presented a painstakingly detailed flow chart that showed the contours of their proposed program, which would involve forging a series of alliances between the representatives gathered. As the duo described the partnership scheme they envisioned, all eyes were fixed on the elaborate map, projected onto the wall via PowerPoint. But before the pair could complete their presentation, the room erupted into factious debate, as participants pointed out the potential pitfalls of their proposal. "This is not the way things would look on the ground!" "Can't we simplify this?" "Our organization would not play the role you depict here!" "Where will you find all these documented migrants?" "Why would any migrant use this device?" "There will be too many *embouteillages* with this plan!" Over the next three hours, the Italian official's tidy diagram and hopeful program were scrutinized and unraveled. One of the primary concerns raised by attendees was that the proposed project was too cumbersome, incorporating too many different actors and steps. Various representatives elaborated in detail the *embouteillages* they envisioned taking shape as dossiers and capital circulated through government ministries, bank headquarters, and IO offices. About halfway through the meeting, a heated debate began about whether the program would even appeal to migrants in the first place. "Let's think for a moment," one frustrated participant interjected. "Why does the informal market [of money transfers] work so well in Senegal? Because the path is simple." As participants voiced hearty agreement with this observation, El Hadji shook his head, clearly amused by the uproar, and whispered into my ear in English (with the hope of remaining somewhat discreet): "It's because of shortcuts." Defeated and visibly concerned, the Italian embassy emissary adjourned the meeting, vowing to return to the drawing board, and participants disappeared into cabs or company cars, retreating headlong into the city's lunchtime bottlenecks. The Italian plan, it became clear, was not the simple "alternative route" to neoliberal economic change that its architects had hoped it would be. Intended to celebrate and harness mobility as a transformative value, to generate capital flows and optimism in an era of bottlenecked development, the project was instead mired in *embouteillages*.

A year after this meeting at the Italian embassy, after my official role as *stagiaire* had come to an end, I returned to APIX to follow up with staff members about the status of this and other migrant-investor programs in the city. During my visit, El Hadji described promising discussions he had recently had with staff members at the Ministry for Senegalese of the Exterior (Ministère de Sénégalais de l'Extérieur) about possible collaborative efforts, and he detailed APIX's ongoing efforts at migrant outreach, all of which had been enthusiastically received, he assured me. But he was most eager to share with me a little piece of interoffice gossip: when Damiano returned to the drawing board to revise the Italian plan, as he had promised, APIX and all of the private-sector partners were left out of the new project. Instead, the IOM and the embassy were primarily working to design a program with a couple of government ministries. The pared-down plan was simpler, certainly. But with a shrewd smile, El Hadji added, "Make sure you include this in that book you will write: I knew this is what would happen. They are being too cautious. Cutting out APIX and the private sector means that the program will remain development-driven. It won't draw in more investors and it will never function or move on its own."

What are we to make of this seemingly stalled program, the collaborations it both fused and loosened, and the lingering debates it stirred? Through their very grounded discussions of simplified paths, *embouteillages*, and shortcuts, meeting participants sought to come to terms with the impact of institutionalizing financial practices that had thrived for so long as part of the informal sector. Officials were well aware that these initiatives have flourished in large part because they are typically situated within the so-called informal economy, where financial transactions and labor practices are not mediated by the state in any direct way. Migrants seeking to invest at home turn to relatively inexpensive and hassle-free mechanisms to transfer money, including MoneyGram and other commercial services, money orders acquired through post offices, cash sent along with compatriots traveling home, or low-cost transfer services overseen by Murid and other global religious brotherhood networks (Riccio 2008). They tap into preexisting personal networks of relatives and friends to oversee start-up and daily operations in their absence. Most "invested" migrants I knew did whatever possible to avoid paperwork and state offices, choosing to rely instead on proven informal methods and trusted personal networks.

The proposed Italian plan, in contrast, would require migrants to navigate a bureaucratic labyrinth with which they likely would not be familiar, and it added formal expectations of business plans, investment registration numbers, office visits and consultations, and deciphering intricate legal codes. Even the seemingly straightforward process of transferring capital from Italy to Senegal would appear too "heavy" (*lourd*), meeting participants worried, when contrasted with the relatively "simple" mechanisms already at migrants' disposal. How could the partnered institutions compete, then, with these attractive and effective informal routes, which were not contingent on a migrant's legal status or business proposal? Particularly illuminative here is El Hadji's comment that people use informal routes to send money and make investments because they involve "shortcuts." It is not simply that informal investment practices are simpler, but that they also enable migrants to navigate around formal routes altogether. That is, transnational migrants used unofficial channels for sending money *because* these routes escaped state monitoring and intervention; rendering these channels "legitimate" would thus devalue or even disable these networks and would proliferate other under-the-radar alternatives. Moreover, formal programs could not easily accommodate undocumented migrants, largely because governing institutions could not sanction extralegal migration practices. This further limited the number of possible participants in these programs, as many Senegalese migrants—particularly in places like Italy—were living and working abroad *sans papiers* (without legal papers). Seen from this perspective, then, replicating popular informal programs and marking them with partnered organizations' formal seal of approval would not necessarily attract migrants to invest or render the state newly relevant. Indeed, those gathered at the meeting—linked and emboldened by discourses of collaboration in the name of development—found themselves facing a predicament: their efforts to formalize migrants' existing strategies through institutional partnerships would very likely fail.

The debates surrounding the Italian plan also exposed broader concerns, then, about "collaboration" as a critical mode of economic governance in Dakar and beyond. As this particular case makes clear, development programs in contemporary Senegal typically bring together a diverse group of partners, sponsors, and affiliated offices from both the public and private sectors. Increasingly, these programs also incorporate the "targets" of their interventions—in this case migrant-investors—as "shareholders" in the project. These often-unwieldy collaborative relationships are sustained, in turn, by a proliferation of brainstorming and planning sessions, map-drawing exercises, conference calls, office visits, and document exchanges. But at the same time that these collaborations produce linkages and movements, they are also deeply unstable, generating distrust, anxiety, resistances, refusals, and heated office gossip, as El Hadji's comments make clear. Programs like the Italian plan, then, rely on cultivating and maintaining complex and very tenuous ties between a multitude of institutions and actors whose interests, goals, and strategies are often at odds with each other. If collaboration is the cornerstone upon which programs like the Italian plan are built, as many of my interlocutors suggested, it is also the force that threatens to unravel their alliances and efforts.

The challenges that characterize migrant-investor programs are by no means unique to Senegal. Just weeks before the Italian plan meeting, I attended a conference in Brussels called DiaForum, billed as a "high profile African diaspora investment forum" that aimed, among other things, to build partnerships among "stakeholders" and to establish "an investment and skills transfer pathway to the continent."[14] DiaForum presenters and participants echoed many of the experiences and concerns that my colleagues in Dakar expressed. In her enthusiastic presentation about the role that diasporic Africans could play as investors in their home countries, one presenter declared, "The road map [for diasporic investment] has been drawn. We have the capital, the intellect, the resources. But we need a road, not just a map." The presenter's observation was met with a boisterous round of applause from an audience composed primarily of well-to-do African emigrants to Europe, local business leaders, embassy officials, and IO and NGO employees. During the coffee break that followed, several diasporic African attendees likewise bemoaned that formal investment routes were lacking or cumbersome, speculating that this had a profound impact on economic development in their home countries. Though there were many plans to launch migrant-investor programs and to create environments favorable to such investment (the "map"), they explained to me, the necessary structures—the "roads"—were either not in place or unreliable. But during the course of this same conversation, my interlocutors also confessed their own very deep distrust in governing authorities in their home countries and their own efforts to circumvent formal financial channels. Such "obstacles" to migrant investment were, unsurprisingly, the focus of several panels that day. It was not only in Senegal, I realized, that the migrant-investor concept was mired in uncertainty.

State Presence after Adjustment

How do we make sense of these ambitious but snarled migrant-investor projects? What do they offer an ethnographic study of economic governance and the state in places like Senegal? In this chapter, I have taken *embouteillage*, a term already in use to describe specific moments of bureaucratic impasse, and retooled and rescaled it as a scholarly device to think about

---

14. See http://www.africanaxis.org/diaforum/diaforum_en.htm.

state governance after structural adjustment. Rather than casting unfinished migrant-investor programs as mere evidence of a "crisis" of state legitimacy and presence in Africa, this chapter offers an ethnographic examination of how bureaucrats confront, conceptualize, and harness institutional bottlenecks and to what effect. Decades of adjustment and liberalization produced a state in suspension, one wedded to mobile aspirations that could not be achieved. State workers found themselves caught up in the very *embouteillages* they sought to dissolve, and they shared many of the anxieties about mobility and the future that other urbanites expressed. But at the very same time, these bureaucratic bottlenecks also generated momentum in APIX's offices. Staff members co-opted existing informal practices, finding ways to turn the ill effects of structural adjustment into possibilities for state presence. They forged tenuous and volatile alliances with other offices and actors that might lead to new programs down the road. They looked for ways to extend APIX's reach, helping this small state office to "occupy space" differently. What emerges is a vision of the ideal structurally adjusted state: a state made presence through its judicious absence from the everyday lives of its citizens, and through its claims to future flows of capital and expertise. Though the migrant-investor programs I describe here were not fully realized or formalized, APIX nonetheless relied on them to articulate future possibilities and expectations for state presence. Meanwhile, the agency benefited from the informal, indeterminable, and sometimes illicit flows that exceeded its institutionalizing grasp, as it was these flows that kept everyday economies afloat. What might first appear as a failed or misguided set of programs, then, proves much more complex upon closer scrutiny.

The bottlenecked programs I discuss in this chapter also produced novel articulations of citizenship, participation, and economic possibility in an era of continued economic austerity. Seen from the perspective of APIX's headquarters, the structurally adjusted state has come to rely upon and extoll the virtues of a new sort of citizen. This ideal citizen lives and works abroad but focuses his energies on "home." He is savvy and self-interested in his pursuit of profit and yet faithful to obligations to kin and country. This conception of participation and presence, in turn, helps to both justify and spur urban residents' fixations on migrating at any cost and despite all odds. What emerges from this bottlenecked bureaucratic landscape, then, is a largely mythical figure—the migrant-investor—whose productive absence shapes everyday life and policy in profound ways.

FIVE

Telling Tales of Missing Men

In the spring of 2007, there emerged in Dakar a fantastic tale about an extraordinary pirogue, a wooden fishing canoe that is ubiquitous on the shores of West Africa. Although I would encounter the story in various guises over several weeks, it was Ousseynou, a taxi driver and one of my most earnest informants, who first related the incredible news: a pirogue named *Le Titanique* (*Titanic*) had suddenly vanished two weeks earlier from the shores of Rufisque.[1] It was the largest pirogue anyone had ever seen, loaded with plentiful food, water and cooking gas; four motors; a sophisticated GPS system; and room for 120 passengers. Ousseynou proudly claimed to have caught a glimpse of the mythic vessel as it was being hewn from a single, massive tree trunk hauled from southern Senegal. An ambitious "entrepreneur" had spent at least 7.8 million FCFA (US$16,000) constructing the pirogue, and hopeful clandestine migrants had individually "invested" (*investir*) more than US$1,200 to secure a spot—an amount that surely exceeded Ousseynou's yearly income. No one was certain where the vessel had gone, but Ousseynou had heard rumors that the now-legendary *Titanique* was en route to the Canary Islands, a key destination for clandestine migrants from West Africa, or perhaps even to the United States. Worried mothers who had not seen their sons began to speculate that they had boarded the famed pirogue before it had departed, and Ousseynou too wondered whether a childhood friend of his had in fact become a *candidat* (candidate or applicant), as hopeful clandestine migrants were commonly called. Alarmed by my informant's tale, I asked Ousseynou if he knew the fate of the original *Titanic*, the

---

1. Prior to and during colonialism, Rufisque was an important port city and trade hub, quite distinct from neighboring Dakar. As Dakar's population grows and expands, Rufisque has declined in importance, and it has become more like a peripheral suburb (*banlieue*) of Dakar.

Figure 9. A street mural depicting a sinking pirogue admonishes potential clandestine migrants: "Wanting to leave does not give you the right to sacrifice yourself."

doomed ship whose maiden voyage had ended in catastrophe. Of course, he replied, everyone knew that story well. The *Titanic* was the boat that had been built too big and that had fallen into the ocean (*tomber dans la mer*) as it crossed the Atlantic. In a tone at once ironic and utterly vacant, he added, "That's probably what happened to this *Titanique*, too." Ousseynou recounted this tale as the two of us navigated the urban labyrinth of Dakar in his ailing cab, snapping photographs of the city's public art that warned against the perils of clandestine migration. I had just climbed back into the taxi after a brief stop at a particularly evocative mural, one painted on a stark white wall with graphic black strokes. It depicted a violent sea swallowing a pirogue and its passengers, and it bore a stern admonition: "Wanting to leave does not give you the right to sacrifice yourself." As Ousseynou spoke, my mind returned to this mural and to the pervasive sense of loss with which it grappled.

Ousseynou's tale and the spectacular mural we visited together were part of a larger social landscape, one in which vanished pirogues and missing men became public preoccupations. In 2006 alone, over thirty thousand migrants were apprehended as they tried to seek illicit passage by pirogue from West Africa to the Canary Islands, an archipelago off the coast of Morocco that is under Spanish jurisdiction (Willems 2008). Another six thousand hopeful migrants are estimated to have died en route, though many officials fear that the actual figures could be much higher. United by the rallying call "Barça walla Barsakh" (Barcelona or death), *candidats* hoped to be processed and sent to mainland Spain, where they aimed to insert themselves into existing migrant networks and find work. Though there were reports of women and even children who joined the voyages, the vast majority of these migrants were men (Mbodji 2008). Most were West African, and more than half were of Senegalese nationality (Willems 2008).[2] Unable to migrate through legitimate channels, pirogue *candidats* were nonetheless not the poorest of the poor, as they could afford the steep "investments" required for participation in the voyages. In dramatic contrast to the diasporic entrepreneurs of the previous chapter, however, the Senegalese state and the international community perceived these particular "invested" migrants as a threat to national development, as a population whose risky movements and shadowy financial transactions required intensive monitoring, containment, and redirection.

Clandestine migration from West Africa into North Africa and Europe is by no means new. Over the past several decades, tens of thousands of West African migrants have attempted clandestine passage across the Sahara, risking their lives to reach "Fortress Europe" (see Andersson 2014). Pirogue voyages, however, garnered an inordinate amount of local and international attention, in part, I suggest, because of the charged sentiments these particular perilous trips evoked. Dakar was a key point of departure for these transnational clandestine flows, and it was, in many ways, the epicenter of loss. My friends and informants routinely scanned the city's beaches, the sea's horizon, and daily newspaper headlines in frantic search of any trace, any mention, any glimpse of these familiar wooden fishing canoes, dubbed "pirogues of hope and of death" by one local journalist.[3] Meanwhile, community organizations and

2. Prior to the 1980s, particular ethnic groups were more likely than others to migrate from Senegal, but emigration figures today generally reflect the ethnic makeup of the general population (see Willems 2008). Nonetheless, many urban residents with whom I spoke saw pirogue voyages as indicative of shifts in particular ethnic groups' interest and involvement in migration. For instance, many people pointed out that the Lebu—considered to be Dakar's first inhabitants and often fishermen by trade—were historically less likely to migrate, but they were thought to be key participants in pirogue voyages. Urban Lebu were often recruited by "owners" to captain the pirogues because of their presumed knowledge of the sea. No official statistics are available that provide information on repatriated migrants' ethnic identification.

3. Yathé Nara Ndoye, "Emigration Clandestine: Les Sénégalais Rallient l'Espagne par la Mer," *Le Quotidien* (Dakar), December 30, 2006.

state offices collaborated on murals and billboards to "sensitize" the public to the dangers of clandestine migration. Radio programs offered updates and estimates of fatalities and repatriations, and public service campaigns were sandwiched between popular evening television dramas. Dozens of development-oriented programs designed to curtail these flows cropped up in state, NGO, and IO offices around the city, and the European Union's Frontex Agency stepped up patrols of the region's coasts by air and by sea (see also Andersson 2014). And yet, even as the media laid bare the risks of pirogue voyages and politicians warned of a deepening "crisis," rumors continued to spread of unemployed sons and disenchanted fathers who had suddenly and inexplicably disappeared. As bodies washed ashore in my neighborhood and urbanites confided in me their desires to migrate at any cost, I found myself deeply troubled: Why participate in this kind of voyage—one that required a steep financial and physical investment—when it was almost certain to end in failure and loss?

Spurred by this nagging question, this chapter examines Dakarois' everyday engagements with these bottlenecked flows, focusing in particular on the vibrant tales of failed clandestine adventure that residents crafted and circulated. The myths I relate here were typically elaborated and circulated within spaces and circumstances of urban *embouteillage*—as urbanites waited for traffic jams to ease, for electricity to return, for long lines to move, for fleeting economic opportunities to appear. As they traveled, these tales drew together and implicated variously positioned urbanites—including myself—and spurred new economies, identities, and relationships. These stories collectively evoked clandestine migrants as *missing*—as disappeared, vanished, absconded, and longed for. In the analysis that follows, I borrow and retool Blackwood's (2005) concept of the "missing man" to consider the gendered assumptions that undergird popular and scholarly reflections on Senegalese migration and nation building. I explore how urbanites' keen attention to the missing man opened up space for debate not just about clandestine migration and its human and economic toll, but rather about life in an era of *embouteillage* more generally—about the gendered imperatives and impossibilities of mobility, about the changing contours of success and masculine presence, about the paradoxes of contemporary urban belonging, and about the vexing challenges facing the contemporary nation, particularly after liberalization. At a moment when mobilities were constricted and resources strained, I argue, these tales paradoxically *enabled* socially marginalized men who could not migrate through legitimate routes to achieve some degree of notoriety, respect, and success for themselves, however fleeting and ambivalent, through their public status as missing men. By attending carefully to the ways these tales of missing men are circulated, interpreted, expounded, and interrupted, this chapter considers how urban residents grappled with and pushed against assumptions about the intertwined "crises"—of clandestine migration, of nation, of masculine adulthood, of the adjusted state—thought to characterize contemporary Senegalese society.

From Enduring Solidarity to National Crisis

In contexts of dramatic social uncertainty, rumors, anecdotes, and tall tales provide urban residents with a means to collectively examine shifting patterns of inequality, political and economic exclusion, national belonging, violence, and corruption (Ellis 1989; Rafael 1997; Smith 2001, 2007). These tales spark debate about what is socially acceptable and what is condemned (Peterson 2009), and they often question the public's complicity in the very acts of exclusion or violence they describe (Smith 2001). Particularly in countries where the media is controlled by the state or otherwise censored—which, it has been argued, is increasingly the case in contemporary Senegal (see, for example, Wittmann 2008)—tales, myths, and rumors make public and visible that which would otherwise remain concealed. Because Senegalese newspaper and radio reports offered rough and sometimes contradictory estimates of numbers of voyages attempted, migrants apprehended and detained, and fatalities en route, tale telling offered the public a valuable source of updated information and helped render visible and tangible the quiet tragedies unfolding off West Africa's shores. Moreover, residents who told such tales often critiqued national and international leadership as they did so, commenting obliquely or frankly on life in an era of proliferating bottlenecks: on the injustices of migration policy shifts, on the collusion of their president in repatriation efforts, on the government's failure to seek concrete solutions to the crisis, and on the dire situation of unemployment and economic stagnation that drove men to migrate in the first place.

A central element of the tales I describe here was the pirogue, long a symbol of the vitality of the Senegalese nation. My first encounter with a pirogue tale took place in 2004, several years before this particular "crisis" of clandestine migration captured public attention. Rather than providing a crash course on the proper forms of greetings, as one might typically expect, my Wolof tutor commenced our introductory lesson by recounting an origin myth: the name *Sénégal*, he explained, was a French interpretation of the Wolof phrase *suñu gaal*, meaning "our pirogue." Prior to colonialism, this oft-told tale goes, everyday life along the coast centered on the pirogue:

Figure 10. A pirogue, worn by age and frequent use, now sits idle. Residents insisted that the pirogue would be sold for use as a vessel for clandestine migration to the Canary Islands.

on the nourishment it provided, the dependable rhythms and complementary gender roles it established, and the sense of collective responsibility it embodied. After independence was achieved, the pirogue was recuperated as a symbol of national unity despite vast ethnic and religious diversity. In order to avoid rocking the metaphorical boat, understood as the nation, the "passengers," assumed to be men, had to suppress their individual desires and work together to address the needs of the community as a whole. Their cooperation and hard work provided not only for the everyday needs of families and communities, this tale implied, but also helped sustain the feeble postcolonial economy, which relied heavily on fishing exports. I heard versions of my tutor's tale, which linked the stability of the nation and the family to the exploits of men, throughout my 2004 stay in Dakar, most often as a means to illustrate the exceptionality of the Senegalese nation in an otherwise tumultuous region.

By the time of my return in 2006, however, a newer generation of pirogue tales depicting a nation in crisis had begun to build on and destabilize these older myths. Some urban residents would refer explicitly to the "old" uses for and meanings of pirogues in order to illustrate how things had changed. In contemporary myths, the fabled solidarity of yore is threatened by the harsh realities of life in uncertain times. As this book has made clear, the state of national "crisis" with which these tales grapple—often symbolized by stormy seas or other challenges—is not new but rather chronic, stretching at least to the global price fluctuations, climbing national debt, and devastating ecological changes that marked the 1970s. Structural adjustment measures enacted in the 1980s, which were aimed at stabilizing Senegal's economy but instead exacerbated circumstances, included a push to open Senegal's maritime frontier to foreign investment and exploitation. This move has had a direct and devastating impact on the country's centuries-old artisanal fishing industry, as the pirogue simply could not compete with hyperefficient foreign fishing supertrawlers. By 2006, experts and government leaders began to publicly express concern for the future of Senegal's waters.[4] As marine populations dwindled and local fishermen abandoned the trade, the pirogue was increasingly retooled as a vehicle for illicit migration and informal economic activity, and it was reconceptualized as a sign of unresolvable crisis. It was not uncommon in 2006 and 2007 for urban residents to link the perceived disappearance of working pirogues from Dakar's shorelines to broader economic and social shifts, like the increasing presence of "Asian" investments in the city, the withering of family occupational legacies, and the restlessness of unemployed youth. This ancient vessel gradually came to stand, then, not for the vitality of a nation but for the endangerment of cherished national livelihoods and values and the fracturing of solidarities. The ostensible decline of the fishing industry is just one small part of a more generalized economic crisis—one that feels both newly urgent and exasperatingly routine. This ongoing economic crisis, in turn, has generated profound social uncertainty, as adulthood, marriage, and the establishment of families are delayed or put on hold indefinitely; gendered roles and normative values are questioned; and the legitimacy of both nation and state are undermined (Buggenhagen 2001; Diouf 2003). The crisis of nation, then, is likewise a crisis of masculinity. Amidst these changes, talk of crisis became a "structuring idiom" through which people narrated, comprehended, and rationalized the uncertainty and absurdity of the everyday (Mbembe and Roitman 1995, 325). And the pirogue emerged

---

4. See Oumar Ndiaye, "Avenir de la Pêche en Afrique de l'Ouest: Des Mesures pour la Sauvegarde des Ressources. *Le Soleil* (Dakar), March 17, 2007.

as one of the most powerful emblems of the paradoxical reasoning to which people turned during these disorienting times.[5]

This new generation of pirogue tales surfaced and circulated, moreover, in a structurally adjusted city where the so-called informal economy employs a large percentage of the able-bodied workforce and offers opportunities that are typically short-term, unreliable, and sometimes illegal. As various other anthropologists have made clear, these seemingly "marginal" activities are in fact *central* to household, urban, and national economies throughout Africa and help call into question what constitutes marginality, illegality, and illicitness in the first place (see, for instance, Larkin 2008; Roitman 2005). Clandestine migration is a complex and integral part of this economic sphere, one that creates unique opportunities for profit, mobility, and prestige in uncertain times, and lures people from throughout the country and the region to Dakar. One of my interviewees, a skilled artisan who had been commissioned to carve a pirogue for explicit use by hopeful migrants, explained to me that this particular contract was "just work" (*liggeey rekk*)—no more unusual, illegal, or alarming than any other project he had been hired to do—and that clandestine migration was just "business" (using the Wolof pidgin term *bizness*). As his assertion demonstrates, the business of clandestine migration presented important economic opportunities that were often deemed acceptable and legitimate (if only temporarily), and it drew in variously positioned individuals looking to make ends meet, to physically escape their current circumstances, or to make a quick and easy profit. Paradoxically, then, it was through participation in the seemingly "marginal" practice of clandestine migration by pirogue that *candidats* hoped to overcome their marginal economic and social positions. Urban residents thus used tale telling to explore the shifting boundaries differentiating legal from illegal and legitimate from illicit that this booming economy imposed.

The Troubling Disappearance of the Migrant Man

When situated within this context, one can read Ousseynou's *Titanic* tale as contributing to public debates about the acceptability of "investment" in clandestine migration in an era of bottlenecked routes. While the name *Ti-*

5. It is interesting to note that even when a different sort of seaworthy vessel was used for clandestine migration—as becomes clear in Souleymane's story, recounted below—it is typically nonetheless cast as a pirogue, likely, at least in part, because of the cultural and historical resonances that this particular vessel provides tale tellers and audiences.

tanique was likely chosen by its architects to celebrate the vessel's extraordinary size (see Tall 2008, 49), my conversation with Ousseynou draws our attention to the alternative meanings and ironies that urban residents generated through this tale. Young Senegalese are familiar with the story of the *Titanic* and its fate, which they encounter through the Hollywood blockbuster of the same name, dubbed in French and sold with other bootleg videos in Dakar's bustling markets.[6] The film's themes of tragic loss, heroic bravery, and sunken fortunes aligned well with discourses in circulation about the dangers and seductions of clandestine migration, and the theatrical quality of the film seemed to capture the sense of surreality that characterized daily life in the city (see Anjaria and Anjaria 2008). Not only was the *Titanique* "built too big" in comparison with the typical pirogue used for clandestine migration, but it was rumored to be headed to the United States, imagined by many Senegalese during this time period as a land of unbridled economic possibility and entrepreneurial self-making. Greedy, too, was the rumored "owner" of the vessel, who built a much larger vessel than usual to accommodate more paying passengers—without concern for consequence.[7] On dozens of previous occasions, Ousseynou himself had dismissed clandestine migration by pirogue as both foolhardy and a waste of money, and several other urban youth with whom I spoke about the tale suggested that they would have put such a large sum of money to better use. Nonetheless, Ousseynou, like many of his peers, spoke frequently of his hopes and plans to migrate and described his own future as contingent on his ability to find work abroad. Ouseynou's story thus aligns well with recent anthropological theorizations of millennial capitalism: wealth conjured from "nothing" is frequently regarded with a rather paradoxical mixture of fear, suspicion, and awe (Comaroff 2001; Geschiere 1997; Masquelier 2000). The tale crystallized as a sort of urban parable that simultaneously expressed a deep ambivalence about economic and physical risk taking and reaffirmed conceptions of the diaspora as a place of almost magical wealth creation.

6. In her work on the shifting politics of marriage payments and migrant remittances in contemporary rural Senegal, Beth Buggenhagen (2004) similarly notes the influence that this film has had in shaping notions of "love" marriage among young Wolof women.

7. Regardless of the success of the voyage, "owners" would profit from the enterprise, as the participants paid before the pirogue departed. Owners used some of this money to purchase the pirogue and outfit the vessel with navigation and cooking equipment, water, and food; to gift *marabouts* (religious men) who prayed for the vessel's safety; and sometimes to make a small payment to the captain or other staff, if this was part of the arrangement. Owners themselves did not take part in the voyages, and they often remained anonymous and thus were impossible to track down. I also heard tales of "owners" who were themselves migrants living in the diaspora, working entirely through local contacts who ran recruitment efforts in their absence.

At the center of fantastic tales like Ousseynou's is the figure of the adventure-seeking migrant, whose historical emergence and profound cultural significance I discuss at length in chapter 1. The migrant was hailed for decades as a national hero due to his presumed (and often imagined) success and wealth, particularly as structural adjustment depleted budgets and opportunities for social status and economic accumulation. Though more and more women and families were participating in transnational flows by the 1990s, migration was nonetheless considered a predominantly masculine activity reliant on networks of "brothers." This point is well illustrated by Ousseynou's own circumstances. About eight months prior to the conversations I recount here, Ousseynou's oldest brother, who was working for one of Senegal's political parties, was invited to attend a political event in Italy that was geared toward building support among the Senegalese diaspora there. At the last minute, this elder brother was unable to attend the event, and so he used his connections to arrange for a visa to send the family's youngest brother in his place. A maternal uncle stepped in to finance the journey of this youngest sibling, who had been chosen as his brother's substitute because he had been unemployed in Dakar. After the political event, this youngest brother was able to secure a residency permit, and he found work as a *commerçant* in an Italian city. With a tinge of regret for his own inability to migrate, Ousseynou described his brother as successful and the pride of his parents, who relied on the money he sent each month via Western Union.

Although quite commonplace in previous decades, Ousseynou's brother's good fortune had become rather exceptional by the time of my research. By casting migrant men as "missing," the pirogue tales that circulated in Dakar in 2006 and 2007 both reflected and stirred public anxiety about the tightening of migration regulations over the past decade and Senegalese men's concomitant failure to migrate. "Before," Ousseynou explained wistfully, "Five brothers in the same household could go abroad. With Diouf [the preceding president], it was easy . . . there were families where most of the working-age men were abroad . . . It all changed with the *alternance*."[8] Ousseynou's comment and the *Titanique* tale point to the increasing tension between contemporary formulations of success and of nation on the one hand and the realities of global migration on the other—tensions that are, of course, at the heart of this book. Since the turn of the millennium, vari-

8. The term *alternance* refers to the victory of Abdoulaye Wade and the Senegalese Democratic Party in the 2000 presidential elections, which ended forty years of de facto single-party rule in Senegal in 2000.

ous legal and extralegal migratory channels that have linked Senegal with the West have been narrowed or blocked. These shifts, which urbanites typically characterized as quite sudden and disorienting, have arisen in an era of deep concern about "security" post–9/11, of the growth of conservative political movements rooted in claims of autochthony, of concerns about dwindling employment opportunities and overburdened state welfare systems, and of competition for visas from "newer" migrants from other parts of the world, including postsocialist Europe. As transnational movements are constricted, some hopeful migrants turn to more dangerous and extralegal means—like clandestine pirogue voyages—to get abroad.

As Ousseynou's claim—that, before 2000, "five brothers in the same family could go abroad"—makes clear, these dramatic shifts were imagined in particular as undermining masculine identities and severing networks of familial and spiritual kin. In fact, the pirogue tales I recount here coincided with heated protests over proposed "illegal immigration reform" measures in the United States and with *immigration choisie* debates in France, a country with one of the largest populations of Senegalese migrants. The immigration reform bill that resulted from French debates made visa policies more exclusive and included a controversial provision that allowed consular officials to require applicants for family reunification visas whose dossiers were deemed dubious to furnish DNA samples to "prove" their kinship ties. Such exclusionary migration policies were perceived in deeply personal terms by my informants in Senegal, a nation whose identity has become so thoroughly imbricated with the itineraries of its migrant citizens. These regulatory shifts both underscored migration as an activity that is generated by and solidifies networks of biological kin, and they legitimized discourses of "choice" and "self-selection" as integral features of contemporary migration regulation.

Once considered a matter of exploiting social networks and seeking brotherly aid, migration is increasingly imagined as an individualized activity, as a matter of chance or luck, and as involving a personal engagement with risk. These shifts in popular conceptions dovetail neatly—and not coincidentally—with development rubrics that privilege entrepreneurial risk taking and future-oriented investment like those I discuss in previous chapters. Like many of my informants who related tales of clandestine passage, Ousseynou explicitly used the French words l'*entrepreneur* and l'*investissement* to describe the activities and characters in his story. In doing so, he brought broader efforts to construct an entrepreneurial citizenry under critical scrutiny. His story called into question the goals and tactics of "owners" who construct pirogues doomed to fail and passengers who seek success and wealth in the diaspora by risking their own lives. For the hopeful migrant, the tales insist, brotherly ties and hard work are no longer sufficient; instead, migration is a matter of luck, chance, and risking one's life savings (or that of family)—and one's life. Success, moreover, is increasingly achieved through involvement in the informal economic sector, often through illegal or otherwise clandestine activities. Through tale telling, urban residents grappled with the realities of bottlenecked flows, which were imagined to threaten family "traditions" of male migration and to spark rampant individualism and personal risk taking. At the very same time that these myths reflect on the failure of masculine networks, however, they also re-center masculine solidarity as crucial to the project of migration and, by extension, the nation.[9] In this way, pirogue stories simultaneously signal new concerns about social presence and the present, and they recuperate and reaffirm as culturally significant older ideas about masculine accomplishment and brotherly aid, reaffirming the centrality of men to the national story. By casting men as "missing," urban residents brought public attention to the predicament of social presence in contemporary Dakar: if male adulthood and success were contingent on migration, and migration regulations and surveillance policies increasingly excluded Senegalese men from participation, urban residents wondered, how were men expected to become "big" (*grand*)—successful and respected adults— within their communities?

Achieving Presence through Tales of Absence

Pirogue mythmaking not only reflected on the situation of missing men who sought urban presence and success through clandestine means; it also *produced* these highly visible national figures and helped to redefine the contours of success in an era of bottlenecked flows. Typically in Senegal, departing migrants are funded, at least in part, by community or family contributions, and

---

9. The notion of masculine solidarity or brotherhood that I critically examine in this chapter is, I argue, a complex and hybrid one. The concept is informed, in part, by the critical role that patrilineal kin ties play among various ethnic groups in Senegal. It also bears the traces of religious belief, though it cannot simply be equated with descriptions of the Murid tariqa and other Sufi orders as "brotherhoods," a translation that has come under increasing scrutiny by scholars (see, e.g., Buggenhagen 2009). My informants did not necessarily speak of "brotherly" relationships in strictly spiritual or kin terms, however. It is likely that the concept was also influenced by a range of local and global influences, including media and popular culture, development policy and rhetoric, and democratization discourses, related at least to some degree to French notions of *fraternité*.

they are sent on their way only after a celebratory meal, one that often involves visits from various supplicants, well-wishers, and spiritual guides. But toward the end of 2006, as death tolls and public anxiety rose, clandestine migration by pirogue became a more hushed affair accomplished through individual investment and less frequently accompanied by public ritual. As one migrant phrased it, by the winter of 2006, no mother would have given her blessing for her son to participate in these voyages, as the risks had become apparent. Instead, I was told, migrants hid their true intentions as they arranged for cash, and they disclosed their plans to few, for fear that hushed rumors might spark police investigations and shut down the clandestine operation. Migrants who survived the voyage placed calls home only after they had successfully arrived at their destinations or once they had been placed in detention. These trips thus signaled a shift in migration tactics and cultural perceptions and also indexed a particular sense of urgency on the part of individual *candidats*.

Men's absence from the household may not have been cause for alarm under ordinary circumstances. Many of Dakar's un- and underemployed men lead ambulatory lifestyles in search of work, seasonal opportunities, extended network connections, or entertainment and adventure, coming and going from the household somewhat unpredictably. Some men in polygamous marriages shuttle between multiple households during the week. Indeed, in many of the households in which I lived or spent time in Dakar, men spent significant periods of time elsewhere, and this was considered thoroughly unremarkable. Amidst the pirogue "crisis" in the city, however, some absent men became hypervisible. This claim is well illustrated, for instance, by Ousseynou's description of frantic mothers who, about two weeks after the vessel's disappearance, began to speculate publicly that their sons had boarded the *Titanique*. He expressed concern for a close friend, too, who had gone missing around the time that the infamous pirogue had disappeared. The *Titanique* tale roused similar reactions from other urban residents, who likewise called attention to neighborhood men whose absences were suspicious. But in fact, reports later surfaced that police in Rufisque had confiscated the *Titanique* before it had ever departed for the United States. The tales that circulated in the city nonetheless served to make spectacularly present men who would otherwise warrant quite little public attention or interest—even though these men, in fact, *never really left*.

Around the same time that *Titanique* tales circulated in the city, I heard incredible stories about a group of young men who had made it to New Jersey in 2006 aboard a pirogue and had recently been repatriated. Through a network of informants, I was introduced to one of these neighborhood celebrities. On the morning of our scheduled meeting, Souleymane, an un-married Dakar native in his midthirties, met me at the corner of his street to escort me to his parents' house. The road had been cordoned off and tables, large speakers, and hundreds of plastic chairs had been set up in preparation for a celebration. Elaborately dressed guests began to crowd the narrow street. As he led me through the crowd, Souleymane spoke above the clamor, explaining that his neighbors were hosting a baptism (*ngénte*), financed by a son who lived and worked abroad. Once we had navigated through the dense crowds and settled in his quiet room, Souleymane's efforts at conversation ended abruptly. He solemnly retrieved a small wooden chest from a dresser in the corner brought it to where I was seated. As he emptied the contents of the chest onto the bed beside me, I had the certain impression that I was witnessing a sort of ritual, a ceremony that had been performed for many other captivated guests before my visit. Carefully arranged on the bed for my inspection was "proof" of the men's legendary voyage—photos of the boat and its captain, Souleymane's friend; assorted processing forms from the detention center in New Jersey; paperwork for obtaining phone cards while at the facility; information about translator services; and a pamphlet detailing the procedures of his return to Senegal.

He then unraveled his tale with the same sort of meticulous care he had used to assemble this exhibit. Before his trip, he explained, he had been employed as a carpenter for a furniture workshop in Medina. His childhood friend, Pape, was the caretaker for a fishing schooner—which, in line with the storytelling conventions I have described, he nonetheless called a "pirogue"— and it was this friend who had come up with idea of taking the vessel to the United States. Pape had worked on fishing pirogues for over a decade, and so Souleymane trusted his friend's ability to get them safely to their destination. Though other participants had to pay for their spots, Souleymane paid nothing because Pape was "like a brother" to him; he would never have been able to migrate otherwise, he explained. They left under the cover of darkness and he told no one of his plans—though his mother immediately noticed his absence. Over the course of an hour, Souleymane offered vivid details of his departure from the shores of Dakar, the challenges the passengers endured at sea, the two months he spent in detention in New Jersey, and his eventual return home. Perhaps most fantastic was Souleymane's description of the passengers' physical confrontations with risk:

SOULEYMANE: The voyage was terrible. Like a nightmare. The pirogue was 18 meters by 10 meters. The sails were destroyed after just a couple of days. We
took on water. We never had enough food to eat and had to collect rainwater

to drink, because our supplies for drinking and cooking were exhausted so quickly. It was hard, hard, hard. One night, we faced a huge storm and the boat was taking on water. It was hard. Several times, we said that we might not survive. But God is great. If I was going to die, I was going to die. In the night, someone went overboard, and the captain [Pape], who could swim well, went to rescue him. I threw them life vests. My friend took a risk to help the man who had been swallowed by the sea. There was panic on the pirogue, too, when it started taking on water, and we all had to work together.

MELLY: Who were the other passengers? Were there women onboard?

SOULEYMANE: Women? Ha! They would never last. They would die. A pirogue is not a place for women.

This interview excerpt and the larger tale of which it is a part cast the missing man—in this case, the narrator himself—as a central participant in a physical and spiritual battle against the sea, described in public discourse as a profoundly volatile and bitter (*naqar*) place, where there is nothing to grip or hold onto (*geej amul banqaas*). This tale meshes well with popular and scholarly accounts of pirogue voyages, in which passengers are pushed to their limits and must work as a team to endure storms, depleted supplies, battered vessels, illness, and accidents. Though there were reports of female *candidats* as well, Souleymane's assertion that a pirogue was "not a place for women" underscored popular assumptions that men were most capable of guiding the pirogue—and, by implication, the nation it symbolized— through tumultuous weather and uncertain waters. These voyages typically took on a deeply spiritual tone, as well. Souleymane had in fact left Dakar only once before, to take part in the annual religious pilgrimage to the Mouride holy city of Touba, which commemorates the exile by colonial authorities of the brotherhood's founder, Cheikh Amadou Bamba.[10] When he boarded the pirogue in hopes of finding work abroad, Souleymane explained, he was inspired by the saintly leader's mantra that hard work was a path to salvation, and he found strength in Bamba's own story of confinement and return. Not only did this pirogue voyage foster brotherly solidarity among participants,

---

10. Grand Magal commemorates the exile of Cheikh Amadou Bamba, the founder of the Mouride Way. Millions of faithful from around the world gather in the holy city of Touba, an autonomous zone outside the control of the Senegalese state, to pray, feast, visit the mosque and other holy sites, and socialize. Because there are no hotels or restaurants in the city, participants must share sleeping quarters, food, and worshipping space with each other. This annual pilgrimage ties up the narrow roads that link Dakar and Touba, but friends and informants who participated in the pilgrimage always insisted that the traffic-clogged roads only added to the sense of collective purpose and religious and national solidarity that Magal inspired.

who risked their lives and (for some) fortunes in violent waters, it also confirmed Souleymane's devotion to a wider brotherhood of Mouride faithful—a group for whom spirituality and migration are inextricably linked. In the previous section, I explored how migration, once a matter of exploiting brotherly networks, is increasingly imagined as an individualized activity, as a matter of chance or luck, and as involving a personal engagement with risk. Souleymane's tale indexes these shifts and draws attention to the emergence of new brotherly networks and masculine identities as others are dismantled. As Zaloom (2004) has noted for risk takers of an entirely different sort—pit traders at the Chicago Board of Trade—active and voluntary engagement with risk shapes both self and community. Through claims of brave encounters with risk, made visible to audiences through descriptions of an enraged sea, *candidats* like Souleymane were able to lay claim to a new sort of identity and to membership in a broader network of "brothers" related through their shared goals and trials.

Despite his participation in this fantastic adventure, Souleymane acknowledged that he was haunted by a sense of shame (*gacce*), as he had not being able to migrate and find work, care for his family, find a wife and afford marriage rituals, or gain respect and become a leader in his community—in his words, to become "big" (*grand*).[11] Brotherly networks had failed to get (or at least keep) Souleymane abroad, and his heroic battle with the seas had only landed him back where he started. The somber tone of our conversation contrasted starkly with the rhythms of the lively baptism celebration, now in full swing, just outside the window. Just an hour before, we had come into contact—in quite corporeal ways—with the impetus that had led Souleymane abroad in the first place. For decades, transnational migration was a crucial strategy for financing traditional rites of passage (see Johnson-Hanks 2007), including the *ngénte*. Unlike his absent neighbor—who was able to migrate, marry, have children, and finance elaborate ceremonies for his family— Souleymane himself was unable to afford the rites of passage that would mark his own transition into full social adulthood.

Despite his anxieties about his failure to migrate and to become big, I argue, Souleymane was able to achieve some degree of social presence, quite paradoxically, through his tale of failed migration. Through his story of survival, Souleymane positioned himself not as a youth who sits and waits (*toog*) for opportunities to come his way but as a man who moves and travels

---

11. Various scholars who have worked more extensively with return migrants likewise describe repatriated migrants as plagued by shame, disappointment, and frustration. See, e.g., Willems 2008.

and sees the world. He and his fellow passengers did not sit passively and wait to arrive at their destination; they battled risk and worked together as brothers. Though Souleymane's efforts to migrate ended in failure, his attempted voyage and subsequent repatriation nonetheless enabled him to achieve social visibility as one who had worked hard, taken risks, and experienced life elsewhere. Moreover, his collection of documents made his presence on American soil a seemingly irrefutable fact, and his dramatic recreation of his adventure produced his absence in spectacular ways for a captive audience. When I asked if he regretted his trip and the difficult period of detention that followed, Souleymane was firm that he regretted nothing: "Time passes quickly, and you must do well with the time that you have, so that your reputation will be good. Your reputation is all you have after death. You have to maintain your reputation, so that people will say, 'He was good and courageous and generous,' because life only lasts so long." Transnational migration not only finances rites of passage; it has also become a key rite of passage *in and of itself*, one that enables men to claim social adulthood and respect (see Mains 2007; 2012a). The social visibility afforded by tales of failed migration is necessarily transitory and always contested, however, and at the time of our meeting, Souleymane had already begun to consider plans for another journey, this time to Europe. He was back to work as a carpenter, he explained, and was saving his money with the hopes of "buying" a visa and moving to Amsterdam, where another "brother" had settled. Though visas were a matter of luck, Souleymane insisted, he was determined to get abroad again.

Critically Engaging the "Crisis" of Missing Men

I have been arguing that pirogue myths enabled public debate about the changing parameters of male social visibility and success in Dakar at the same time that they paradoxically recast as spectacularly present men who had *failed* to achieve by these social standards. Since most *candidats* were men, an uncritical analysis of these tales might initially suggest that women were helpless bystanders to these events and practices—that they were left to wait, watch, agonize, and mourn as men actively confronted financial and physical risks. To some degree, these tales and rumors did indeed recuperate older themes central to pirogue mythologies: that men face the daunting seas while women wait on shore, eager to collect and prepare their catch, and that family, community, and nation are dependent on their success. In many contemporary pirogue tales as in other popular and even scholarly migration accounts, women wait for remittances made possible by clandestine pirogue journeys, or they wait for the return of their husbands and sons—through repatriation or in the recovery of their bodies. In both Ousseynou's and Souleymane's renditions, moreover, it is women—particularly mothers and wives—who initially bring public attention to the absence of men. At first glance, then, these tales seem to suggest that urban women play mere supporting roles to the "missing" men they evoke, men whose spectacular sacrifices are aimed at bringing about alternative futures. In this sense, men are not only missing in that they have disappeared and cannot be found; these tales also suggest that men are *missed*, that they leave behind incomplete and fractured households (Blackwood 2005), neighborhoods, and nations.

But in fact, many men in Senegalese society are already "absent" in various ways from the home. For generations, many have participated in urban-rural migration currents that keep them away for periods of the year. They frequently do not have absolute authority over household budgeting or decision-making but instead hold roles that are distinct from but complementary to those of women. And, particularly in Dakar, men in polygamous marriages often live separately from their wives and are only present for parts of the week. These social realities suggest that men's absence from the household is not necessarily extraordinary, nor are men who spend time elsewhere necessarily "missed." Scholars working in the context of Senegal have furthermore demonstrated that women have in fact long claimed *central* roles in shaping male migrants' itineraries and decisions, and that they have actively established personal autonomy and social prestige through their husbands' and sons' absence and earnings (Buggenhagen 2001; Bouilly 2008). Though they depend on male remittances to finance religious ceremonies, engage in ostentatious consumption practices, and furnish family homes, women also increasingly provide for households themselves by working outside the home. Others are themselves migrants, and many of these women work to construct homes for their families or for rent. And yet, although female-headed households have become rather commonplace in contemporary Senegal, they are nonetheless frequently imagined as contingent on the "absent presence" of the male migrant (Battaglia 1997, 631). The social status of these missing men, however, is always contested and ambivalent. Though *candidats* garner social presence through their absence—especially, I have shown, through urban mythmaking practices—this presence is also challenged through this same act of tale telling. In this section, I turn my attention to a tale told by two women, one that belied gendered assumptions that men were really "missing" at all.

In February 2007, I hosted a dinner party for two dear friends, Aïda and Yaye. Both women were in their early thirties, were well educated, and worked in the private sector. The occasion was intended in part to celebrate Aïda's recent—and quite sudden—marriage to a man I had not yet met. Just about six months earlier, Aïda's first marriage had dissolved when her husband, who lived and worked in France, announced the arrival of his new infant son—fathered by a girlfriend whom Aïda had not known existed.[12] When Aïda called to tell me the news of her remarriage, she was eager to pass the phone to her new husband, an employee at the American embassy in Dakar, explaining that he was working hard at the embassy in order to migrate and that he wanted to speak to me about life in America.[13] In contrast, Yaye, one of Aïda's closest friends, had never been married. She lived at home with her aging adoptive mother, a divorcée who had rescued Yaye from rural poverty and had cared for her since her youth. Yaye wanted desperately to marry so that she could establish her own home and be relieved of some of her care-taking duties, but suitable male partners were lacking, and Yaye's enormous household responsibilities left her with little time to socialize.

As we dined by candlelight in the throes of one of Dakar's routine power outages, the three of us talked about Aïda's new husband before the conversation shifted to politics and the upcoming presidential election. Both women were outspoken critics of President Wade, and on this particular evening, they slammed his administration for its *laissez-faire* attitude toward unemployment. Yaye herself had spent nearly half of the previous year searching for work—despite a stellar résumé and a *diplôme* from a reputable business school in the city—and her assessment of Wade's campaign promises and performance was particularly pointed. These women regarded unemployment as part of a broader social crisis, one that impacted not just men's identities and strategies but women's as well. As the lively debate faded into a brooding silence, Aïda suddenly became gleeful, as she recalled a pirogue tale she had heard a week earlier, one with which we were all familiar. The plot centered on a lucrative scheme concocted by a few youth in Dakar who allegedly charged hopeful migrants from rural West Africa

12. Divorce is increasingly common in Dakar, but an estimated 90 percent of women who divorce remarry within five years. For more on marriage and divorce in Dakar, see Dial 2008.

13. Aïda's new husband's high hopes were not entirely unfounded. An American embassy official confirmed that, in extraordinary cases, truly exemplary employees who have contributed many years' service at the embassy may be considered for an American green card in recognition of their dedication.

and Asia for a trip to the Canary Islands. Their pirogue, stocked with food, medicine, and water, departed from Dakar in the darkness of the night. The passengers, who were neither well educated nor well traveled, had not realized that they were taken instead to Saly Portugal, a tourist enclave about sixty-five miles south of Dakar frequented almost exclusively by Europeans. Aïda was dismissive of the gullible *villageois* and foreigners, while Yaye, whose reaction to the tale was more subdued, added her disapproval of the urban tricksters who had become rich at the expense of others. My friends marveled together at how far the *candidats* had traveled and at how much money they had "invested" to engage in an activity seemed to make so little sense. The women, who had just slammed Wade's administration for doing so little to counteract unemployment, now took pleasure in the rumored predicament of the men, whose desperate search for masculine adulthood and global mobility had landed them back where they started. The two erupted into laughter as Aïda exclaimed, "I hear that they are still wandering around, thinking they are in Europe!"

In contrast to Souleymane's and Ousseynou's *candidats*, Aïda and Yaye's central characters were seduced by a mirage, one that made migration and social success seem within their reach despite the odds. Aïda and Yaye did not describe mysterious voyages, heroic pursuits, or clandestine movements that brought public visibility to marginalized men; they focused instead on the fact that these men ended up back where they started. These women did not romanticize brotherhood or masculine solidarity, nor did they frame *candidats'* efforts as valiant, cunning, or productive. Instead they described a motley group of missing men who found themselves, by chance, in the same boat. Their tale thus called into question the implicit (and sometimes explicit) framing of pirogue voyages as opportunities for marginalized men to reclaim their role in the nation's future, highlighting instead the transnational character of the voyage. These were not national adventurers working toward a shared goal, Aïda and Yaye suggested, but a group of unrelated men with few other options. The pirogue itself was not an imposing vessel (like Ousseynou's *Titanique*), a site where men reinvented themselves (as Souleymane had claimed), or a symbol of national unity and struggle (as both men's stories suggested). It was simply an ordinary wooden fishing boat, one that never strayed too far from shore. The pirogue's passengers were not cosmopolitan adventurers, the women asserted, and the foreign paradise these *candidats* found so dazzling was actually just a short drive from Dakar. These wandering men were neither knowledgeable investors nor risk-taking entrepreneurs but instead were pawns in a lucrative scheme designed to capitalize on their marginality and desperation. They were not missed but *lost*, led astray by spectacular but shallow promises of wealth and success. Aïda's triumphant final addition to the tale—that they were *still* wandering around—suggests that the duped men were the last to realize their own failures, clinging instead to false conceptions of their own worth and futures.

I listened uncomfortably that night to my friends' lighthearted account of this voyage to nowhere, searching for an opportunity to redirect the conversation. In a context of ongoing crisis and profound loss, their amusement seemed rather inappropriate and insensitive, particularly given the relative class status the two enjoyed. But in the days and weeks that followed, I came to understand Aïda and Yaye's seemingly flippant tale as marked instead by a sense of deep ambivalence. As Mbembe and Roitman have pointed out in their reflections on crisis in Cameroon, "Fear, and the laughter it provokes, are often an effect of the ambiguity of lived experience: one is subject to this violence and yet, often in spite of oneself, one participates in its very production" (1995, 351). Aïda and Yaye were likewise grappling with their own experiences of privilege and marginality in a city caught in "crisis." Both women were economically independent and used their salaries to support larger households. Yaye in particular had spent her adult life caring financially and emotionally for her adoptive mother, whose two sons lived with their families abroad. Aïda had recently traveled to the United States as part of a distinguished program run by the American government, and she claimed upon her return that she could have stayed more permanently had she not had so many responsibilities at home. In contrast to the wandering men they evoke, then, Aïda and Yaye expressed attainable goals, fulfilled duties and expectations, traveled abroad, and sacrificed themselves for the good of their families. Yet it was migrant men—and even men who failed to migrate—whose activities and absences seemed to garner attention on the city's walls, on news programs, in public chatter, and in high-level international meetings. At the same time, despite their independence and resourcefulness, both women acknowledged on many occasions that having a migrant husband was central to the life she imagined for herself. It was not necessarily *men themselves* whom these women missed, however, but the opportunities and alternative futures opened up through men's productive absence, through their marriage to migrants.

My friends' tale does not stand in any straightforward way for the perspectives and experiences of women in Dakar, many of whom would have experienced and narrated these events quite differently. Instead, like Ousseynou and Souleymane, Aïda and Yaye drew on their own complex, situated experiences dealing with men, migration, and economic uncertainty as they recounted this urban myth. These two women were not the only ones who expressed skepticism about pirogue voyages, their causes, and their effects; rather, their doubts were echoed by many urban residents, rich and poor, male and female. This tale is instructive, then, not because it offers an essentialized "women's perspective" on clandestine migration but because it foregrounds the frictions and ambivalences that characterized public debate about "missing men" more generally. Through their tale and the laughter and unease it provoked, Aïda and Yaye disrupted nostalgic representations that romanticized pirogue voyages and rendered "missing men" hyperpresent. In doing so, they pointed instead to the deceptions and gendered exclusions that these tales both relied upon and enacted. Just as Souleymane could claim some degree of social presence by narrating his treacherous voyage to the United States, Aïda and Yaye used tale telling to position themselves as legitimate participants in urban debates about gender, class, and nation in an era of bottlenecked flows. In doing so, they revealed "crisis" not as a simple fact or as a reason for swift intervention but as contested social claim that had real effects on everyday urban lives.

The Inadvertently Invested State

It was not just urban residents who expressed ambivalence about vanishing pirogues and missing men. The Senegalese government likewise had a remarkably fraught relationship with clandestine migration and the economic and social forms it generated. The public often saw missing men as the victims of state withdrawal and economic liberalization; youth were willing to endanger their lives, quite simply, because the state had failed to produce viable opportunities for them. City residents accused the government of funneling large sums of money into infrastructural projects that benefited elites and foreigners but made everyday urban lives more difficult and disconnected, as I explored in chapter 2. Stories abounded, too, of national leaders who quietly pocketed kickbacks from foreign governments for their complicity in staving off clandestine flows. There was some truth to these suspicions. Pirogue voyages were indeed remarkably generative for Wade's administration: European countries earmarked significant funds for economic development in Senegal in exchange for the rights to patrol West African coasts and repatriate Senegalese nationals who tried to migrate illicitly. These funds spurred a proliferation of microcredit programs and rural development projects that promoted investment in the nation's youth as a means to address Senegal's clandestine migration crisis.[14] In stark contrast to the Entrepreneurial Diaspora program under construction at APIX, which I discussed in the previous chapter, this flurry of antimigration projects cast certain kinds of global mobility as gravely concerning and counterproductive. These investment programs thus produced two radically different kinds of mobile, missing men: those whose absence inspired national development, and those whose movements drained resources and required vigilance, containment, and heavy-handed paternalism.

But these antimigration youth programs were also rumored to have had remarkable unintended consequences. In 2006 and 2007, tales circulated of young urbanites who had used microcredit loans to invest in the very same clandestine voyages these funds were intended to deter. The program at the center of many of these rumors, Tout Petit Crédit, was administered by the state-run organization Fonds National de Promotion de la Jeunesse (FNPJ; National Fund for the Promotion of Youth). It offered microloans of 20,000–500,000 FCFA (roughly US$40–$1,000) to young men and women who proposed projects like launching *cybercafés* or opening small sewing shops. These rumors brought me to the office of Samba, a project manager at FNPJ, in April 2007. Seated behind an imposing wooden desk beneath a large framed portrait of President Wade, Samba explained his daily work with enthusiasm. Established in 2000 by a newly elected President Wade, FNPJ was charged with developing instruments to address the high rates of youth unemployment that had helped catapult him to office in the first place. "Our organization turns idle youth into entrepreneurs!" Samba beamed, as he patted a thick stack of pink-sleeved investor dossiers on his desk. The Tout Petit Crédit program was created in 2006 to respond to the uptick in clandestine migration, he explained, and it had proven wildly popular with urban youth because it boasted streamlined application

14. Launched in July 2006, Plan REVA (Retour Vers l'Agriculture, or Return to Agriculture) was one of the most visible and controversial of these development programs. It claimed as its goal "fixing" (*fixer*) youth in place, particularly those who had migrated or had been repatriated, by reinvesting in the country's long-neglected agricultural hinterlands. These same rural regions have provided unskilled and semiskilled labor to Europe's fields and factories for generations. This program thus signaled a forceful rupturing of transnational linkages that have fortified households and villages for decades, one that many Senegalese found unsettling and deeply suspect. Many state and other bureaucratic workers saw REVA as a (dubious) move away from entrepreneurial-focused development initiatives like microcredit (which often targeted women as ideal participants) and a "return" to more communally focused development models of past decades. For more on Plan REVA and the broader sphere of agricultural reinvestment of which it is a part, visit the Initiative Prospective Agricole et Rurale website at http://www.ipar.sn /Nouvelle-orientation-de-la.html.

procedures and a decentralized reporting system. When I mentioned the rumors circulating about the program in the city, Samba acknowledged that the office's decentralized approach, the large volume of applications received, and an overworked staff had indeed made it difficult to keep up with and monitor individual loan cases. In the interim, some recipients had simply disappeared, leaving their debts unpaid. These delinquent youth were not true "investors," Samba said sternly, and his office was working hard to promote a culture of economic risk taking and debt repayment that would uproot stubborn conceptualizations of the state as a giver of *cadeaux* (gifts).

How do we make sense of this particular cohort of "missing men" and their relationship to the state? What realities does the Tout Petit Crédit rumor bring into view and produce? In some ways, the characters in this tale appear to be ideal neoliberal subjects. They dream big, choosing to invest their loans—and their lives—in risky, future-focused endeavors rather than channeling cash into more modest local initiatives. By setting their sights on opportunities abroad, these young entrepreneurs challenged state-spun narratives of Senegal's imminent emergence as a global investment hotspot. Moreover, they rebuked state efforts to privilege certain kinds of mobility while preventing others. Samba, in contrast, pushed against these public narratives of risk taking, investment, and unrestrained mobility, using the Tout Petit Crédit rumors to instead reassert the boundaries of licit, legal, and productive economic practice. Casting these "missing men" as misguided youth who had naively mistaken loans for gifts, this bureaucrat reasserted the central role of the state in defining, producing, and managing mobility as a national wealth and cultural value. In this way, Samba's words echoed the message of the mural I described at the start of this chapter. And yet even as the state worked with foreign governments to deter clandestine flows, it relied on and profited from them. The program would not exist, after all, without these errant migrants; these clandestine flows thus gave this ministry office a renewed sense of purpose and social presence. One of the reasons that urbanites found this rumor so captivating was precisely because it publicly implicated the state as an investor, however inadvertent, in the very same flows it sought to disrupt. Narrators like Ousseynou used this particular tale to cast the adjusted state—rather than the hopeful migrants themselves—as misguided, naïve, lacking intention, and spectacularly *missing* from its own affairs. Neglected by a state mired in its own crises of identity and presence, the rumor suggests, these enterprising youth were left to forge new paths and generate new economic opportunities for themselves. Telling tales thus gave urbanites an opportunity to debate the remarkably ambiguous relationship between the state and its "missing" citizens.

But there is one final layer to this particular mythmaking story, one that helps to further complicate the assumed opposition between state and hopeful migrant. The evening after our meeting, I received an unexpected phone call from Samba. We had exchanged business cards before I left his office that day, as I usually did with interviewees. He explained that he had called to thank me for my interest in FNPJ's programs and to invite me to return for a follow-up discussion anytime. Over the course of the next half hour, we chatted a little about politics and my research before discussing at some length his interest in some day traveling to the United States. The conversation ended rather abruptly, however, when Samba asked about my living circumstances in the city, and I explained that my husband had also moved with me to Dakar. This was not the first time I had received this sort of phone call after an interview, nor was it the first time that migration—and, indeed, my marital status—appeared to be at the heart of the conversation; in fact, it is the remarkable *ordinariness* of this conversation that makes it worth discussing. In contrast to Ousseynou and Souleymane, Samba claimed a university degree and a dependable salary, and he had spoken enthusiastically about his work with FNPJ during our meeting that morning. Why, then, was this state functionary—whose relatively successful career would have been the envy of many of my interlocutors, and who himself worked to create viable local alternatives to migration—looking to migrate abroad? These seeming inconsistencies were not evidence that Samba (or, by extension, the Senegalese state) was hypocritical or insincere or that his "personal" aspirations conflicted with his "official" goals and responsibilities as a state functionary. Instead, this postscript to the Tout Petit Crédit tale underscores the dramatic instability of all kinds of mobility-focused projects in an era of *embouteillage*. Amidst chronic uncertainty, both the Senegalese state and its citizens invest their hopes and resources in various—sometimes contradictory—projects, guided by the certainty that some of their future-focused efforts will be snarled. In the process, the boundaries between failure and generation are blurred as urbanites work relentlessly to hedge their bets, salvage opportunities, and strengthen their claims on the future.

My evening conversation with Samba also foregrounds my own participation—however inadvertent—in producing Dakar's mobile fixations. The urbanites with whom I lived and worked every day did not merely (or even primarily) see me as a foreign researcher who had come to ask questions and collect data; they also regarded me as a young woman and as a transnational elite caught up in the very same practices, circulations, and asymmetries I had come to study. The relative ease with which I moved between California and Dakar was a frequent topic of conversation throughout my research years. Urban men in particular often explained their circumstances by contrasting their movements with my own, and some saw me as a conduit to alternative futures, as I discuss in chapter 2. My personal relationships with Ousseynou, Samba, and others were profoundly shaped by my gender, class, race, and nationality. They are not tangential but instead *integral* to the tale-telling practices I describe in this essay. Indeed, contending ethnographically with the realness of chronic economic and social uncertainty in Dakar requires centering these often awkward, always asymmetrical relationships with my urban interlocutors. Seen from this perspective, Samba's after-hours phone call is critical if we want to make sense of ways these rumors circulate, of the work they do in the city, and of the realities and relationships they cement as they move.

Querying the Missing Man

The pirogue tales I have related here are neither fictions nor fantasies but rather part of a rich tradition of public commentary and engagement, one that is particularly notable in postcolonial Africa. They were carefully crafted by variously positioned urban residents—by men and women, by educated professionals and the unemployed, by hopeful migrants themselves and outspoken critics of clandestine migration—all of whom were moved in some way by the events unfolding in 2006 and 2007. These tales surfaced throughout the city—around shared bowls of rice and fish, on radio call-in shows, in shops and markets, in newspaper stories, among passengers on *cars rapides* stuck in *embouteillages*—and they both reflected and generated a general sense of anxiety and anticipation. They were deeply personal accounts, inextricable from the everyday experiences and expectations of their narrators and audiences. They were at once cautionary and celebratory, mournful and eerily hopeful, nostalgic and future-focused. In contrast to "official" reports, which offered only vague and impersonal estimates of voyages and fatalities, pirogue tales rendered the crisis visible and real and helped residents to give voice to the unspeakable (Vicente 1997). Though the four tales I describe here are all documented officially in some way, my interest has not been in evaluating the veracity of residents' claims or in using these myths to fill in gaps left by more "legitimate" sources. Nor are my readings of these tales and their contexts the only interpretations possible, as I have tried to make clear. Instead, these tales offer an array of ethnographic entry points for examining deepening collective anxieties about migration—as a means to accumulate wealth, as sanctioned or hindered by the state, as crucial to the continuation of the family and the nation, as frequently linked to discourses of entrepreneurialism, and as governed by increasingly exclusionary regulations. Moreover, pirogue tales did not just reflect (on) the conditions of male social presence; they also transformed these conditions. The tales themselves took on a "runaway agency," as Faier (2008) has aptly phrased it, shaping the behaviors, strategies, and perspectives of the same actors who gave them life and meaning. They engendered and privileged certain forms of belonging while marginalizing or rendering invisible other residents' claims to participation, as not all men and very few women were able to participate in these voyages. But these elaborate stories also helped forge a postcolonial public, one that offered nonmigrants an active role in defining social norms, values, and expectations in the bottle-necked city.

My specific focus in this chapter has been on how these urban tales portrayed both pirogues (cherished symbols of the Senegalese nation) and men (whose transnational movements are thought to bring about the nation) as missing, vanished, or threatened. As Debbora Battaglia (1997) has convincingly argued, the act of making an absence tangible—of regarding absence itself as a sign, rather than as the lack of a sign—impels people to confront fundamental questions about what it means to be present, both temporally and physically. Foregrounding absence makes hyperpresent that which is displaced or invisible, and it renders the present dubious, slippery, unstable. By telling tales of missing men and vanished pirogues, urban residents raised crucial questions about what it meant to belong to, govern, and shape the city in an era of bottlenecked flows. To cast men as "missing" was thus to bring critical attention to several troubling paradoxes that animated contemporary urban life: that men claim social presence through their absence; that marginality can be overcome through participation in a purportedly legally and socially "marginal" practice; that the state is in fact complexly entangled with and invested in these illicit flows; and that even in their failure to migrate, men stake some passing claim to success. What many of these tales shared in common was their profound ambivalence about the "crises" that captivated Dakar. These tales challenged the relevancy of the social norms that governed individual success and nation building at the same time that they nostalgically reaffirmed these same ideals and values. Like the mural that I describe at the start of this chapter—whose ostensibly black-and-white message admonishes clandestine migrants while also publicly affirming these voyages as acts of sacrifice—these tales concretize absence, rendering otherwise invisible men spectacularly and paradoxically present.

Throughout this book, we have encountered "missing men" of all sorts—investors, leaders, builders—whose absence abroad is thought to bring them social presence and a claim to permanence in the country they have left behind. As global mobility becomes both more critical to urban life and more impossible, those left behind grapple with what it really means to be present (or absent) after all. It is this sense of predicament with which pirogue myths grapple. It is important to note that in the narratives I have presented here, men are not necessarily "missing" at all, a point that Aïda and Yaye make clearest. Their tale in particular undermines both popular and scholarly accounts of the impacts that migration has had on Senegalese society, which often uncritically or unwittingly produce men as spectacularly and productively absent. In her work on woman-headed Afro-Caribbean households, Evelyn Blackwood (2005) is troubled by the absent presence of a similar sort of "missing man." She draws our attention to a central assumption that animates both public perceptions and policies *and* anthropological theorization of matrifocality: matrifocal households are assumed to be those where men—as fathers and husbands—are *absent*. Yet this stands in stark contrast to actual anthropological findings on the dynamics of Afro-Caribbean households, which indicate that "these families were groups of kin and close friends that included men and were not defined by the entry or exit of a man in a heterosexual relationship" (2005, 9). Both public debates about and anthropological theorizations of contemporary marriage, Blackwood suggests, rely on the assumption that families, households—and, by extension, nations—are brought about by and given meaning through male action and presence.[15] In my analysis here, therefore, I have sought to extend Blackwood's keen observation to consider how both public and scholarly reflections on postcolonial nation building and male migration constantly re-center male movements and actions—even when these pursuits end in failure. What comes into view when we do this, I suggest, is not some sort of reawakening of masculine solidarity born by a sudden state of crisis, but instead the emergence of various gendered and classed hierarchies predicated on certain forms of mobility. These fantastic tales of failed migration thus oblige a critical examination of "crisis" more broadly, one that considers the predicaments and possibilities faced by both state and citizen after structural adjustment.

15. Blackwood's assertions overlap in interesting ways with Helmreich's (1992) insistence that diaspora has been conceptualized as a "system of kinship reckoned through men" (245).

Embouteillage and Its Limits

What are the limits of the concept of *embouteillage*? In these final pages, I consider this important question from two different vantage points: first, from Dakar, in the years after the urban segments of the road construction projects had concluded; and then from the United States, where concerns about economic crisis shaped everyday life and policy.

Dakar, Senegal / 2010

How durable is the concept of *embouteillage*? To what degree do bottlenecks of all kinds continue to shape everyday life and policy Dakar? These questions led me to return to the city in January 2010. What I found when I arrived was a city preoccupied with "renaissance." During my field research years, while dozens of other much more visible construction projects captured public attention, I had watched a team of laborers quietly clear a modest hill in the city's Ouakam neighborhood. Now, that bare patch of land boasted the Monument de la Renaissance Africaine, a 160-foot bronze colossus executed in a style reminiscent of Soviet-era state projects. Taller than the Statue of Liberty, the monument depicts the entangled figures of a man, a woman, and a small child, who sits perched atop the man's shoulder and points emphatically toward the Atlantic Ocean in the distance. The project had cost US$27 million and was made possible through a curious relationship between Senegal's President Wade, a local artist, and a crew of North Korean laborers.

For many months, I followed media coverage of the construction from Massachusetts, intrigued by the various controversies that swirled around the project. Urban residents, it seemed, had turned their attention from the city's road projects to the gleaming statue that rose just a few kilometers from the city's airport. Some denounced the half-clothed figures as idolatrous while others unfavorably compared them to Christian sculptures of the Holy Family. Other critics blasted Wade's investment as both arrogant and excessive, especially as news outlets reported that the president had brazenly declared intellectual property rights and insisted that he deserved a share of the monument's future profits. While some media accounts celebrated Wade's vision and the international attention it brought to the city, many others wondered what kind of "renaissance" the structure was meant to celebrate anyway.

Now, as my plane touched down just a few kilometers away, I caught my first glimpse of the contentious construction. My face pressed against the glass, I found myself riveted by the forward rush of the figures and by the young child's unwavering gesture across the ocean toward new horizons. The statue, which was to be formally dedicated on the fiftieth anniversary of Senegal's independence from France, was meant to herald a new era in the nation's history. Claims of renaissance were nothing new in this postcolonial capital city, of course. Once-grand boulevards, cultural venues, government buildings, and monuments stand today as a testament to the Pan-African ideals that animated politics in the independence era. In contrast to these projects, however, the Monument de la Renaissance Africaine celebrated a nation reborn through global collaboration and unfettered capital flow, one linked not only to other African countries but also to the West, Asia, and the Middle East. This was a nation whose historically anemic economy would find new life through infrastructural expansion and the opportunities for global consumption it entailed. It was a nation on the verge of technological revolution, where investments in information and communications technologies had begun to surpass those made by economic giants Kenya (Africa's "Silicon Savannah"), South Africa, and Egypt.[1] By the time I arrived that January, plans were in motion for a new technology park in the town of Diamniadio, which would be connected to Dakar by the autoroute. Startup companies and technology firms were cropping up throughout the city, and development policy was rapidly shifting to centralize the logics of technological enterprise. In this way, the monument was built not so much on gloried pasts and postcolonial expectations but instead on high speed, capital-infused futures.

1. Samantha Spooner, "Viva Senegal: How this West African Nation Became Africa's Quiet High Tech Titan," *Mail and Guardian Africa*. June 19, 2015. http://mgafrica.com/article/2015-06 -17-senegal-silicon-valley.

Wade's vision of renaissance seemed remarkably persuasive that January morning, as I hailed a cab and headed to my temporary lodging in Plateau. The urban phase of the autoroute project had come to an end, and traffic along this circuit had eased. The Route de la Corniche had been completed, too, and the Organization of Islamic Cooperation Conference had come and gone. I marveled at the ease of our journey along the seaside Corniche and at the luxury hotels, restaurants, and apartment complexes tucked from easy view. As we moved along these smooth surfaces, it was tempting to conclude that *embouteillages* had indeed given way to mobile futures, just as politicians and bureaucrats had promised during my fieldwork years. Perhaps *embouteillage* had lost its cultural and analytical force, I thought, as these new spaces took shape.

But over the coming days and weeks, as I reconnected with friends and hurried to appointments scattered across the city, a clearer picture of life in this era of urban renaissance would emerge. During follow-up discussions at APIX, staff members griped about persistent bureaucratic bottlenecks and stalled programs. Urban residents complained to me about sewage leaks, electricity outages, traffic jams, and shoddy roads. Employment was just as difficult to find as it had been, and young men and women continued to imagine futures contingent on leaving this city. As Dakarois engaged with each other and the shifting urban landscape, they launched a critique of state monumentalism, one they were eager to share with me. The Monument de la Renaissance Africaine was for many of these urbanites a startling sign of the hollowness of President Wade's proclamations of grand change and of his detachment from the needs of a struggling majority. Though the term had fallen out of ubiquitous use by this time, *embouteillage*—as an urban condition and a means of public critique—had in no way disappeared. By their very definition, bottlenecks were not eternal: they hampered and swallowed flows, only to dissipate and take form elsewhere.

This became particularly clear to me a few days after my arrival in the city, as I headed to visit the generous hosts I now call family in Parcelles Assainies. The cab moved with startling ease along smoothly paved roads, up the connector segment of the autoroute. As soon as we entered Parcelles, however, the road surfaces changed dramatically and traffic—of vehicles, animals, people—slowed. Along particularly difficult stretches of road, motorists avoided the designated road surfaces altogether, driving instead along the unpaved shoulders of the road because they were less treacherous. As we approached the home in which I once lived, built largely with funds from the diaspora, we passed the shuttered Sandwich'rie shop. The small, vacant snack shop was once owned and operated by Laurent, the son of a Togolese mother and a Senegalese father. He had been born and raised in Dakar but had spent the past several years working and studying in Europe and the United States. He returned from Paris in late 2005 because, he said, Wade had given him hope. It wasn't so much Wade's political party or platform, Laurent explained to me in 2006, but instead his concrete commitment to change. While living abroad, he had read of Wade's plans for the city—of his desire to build new roads, in particular—and he returned with his wife, armed with optimism and a plan to open a business and start a family in his natal Dakar. His Sandwich'rie shop featured the "Philadelphia-style" sandwiches he'd discovered during his years in Pennsylvania, which he was sure would appeal to the quartier's globally focused youth. By late 2006, however, the enthusiasm of this "diasporic entrepreneur" had deflated. He pointed to the insalubrious street as evidence of despair as we spoke one summer afternoon, worried that the sewage that constantly overflowed just outside the restaurant was discouraging customers. Drivers had to navigate carefully around the mess that it made. Pedestrians increasingly avoided the segment of road altogether if they could. Laurent no longer indexed Wade's roads as a source of hope but saw them instead as a sign of the president's questionable priorities and empty promises of long-term "change." Laurent had abruptly abandoned his enterprise by early 2007, around the time of Wade's reelection. He had emailed me from France to explain that he had returned to the Alps to work at a ski resort. Three years after his departure, the Sandwich'rie sign remained affixed to an empty storefront, and residents continued to complain of cycles of infrastructural breakdown and government apathy.

The shuttered sandwich shop indexes the endurance of the bottleneck as an urban reality and a conceptual framework, even after the urban road projects were completed and traffic had eased. Like the other urban residents whose perspectives I have shared in this book, Laurent's itinerary was profoundly shaped by the roads themselves—by their powerful vocabularies and imaginaries, by the possibilities they opened up and by those they foreclosed. As local infrastructures languished in the shadow of more monumental projects, Laurent found his financial resources and his hopes quickly depleted, and this "diasporic entrepreneur" saw another move abroad as his only viable alternative. It is tempting, then, to interpret Laurent's abandoned enterprise as a sign of the *failures* of the Wade administration and indeed as the antithesis of the project of urban and national renaissance. For most urban dwellers, however, renaissance was neither the opposite of *embouteillage* nor its ultimate resolution. Quite to the contrary, *embouteillage*

Figure 11. Laurent's shuttered Sandwich'rie shop. In 2006 it was a popular hub for neighborhood youth, who came to enjoy "Philadelphia-style" sandwiches. By 2007, the shop stood vacant, as Laurent had left for other opportunities abroad.

and renaissance were inextricable and sometimes indistinguishable from each other.

Riverside County, California / 2007

Embouteillage, I have been arguing, continued to provide a meaningful lens for thinking about life in contemporary Dakar even after the road projects had drawn to a close. Indeed, one of the defining features of bottlenecks is that they dissolve only to take shape elsewhere. Where else, then, might they take shape? How adaptable is the concept of *embouteillage*, in other words, for speaking of predicaments unfolding on other terrains? In the fall of 2007, as the car in which I traveled moved from traffic-clogged highways onto winding side roads, I found myself asking precisely this question. My husband and I had just recently resettled in Orange County, California, after nearly two years of fieldwork in Dakar, and we were slowly reacquainting ourselves with the "home" we had left behind. On this particular Sunday afternoon, we were on our way to visit friends who lived in Corona, a city in

Riverside County. In our absence, the so-called subprime mortgage crisis had begun to gather momentum, and Riverside County was one of the epicenters of this economic disarray. From our apartment in Dakar, I had closely followed media coverage of the unfolding financial crisis at home. In the United States, houses are a means of storing wealth and generating value, of course, just as they are in Dakar. For years, investing in a house was considered a safe bet, as home values seemed to climb without end. Fueling this spectacular growth were adjustable-rate mortgages, schemes that transferred the lion's share of economic risk from lender to borrower. Through these mortgages, many individuals and families with little savings or poor credit ratings were able to realize their dreams of homeownership. Towns like Corona had existed long before this modern housing boom, of course, but they grew rapidly and dramatically as buyers took advantage of readily available credit. Our friends had likewise made the most of this easy credit, not only buying and furnishing a spectacular, sprawling home but also taking out home equity loans to finance family vacations and car purchases. During my fieldwork years, however, home prices began their precipitous decline, and borrowers quickly found themselves trapped in sinking investments. Now, once-lively neighborhoods were overwhelmed by vacant homes. All around us, signs noted bank-owned properties and dramatic price reductions. Unkempt landscaping seemed to swallow houses. "Untended Properties Become Eyesores," a *Los Angeles Times* subheading declared. "Then there are the uninvited guests: mosquitoes, vandals and squatters."[2]

As we navigated these streets, my thoughts returned to the inside-out houses that had occupied so much of my attention in Dakar. As I have discussed, urban residents and politicians regarded the city's migrant-built houses as unnecessarily lavish and as illogical investments; President Wade even blamed these constructions for helping to fuel the nation's clandestine migration crisis. Likewise, while some American politicians and media outlets pointed fingers at the irresponsibility of titan banks, there was also plenty of blame laid on homeowners themselves, who had naively accepted the terms of mortgages they could not afford, or who had greedily used home equity loans to finance car purchases or vacations. For many, this emergent foreclosure crisis was a sign of deep economic dysfunction, not only within the banking system but also within American households themselves.[3]

2. David Streitfeld, "Blight Moves In after Foreclosures," *Los Angeles Times*, August 28, 2007. http://www.latimes.com/la-fi-vacant28aug28-story.html.
3. For a thought-provoking discussion of the Great Recession and the concept of crisis, see Roitman 2013.

But like the half-built structures that defined Dakar's landscape during my research years, these foreclosed homes indexed more than soured investments and irrational risk-taking. Journalists told tales of a much deeper, much more pervasive sense of predicament that gripped towns like Corona. They related stories of immigrant families, first-generation homeowners, and single mothers who had regarded home ownership as a critical means of establishing social presence, of sheltering and nurturing families, and of making some claim on the future. They described couples and individuals caught in a sea of unforeseen health woes and mounting medical bills, of lost jobs and unemployment checks, of refinancing and remodeling projects—and, of course, of fickle mortgage rates and plunging real estate values. Buying one's first home, seen as a crucial rite of passage into adulthood and the essence of the American dream, was endangered. Families were sent packing, marriages dissolved, and middle-class couples suddenly found themselves relying on handouts, food banks, and shelters. The very essence of "family" was in jeopardy, many journalists hinted, as households were emptied and real estate values sunk. At the same time, the media featured stories of families who defied eviction notices and continued living in their homes, and of people squatting on sprawling, vacant properties, thus generating new claims to land and to inclusion. Far from a quiet, forgotten neighborhood touched by private misfortunes, this tangle of California streets slowly came into view as a charged political terrain, as a site where belonging and authority were being debated, contested, and redefined not only by residents but by the nation itself.

What would it mean to conceptualize Corona's emptied houses as turned inside out? What connections can we make between these spaces and Dakar's landscape in process? To be certain, these foreclosed properties were quite different from the migrant-built structures I describe in chapter 3. They were produced by a different constellation of factors and forces, both local and global, that I cannot explore in detail here. And yet, there were important resonances between these seemingly distinct spaces. Exposed by the media and open to public scrutiny, Corona's hypervisible structures had likewise come to stand for the predicaments of life in a particular place, at a particular moment in time. They offered neighborhood residents, politicians, and the American public more generally a concrete means of discussing and debating the unfolding economic crisis and its reverberations. More than merely *signs* of an era, these languishing structures were actively transforming not only the built environment but also the landscape of belonging itself. As these foreclosed homes frequently moved to the center of conversation later that afternoon, I wondered: What would it mean to see Dakar's bottlenecked houses not as aberrant or parochial, but as the global standard by which we might understand house practices and structures more generally? Moreover, what potential might the concept of *embouteillage* hold for thinking about lives lived elsewhere, particularly in times of "crisis"?

Northampton, Massachusetts / 2008

These questions would surface again in the months and years after I left California. In the fall of 2008, I had just settled into a new faculty position at Smith College, a women's liberal arts college located in western Massachusetts. Our arrival in the town of Northampton coincided with the collapse of Lehman Brothers, a major investment firm, and with the plummeting of the stock market and subsequent cycles of government bailout. These were the ripple effects of the economic crisis that had begun to shake California's housing market years before. In the media, among politicians, and in American homes, there was talk of an economy that had been "built too big." Rationality had given way to irrationality, the narrative went, and sound and measured investment practices had been trampled by greed. What we were witnessing, economists explained, was the "Great Recession," a time of rising debt, sinking global trade, massive layoffs, and widespread home foreclosures. The effects of this recession were felt far and wide and would linger for years, long after the official crisis had ended.

Tucked away among rolling hills and quiet lakes, Smith's bucolic campus seemed a world away from the frenzy of falling stock markets and foreclosed homes. It seemed, too, quite distant from Dakar's bottlenecked streets and failed clandestine flows. As the snow fell heavily and the spring semester began, I wondered how I might bridge this apparent distance in my Globalization in Africa course. Like many of my colleagues who teach undergraduate-level courses on Africa, I want my students to emerge from my class with an appreciation of the continent as both vastly diverse and as indisputably global. After offering a crash course on the concept of neoliberalism, I assigned several readings on African urban youth and economic uncertainty. Before we discussed the readings, I spoke a bit about my own work in Dakar and introduced them to the concept of *embouteillage* that had proven so useful to me as an ethnographer. As discussion ensued, it quickly became clear that the students did not perceive African predicaments to be strange or distant at all. In fact, a singular sentiment rose quickly in the room: embouteillage *describes our lives, too.* Dwindling job prospects, constant economic uncertainty, the eroding value of a university diploma, moving in with mom and dad after graduation, declining marriage rates, delaying or altogether rethinking parenthood, forestalled adulthood: these were the realities of American youth, too, they insisted.

It is easy to dismiss this animated assertion as my students' failure to engage with African realities as historically and socially situated, or as my own failure to properly contextualize these readings and concepts. Indeed, at the start of the discussion, I found myself unsettled. I worried that the connections we were making might remain too superficial to be effective, eroding all sense of difference and specificity. Surely, the concept of *embouteillage* could not be so easily trafficked, particularly to think about the predicaments of coming of age at an elite American liberal arts college? And yet, those who spoke were quite well aware of their relative privilege. They were nuanced in their arguments, drawing on course readings about postcolonialism, structural adjustment, gender, urban life, and race to make important distinctions between the experiences of youth in the United States and in urban Africa. What this group of students succeeded in doing, then, was placing American and African experiences of coming of age into productive tension, noting the transnational currents that linked these twin "crises" in interesting ways. Their theories were at times shaky, but they were also provocative, bringing to the surface new ways of thinking about life lived on two different continents.

In these pages, I have focused on the predicaments of life and policy in Dakar, Senegal, at a very particular moment in the city's contemporary history. Indeed, one of the reasons that I found *embouteillage* to be such a compelling framework for this book was that it emerged from urban residents' very located engagements with the city's landscape, with institutions, and with each other. It reflected concerns about mobility that were, in many ways, expressly Senegalese and that were complexly woven into urban life, national and personal histories, and approaches to governance. As one American embassy official had noted during an interview, it was only during her post in Iraq in 2002—on the cusp of American invasion—that she had encountered a more fervent desire to migrate abroad. *Embouteillage*, as I have tried to make clear in this book, is the product of historical and cultural circumstances, and it produces a very situated, material effect. *Embouteillage* was felt acutely and in deeply embodied ways on the city's streets, in embassy lines, in bureaucratic offices, and in the city's pulsing neighborhoods. To speak of *embouteillage* was to describe a very localized experience of suspension and also to underscore one's expectation for renewed movement and connection. In this way, my use of the bottleneck as an ethnographic concept is firmly in line with anthropology's centuries-old work to relentlessly contextualize, specify, and resist all sorts of generalization (see Ferguson 2006; Myers 2011). It resonates, too, with postcolonial methodologies that eschew grand theory in favor of grounded, intimate theories predicated upon fragmentation and difference.

But to see *embouteillage* as merely parochial, as an effect of very local preoccupations with mobility and its impossibilities, would be to ignore Dakarois' own adamant assertions to the contrary. In using the term *embouteillage*, urban residents were necessarily and even primarily making sense of the transnational movements, alliances, and priorities that defined their everyday lives. The term, derived from the language of Senegal's former colonizer, is itself a product of a dense traffic that has linked the global north and south for centuries. As it is absorbed into Dakar's lexicon, *embouteillage* accumulates vibrant new linguistic sounds, meanings, and uses. In this way, it provided a compelling framework for thinking about one's place in a rapidly changing city and world. To identify and engage with a particular moment or space as bottlenecked was to position that moment or space as part of the world—despite, or even *because of*, its disconnection from global networks. Talk about *embouteillage* was thus an effort to foreground the ambivalence and contradiction that characterized life and policy in global Dakar. It offered urban residents and bureaucrats a means of placing their own deeply located experiences of predicament within a much broader and more dynamic context, to indeed *claim* a kind of globalness that seemed otherwise denied to them.

What might it mean, then, to embrace the bottleneck as an anthropological tool, one elaborated in the global south but nonetheless useful for thinking about life as it is lived elsewhere? This move does not entail an erasure of difference; quite to the contrary, the framework of *embouteillage* necessitates claiming a perspective that is situated, embodied, and always partial (see Haraway 1988), as I discussed in the introduction to this book. Nonetheless, I want to suggest here that *embouteillage* might indeed travel, and perhaps with revealing results. For centuries, scholars and policy makers have studied topics like development, urbanization, governance, belonging, and crisis—topics at the heart of this book—by applying terms and paradigms derived in the global north. As a result, African cities have long been considered "cities with an asterisk," as Garth Myers so provocatively puts it. We hesitate to see them as "cities" in a full and normative sense, since there are many ways they do not seem to conform to Western models and definitions (2011, xi). There is more at stake here than simply removing that asterisk and recognizing African cities as authentically urban. Rather, a growing number of scholars have suggested that the cities of the global south might in fact have something to teach us about Western cities (see, for example, Comaroff and Comaroff 2011; Simone 2008, 2010)—that it is, perhaps, amidst *embouteillage* that we come to piece together conceptual tools for thinking about both the particularities and the generalities of urban life.

Rather than perceiving *embouteillage* as evidence of Africa's failure, detachment, or incompleteness, the students in my Globalization in Africa course saw the concept as a means of deprovincializing African experiences and making new sense of American life, producing generative debate about economic and social crisis in the process. In some ways, their efforts echoed Dakarois' own seemingly loose use of the term to refer to traffic clogged streets, bureaucratic lags, elusive visas, unreliable infrastructures, and even the city itself. In this book, I likewise work to stretch and repurpose the term in an effort to draw comparisons between unfinished houses and stalled state programs, for instance. The bottleneck concept offers a means of likening things that are not, in their essence, the same. In doing so, the term produces new debates and new ways of seeing, understanding, and inhabiting the worlds in which we live.

REFERENCES

Allison, Anne. 2013. *Precarious Japan*. Durham, NC: Duke University Press.

Anand, Nikhil. 2011. "Pressure: The Politechnics of Water Supply in Mumbai." *Cultural Anthropology* 26, no. 4: 542–64.

———. 2012. "Municipal Disconnect: On Abject Water and Its Urban Infrastructures." *Ethnography* 13, no. 4: 487–509.

Andersson, Ruben. 2014. *Illegality, Inc.: Clandestine Migration and the Business of Bordering Europe*. Berkeley: University of California Press.

Anjaria, Ulka, and Jonathan Shapiro Anjaria. 2008. "Text, Genre, Society: Hindi Youth Films and Postcolonial Desire." *South Asian Popular Culture* 6, no. 2: 125–40.

Appadurai, Arjun, and James Holston. 1996. "Cities and Citizenship." *Public Culture* 8, no. 2: 187–204.

Appel, Hannah. 2012a. "Offshore Work: Oil, Modularity, and the How of Capitalism in Equatorial Guinea." *American Ethnologist* 39, no. 4: 692–709.

———. 2012b. "Walls and White Elephants: Oil Extraction, Responsibility, and Infrastructural Violence in Equatorial Guinea." *Ethnography* 13, no. 4: 487–509.

Apter, Andrew. 2005. *The Pan-African Nation: Oil and the Spectacle of Culture in Nigeria*. Chicago: University of Chicago Press.

Asad, Talal, ed. 1973. *Anthropology and the Colonial Encounter*. London: Ithaca Press.

Ba, Awa. 2008. "Les Femmes Mourides à New York: Une Renégociation de l'Identité Musulmane en Migration." In Diop 2008, 389–408.

Babou, Cheikh Anta. 2002. "Brotherhood Solidarity, Education and Migration: The Role of the Dahiras among the Murid Muslim Community of New York." *African Affairs* 101, no. 403: 151–70.

———. 2005. "Contesting Space, Shaping Places: Making Room for the Muridiyya in Colonial Senegal, 1912–45." *Journal of African History* 46, no. 3: 405.

———. 2008. "Migration and Cultural Change: Money, "Caste," Gender, and Social Status among Senegalese Female Hair Braiders in the United States." *Africa Today* 55, no. 2: 3–22.

Banégas, Richard, and Jean-Pierre Warnier. 2001. "Nouvelles Figures de la Réussite et du Pouvoir." *Politique Africaine* 2:5–23.

Barro, Issa. 2008. "Émigrés, Transferts Financiers et Création de PME dans l'Habitat." In Diop 2008, 133–52.

Battaglia, Debbora. 1997. "Ambiguating Agency: The Case of Malinowski's Ghost." *American Anthropologist* 99, no. 3: 505–10.

Bayart, Jean-François. 2000. "Africa in the World: A History of Extraversion." *African Affairs* 99, no. 395: 217–67.

———. 2007. *Global Subjects: A Political Critique of Globalization.* Cambridge: Polity Press.

———. 2009. *The State in Africa: The Politics of the Belly.* Cambridge: Polity Press.

Bendech, Mohamed, Michel Chauliac, Pascal Gerbouin-Rerolle, Nianguiny Kante, and Denis Malvy. 1997. "Devaluation of the CFA franc and Feeding Strategies of Families in Bamako (Mali)." *Cahiers d'Etudes et des Recherches Francophones / Santé* 7, no. 6: 361–71.

Benoit-Cattin, Michel. 1991. "Ideological and Institutional Antecedents of the New Agricultural Policy." In Delgado and Jammeh 1991.

Berthélemy, Jean-Claude, Abdoulaye Seck, and Ann Vourc'h. 1996. *Growth in Senegal: A Lost Opportunity?* Organization for Economic Cooperation and Development (OECD) Publishing.

Bernal, Victoria. 2014. *Nation as Network: Diaspora, Cyberspace, and Citizenship.* Chicago: University of Chicago Press.

Besnier, Niko. 2011. *On the Edge of the Global: Modern Anxieties in a Pacific Island Nation.* Palo Alto, CA: Stanford University Press.

Betts, Raymond. 1971. "The Establishment of the Medina in Dakar, Senegal, 1914." *Africa: Journal of the International African Institute* 14, no. 2: 143–52.

Blackwood, Evelyn. 2005. "Wedding Bell Blues: Marriage, Missing Men, and Matrifocal Follies." *American Ethnologist* 32 , no. 1: 3–19.

Blum, Françoise. 2012. "Sénégal 1968: Révolte Etudiante et Grève Générale." *Revue d'Histoire Moderne et Contemporaine* 2: 144–77.

Boone, Catherine. 1990. "State Power and Economic Crisis in Senegal." *Comparative Politics* 22, no. 3: 341–57.

Bop, Lamine. 1983. "The 'Improved Parcels of Land' Project. In *Reading the Contemporary African City*, edited by Brian Brace Taylor, 129–30. Singapore: Concept Media.

Bouilly, Emmanuelle. 2008. "Les Enjeux Féminins de la Migration Masculine: Le Collectif des Femmes pour la Lutte Contre l'Immigration Clandestine de Thiaroye-Sur-Mer." *Politique Africaine* 109.

Bourdieu, Pierre. 1970. "The Berber House or the World Reversed." *Social Science Information* 9, no. 2: 151–70.

Bredeloup, Sylvie. 2008. "L'Aventurier, Une Figure de la Migration Africaine." *Cahiers Internationaux de Sociologie* 2:281–306.

Bruck, Gabriele Vom. 1997. "A House Turned Inside Out: Inhabiting Space in a Yemeni City." *Journal of Material Culture* 2, no. 2: 139–72.

Buggenhagen, Beth. 2001. "Prophets and Profits: Gendered and Generational Visions of Wealth and Value in Senegalese Murid Households." *Journal of Religion in Africa* 31, no. 4: 373–401.

———. 2004. "Domestic Object(ion)s: The Senegalese Murid Trade Diaspora and the Politics of Marriage Payments, Love, and State Privatization. *Studies on Religion in Africa* 26:21–53.

———. 2009. "Beyond Brotherhood: Gender, Religious Authority, and the Global Circuits of Senegalese Muridiyya." In *New Perspectives on Islam in Senegal: Conversion, Migration, Wealth, Power, and Femininity*, edited by Mamadou Diouf and Mara Leichtman, 189–210. New York: Palgrave Macmillan.

———. 2011. "Are Births Just 'Women's Business'? Gift Exchange, Value, and Global Volatility in Muslim Senegal." *American Ethnologist* 38, no. 4: 714–32.

———. 2012. *Muslim Families in Global Senegal: Money Takes Care of Shame.* Bloomington: Indiana University Press.

Bugnicourt, Jacques. 1983. "Dakar without Bounds." In *Reading the Contemporary African City,* edited by Brian Brace Taylor, 27–42. Singapore: Concept Media.

Bugnicourt, Jacques, and Amadou Diallo. 1991. *Set Setal, Des Murs Qui Parlent: Nouvelle Culture Urbaine à Dakar.* Dakar: ENDA.

Caldeira, Teresa. 2000. *City of Walls: Crime, Segregation, and Citizenship in São Paulo.* University of California Press.

Carse, Ashley. 2014. "The Year 2013 in Sociocultural Anthropology: Cultures of Circulation and Anthropological Facts." *American Anthropologist* 116, no. 2: 390–403.

Carsten, Janet, and Stephen Hugh-Jones, eds. 1995. *About the House: Lévi-Strauss and Beyond.* New York: Cambridge University Press.

Carter, Donald Martin. 1997. *States of Grace: Senegalese in Italy and the New European Migration.* Minneapolis: University of Minnesota Press.

Certeau, Michel de. 1984. *The Practice of Everyday Life.* Translated by Steven Rendall. Berkeley: University of California Press.

Chalfin, Brenda. 2010. *Neoliberal Frontiers: An Ethnography of Sovereignty in West Africa.* Chicago: University of Chicago Press.

———. 2014. "Public Things, Excremental Politics, and the Infrastructure of Bare Life in Ghana's City of Tema." *American Ethnologist* 41, no. 1, 92–109.

Chu, Julie. 2010. *Cosmologies of Credit: Transnational Mobility and the Politics of Destination in China.* Durham, NC: Duke University Press Books.

———. 2014. "When Infrastructures Attack: The Workings of Disrepair in China." *American Ethnologist* 41, no. 2: 351–67.

Clark, Gracia. 2005. "The Permanent Transition in Africa." *Voices* 7, no. 1: 6–9.

Clifford, James. 1997. *Routes.* Cambridge, MA: Harvard University Press.

Cole, Jennifer. 2005. "The Jaombilo of Tamatave (Madagascar), 1992–2004: Reflections on Youth and Globalization." *Journal of Social History* 38, no. 4: 891–914.

———. 2010. *Sex and Salvation: Imagining the Future in Madagascar.* Chicago: University of Chicago Press.

Cole, Jennifer, and Deborah Durham, eds. 2007. *Generations and Globalization: Youth, Age, and Family in the New World Economy.* Vol. 3. Bloomington: Indiana University Press.

Comaroff, Jean, and John Comaroff. 1999. "Occult Economies and the Violence of Abstraction: Notes from the South African Postcolony." *American Ethnologist* 26, no. 2: 279–303.

———. 2001. "Millennial Capitalism: First Thoughts on a Second Coming." In *Millennial Capitalism and the Culture of Neoliberalism,* edited by Jean Comaroff and John Comaroff. Durham, NC: Duke University Press.

———. 2012. "Theory from the South: Or, How Euro-America is Evolving toward Africa." *Anthropological Forum* 22, no. 2: 113–31.

Cooper, Frederick. 1996. *Decolonization and African Society: The Labor Question in French and British Africa.* New York: Cambridge University Press.

Coquery-Vidrovitch, Catherine. 2001. "Nationalité et Citoyenneté en Afrique Occidentale Français: Originaires et Citoyens dans le Sénégal Colonial." *Journal of African History* 42, no. 02: 285–305.

Coutin, Susan. 2007. *Nations of Emigrants: Shifting Boundaries of Citizenship in El Salvador and the United States.* Ithaca, NY: Cornell University Press.

Cross, Jamie. 2010. "Neoliberalism as Unexceptional: Economic Zones and the Everyday Precariousness of Working Life in South India." *Critique of Anthropology* 30, no. 4: 355–73.

Cruise O'Brien, Donal B. 1996. "A Lost Generation? Youth Identity and State Decay in West Africa." In *Postcolonial Identities in Africa*, edited by Richard Werbner and Terence Ranger, 55–74. London: Zed Books.

Czeglédy, André. 2004. "Getting around Town: Transportation and the Built Environment in Post-Apartheid South Africa." *City & Society* 16, no. 2: 63–92.

Dahou, Tarik, and Vincent Foucher. 2009. "Senegal since 2000: Rebuilding Hegemony in a Global Age." In *Turning Points in African Democracy*, edited by Abdul Raufu Mustapha and Lindsay Whitfeld, 13–30. Suffolk, UK: James Currey Publishers.

Das, Veena, and Deborah Poole, eds. 2004. *Anthropology in the Margins of the State*. Suffolk, UK: James Currey Publishers.

DeHart, Monica. 2010. *Ethnic Entrepreneurs: Identity and Development Politics in Latin America*. Palo Alto, CA: Stanford University Press.

De Jong, Ferdinand, and Vincent Foucher. 2010. "La Tragédie du Roi Abdoulaye? Néomodernisme et Renaissance Africaine dans le Sénégal Contemporain." *Politique Africaine* 2:187–204.

Delgado, Christopher, and Sidi Jammeh, eds. 1991. *The Political Economy of Senegal under Structural Adjustment*. Westport, CT: Praeger.

Dial, Fatou Binetou. 2008. *Mariage et Divorce à Dakar: Itineraires Feminins*. Paris: Karthala.

Diatta, Marie Angelique, and Ndiaga Mbow. 1999. "Releasing the Development Potential of Return Migration: The Case of Senegal." *International Migration* 37, no. 1: 243–66.

Diop, Momar-Coumba, ed. 2004. *Gouverner Le Sénégal: Entre Ajustement Structurel et Développement Durable*. Paris: Karthala.

———, ed. 2008. *Le Sénégal des Migrations: Mobilités, Identités, et Sociétés*. Paris: Karthala.

Diouf, Makhtar. 1992. "La Crise de l'Ajustement." *Politique Africaine* 45:62–85.

Diouf, Mamadou. 1992. "Fresques Murales Écriture de l'Histoire: Le Set/Setal à Dakar." *Politique Africaine* 46:41–54.

———. 1996. "Urban Youth and Senegalese Politics: Dakar 1988–1994." *Public Culture* 8, no. 2: 225–49.

———. 1998. "The French Colonial Policy of Assimilation and the Civility of the Originaires of the Four Communes (Senegal): A Nineteenth Century Globalization Project." *Development and Change:* 29, no. 4: 671–96.

———. 2000. "The Senegalese Murid Trade Diaspora and the Making of a Vernacular Cosmopolitanism." Translated by Stephen Rendall. *Public Culture* 12, no. 3: 679–702.

———. 2003. "Engaging Postcolonial Cultures: African Youth and Public Space." *African Studies Review* 46, no. 2: 1–12.

Diop, Momar-Coumba, ed. 2008. *Le Sénégal des Migrations: Mobilités, Identités et Sociétés*. Paris: Karthala.

Ebin, Victoria. 1992. "A la Recherche de Nouveaux 'Poissons': Stratégies Commercials Mourides par Temps de Crise." *Politique Africaine* 45:86–99.

Ellis, Stephen. 1989. "Tuning in to Pavement Radio." *African Affairs* 88, no. 352: 321–30.

Elyachar, Julia. 2002. "Empowerment Money: The World Bank, Non-Governmental Organizations, and the Value of Culture in Egypt." *Public Culture* 14, no. 3: 493–513.

———. 2005. *Markets of Dispossession: NGOs, Economic Development, and the State in Cairo*. Durham, NC: Duke University Press.

———. 2010. "Phatic Labor, Infrastructure, and the Question of Empowerment in Cairo." *American Ethnologist* 37, no. 3: 452–64.

Englund, Harri. 2002. "Ethnography after Globalism: Migration and Emplacement in Malawi." *American Ethnologist* 29, no. 2: 261–86.

Faier, Lieba. 2008. "Runaway Stories: The Underground Micromovements of Filipina *Oyomesan* in Rural Japan." *Cultural Anthropology* 23, no. 4: 630–59.

Featherstone, Mike, Nigel Thrift, and John Urry, eds. 2005. *Automobilities*. London: Sage Publications.

Fehérváry, Krisztina. 2011. "The Materiality of the New Family House in Hungary: Postsocialist Fad or Middle-Class Ideal?" *City and Society* 23, no. 1: 18–41.

Ferguson, James. 1999. *Expectations of Modernity: Myths and Meanings of Urban Life on the Zambian Copperbelt*. Berkeley: University of California Press.

———. 2006. *Global Shadows: Africa in the Neoliberal World Order*. Durham, NC: Duke University Press.

Fioratta, Susanna. 2015. "Beyond Remittance: Evading Uselessness and Seeking Personhood in Fouta Djallon, Guinea." *American Ethnologist* 42, no. 2: 295–308.

Fischer, Michael. 2005. "Technoscientific Infrastructures and Emergent Forms of Life: A Commentary." *American Anthropologist* 107, no. 1: 55–61.

Fisch, Michael. 2013. "Tokyo's Commuter Train Suicides and the Society of Emergence." *Cultural Anthropology* 28, no. 2: 320–43.

Foley, Ellen. 2009. *Your Pocket is What Cures You: The Politics of Health in Senegal*. New Brunswick, NH: Rutgers University Press.

Foley, Ellen, and Cheikh Anta Babou. 2011. "Diaspora, Faith, and Science: Building a Mouride Hospital in Senegal." *African Affairs* 110, no. 438: 75–95.

Foster, Vivien, and Cecilia Briceño-Garmendia. 2010. "Africa's Infrastructure: A Time for Transformation." Washington DC: World Bank.

Foucher, Vincent. 2007. "'Blue Marches': Public Performance and Political Turnover in Senegal." In *Staging Politics: Power and Performance in Asia and Africa*, edited by Julia Strauss and Donal Cruise O'Brien, 111–33. London: I.B. Tauris Publishers.

Fouquet, Thomas. 2007. "Imaginaires Migratoires et Expériences Multiples de l'Altérité: Une Dialectique Actuelle du Proche et du Lointain." *Autrepart* 1:83–98.

———. 2008. "Migrations et 'Glocalisation' Dakaroises." In Diop 2008, 241–76.

Fredericks, Rosalind. 2014. "Vital Infrastructures of Trash in Dakar." *Comparative Studies of South Asia, Africa, and the Middle East* 34, no. 3: 532–48.

Galvan, Dennis C. 2001. "Political Turnover and Social Change in Senegal." *Journal of Democracy* 12, no. 3: 51–62.

Gellar, Sheldon. 1976. *Structural Changes and Colonial Dependency: Senegal, 1885–1945*. London: Sage Publications.

———. 1995. *Senegal: An African Nation between Islam and the West*. Boulder, CO: Westview Press.

Gellar, Sheldon, Robert B. Charlick, and Yvonne Jones. 1980. *Animation Rurale and Rural Development: The Experience of Senegal*. Special Series on Animation Rurale. Ithaca, NY: Cornell University, Rural Development Committee.

Gersovitz, Mark. 1987. "Some Sources and Implications of Uncertainty in the Senegalese Economy." In Waterbury and Gersovitz 1987, 15–46.

Geschiere, Peter. 1997. *The Modernity of Witchcraft: Politics and the Occult in Postcolonial Africa*. Charlottesville: University Press of Virginia.

Graham, Stephen, and Simon Marvin. 2001. *Splintering Urbanism: Networked Infrastructures, Technological Mobilities and the Urban Condition*. Hove, UK: Psychology Press.

Grillo, Ralph, and Bruno Riccio. 2004. "Translocal Development: Italy–Senegal." *Population, Space and Place* 10, no. 2: 99–111.

Gupta, Akhil. 2012. *Red Tape: Bureaucracy, Structural Violence, and Poverty in India*. Durham, NC: Duke University Press.

Gupta, Akhil, and James Ferguson. 1997. *Anthropological Locations: Boundaries and Grounds of a Field Science*. Berkeley: University of California Press.

Gürsel, Zeynep. 2012. "The Politics of Wire Service Photography: Infrastructures of Representation in a Digital Newsroom." *American Ethnologist* 39, no. 1: 71–89.

Guyer, Jane. 2007. "Prophecy and the Near Future: Thoughts on Macroeconomic, Evangelical, and Punctuated Time." *American Ethnologist* 34, no. 3: 409–21.

Hage, Ghassan. 2009. "Waiting Out the Crisis: On Stuckedness and Governmentality." In *Waiting*, edited by Ghassan Hage, 97–106. Melbourne: Melbourne University Press.

Hansen, Thomas Blom. 2006. "Sounds of Freedom: Music, Taxis, and Racial Imagination in Urban South Africa." *Public Culture* 18, no. 1: 185–208.

Harms, Eric. 2013. "Eviction Time in the New Saigon: Temporalities of Displacement in the Rubble of Development. *Cultural Anthropology* 28, no. 2: 344–68.

Haraway, Donna. 1988. "Situated Knowledges: The Science Question in Feminism and the Privilege of Partial Perspective." *Feminist Studies* 14, no. 3: 575–99.

Harvey, David. 1989. "From Managerialism to Entrepreneurialism: The Transformation in Urban Governance in Late Capitalism." *Geografiska Annaler* 71 B, no. 1: 3–17.

———. 2005. *A Brief History of Neoliberalism*. Oxford: Oxford University Press.

Heidegger, Mark. 1971. "Building, Dwelling, Thinking." In *Poetry, Language, Thought*. New York: Harper & Row.

Helmreich, Stefan. 1992. "Kinship, Nation, and Paul Gilroy's Concept of Diaspora." *Diaspora* 2, no. 2: 243–49.

Hernandez, Esther, and Susan Coutin. 2006. "Remitting Subjects: Migrants, Money, and States." *Economy and Society* 35, no. 2: 185–208.

Hetherington, Kregg. 2014. "Waiting for the Surveyor: Development Promises and the Temporality of Infrastructure." *The Journal of Latin American and Caribbean Anthropology* 19, no. 2: 195–211.

Hibou, Béatrice. 2004. *Privatizing the State*. New York: Columbia University Press.

Holston, James, ed. 1999. *Cities and Citizenship*. Durham, NC: Duke University Press.

———. 2008. *Insurgent Citizenship: Disjunctions of Democracy and Modernity in Brazil*. Princeton, NJ: Princeton University Press.

Howell, Signe. 2003. "The House as Analytic Concept: A Theoretical Overview." In Sparkes and Howell 2003, 16–33.

International Fund for Agricultural Development (IFAD). 2009. "Sending Money Home to Africa: Remittance Markets, Enabling Environment and Prospects." Rome: International Fund for Agricultural Development.

International Monetary Fund (IMF). 2012. "World Economic Outlook: Growth Resuming, Dangers Remain." World Economic and Financial Surveys.

Isotalo, Riina. 2010. "Politicizing the Transnational." In *Migration, Development, and Transnationalization: A Critical Stance*, edited by Nina Glick Schiller and Thomas Faist, 100–41. New York: Berghahn Books.

Jeffrey, Craig. 2010. *Timepass: Youth, Class, and the Politics of Waiting in India*. Palo Alto, CA: Stanford University Press.

Johnson, G. Wesley. 1971. *Emergence of Black Politics in Senegal: The Struggle for Power in the Four Communes, 1900–1920*. Stanford, CA: Hoover Institution on War, Revolution, and Peace, Stanford University Press.

Johnson-Hanks, Jennifer. 2006. *Uncertain Honor: Modern Motherhood in an African Crisis*. Chicago: University of Chicago Press.

———. 2007. "Women on the Market: Marriage, Consumption, and the Internet in Urban Cameroon." *American Ethnologist* 34, no. 4: 642–58.

Kane, Abdoulaye. 2002. "Senegal's Village Diaspora and the People Left Ahead." In *The Transnational Family: New European Frontiers and Global Networks*, edited by Deborah and Vuorela Bryceson Ulla, 245–63. New York: Berg Publishers.

Keane, Webb. 1995. "The Spoken House: Text, Act, and Object in Eastern Indonesia." *American Ethnologist* 22, no. 1: 102–24.

Lambert, Michael. 1993. "From Citizenship to Negritude: 'Making a Difference' in Elite Ideologies of Colonized Francophone West Africa." *Comparative Studies in Society and History* 35, no. 2: 239–62.

———. 2002. *Longing for Exile: Migration and the Making of a Translocal Community in Senegal*. Portsmouth: Heinemann.

Lane, Carrie. 2009. "Man Enough to Let My Wife Support Me: How Changing Models of Career and Gender are Reshaping the Experience of Unemployment." *American Ethnologist* 36, no. 4: 681–92.

Larkin, Brian. 2008. *Signal and Noise: Media, Infrastructure, and Urban Culture in Nigeria*. Durham, NC: Duke University Press.

———. 2013. "The Politics and Poetics of Infrastructure." *Annual Review of Anthropology* 42:327–43.

Lave, Jean. 1988. *Cognition in Practice: Mind, Mathematics and Culture in Everyday Life*. Cambridge: Cambridge University Press.

Lawuyi, Olatunde Bayo. 1988. "The World of the Yoruba Taxi Driver: An Interpretive Approach to Vehicle Slogans." *Africa: The Journal of the International African Institute* 58, no. 1: 1–13.

Lefebvre, Henri. 1991. *The Production of Space*. Oxford: Blackwell.

Leichtman, Mara. 2002. "Transforming Brain Drain into Capital Gain: Morocco's Changing Relationship with Migration and Remittances." *Journal of North African Studies* 7, no. 1: 109–37.

Leinaweaver, Jessaca. 2009. "Raising the Roof in the Transnational Andes: Building Houses, Forging Kinship." *Journal of the Royal Anthropological Institute* 15, no. 4: 777–96.

Lévi-Strauss, Claude. 1982. *The Way of the Masks*. Seattle: University of Washington Press.

———. 1987. *Anthropology and Myth: Lectures 1951–1982*. Oxford: Basil Blackwell.

Liechty, Mark. 2003. *Suitably Modern: Making Middle-Class Culture in a New Consumer Society*. Princeton, NJ: Princeton University Press.

Lukose, Ritty. 2009. *Liberalization's Children: Gender, Youth, and Consumer Citizenship in Globalizing India*. Durham, NC: Duke University Press.

Mains, Daniel. 2007. Neoliberal Times: Progress, Boredom, and Shame among Young Men in Urban Ethiopia. *American Ethnologist* 34, no. 4: 659–73.

———. 2012a. *Hope is Cut: Youth, Unemployment, and the Future in Urban Ethiopia*. Philadelphia: Temple University Press.

———. 2012b. "Blackouts and Progress: Privatization, Infrastructure, and a Developmentalist State in Jimma, Ethiopia." *Cultural Anthropology* 27, no. 1: 3–27.

Manchuelle, François. 1997. *Willing Migrants: Soninke Labor Diasporas 1848–1960*. Athens: Ohio University Press.

Markovitz, Irving. 1991. "Animation Rurale: Biography of an African Administrative Agency." In Delgado and Jammeh 1991, 69–84.

Masquelier, Adeline. 2000. "Of Headhunters and Cannibals: Migrancy, Labor, and Consumption in the Mawri Imagination." *Cultural Anthropology* 15, no. 1: 84–126.

———. 2013. "Teatime: Boredom and the Temporalities of Young Men in Niger." *Africa* 83, no. 3: 470–91.

Mbembe, Achille, and Sarah Nuttall. 2004. "Writing the World from an African Metropolis." *Public Culture* 16, no. 3: 347–72.

Mbembe, Achille, and Janet Roitman. 1995. "Figures of the Subject in Times of Crisis." *Public Culture* 7, no. 2: 323–52.

Mbodji, Mamadou. 2008. "Imaginaires et Migrations: Le cas du Sénégal." In Diop 2008, 305–19.

Mbodji, Mohamed. 1991. "The Politics of Independence: 1960–1986" In Delgado and Jammeh 1991.

McDowell, Linda. 2000. "The Trouble with Men? Young People, Gender Transformations and the Crisis of Masculinity." *International Journal of Urban and Regional Research* 24, no. 1: 201–9.

McFarlane, Colin. 2008. "Urban Shadows: Materiality, the 'Southern City' and Urban Theory." *Geography Compass* 2, no. 2: 340–58.

McKinnon, Susan. 2000. "The Tanimbarese *Tavu*: The Ideology of Growth and the Material Configurations of Houses and Hierarchy in an Indonesian Society." In *Beyond Kinship: Social and Material Reproduction in House Societies*, edited by Rosemary A. Joyce and Susan D. Gillespie, 161–76. Philadelphia: University of Pennsylvania Press.

McLaughlin, Fiona. 2001. "Dakar Wolof and the Configuration of an Urban Identity." *Journal of African Cultural Studies* 14, no. 2: 153–72.

Melly, Caroline. 2010. "Inside-Out Houses: Urban Belonging and Imagined Futures in Dakar, Senegal." *Comparative Studies in Society and History* 52, no. 1: 37–65.

———. 2011. "Titanic Tales of Missing Men: Reconfigurations of National Identity and Gendered Presence in Dakar, Senegal." *American Ethnologist* 38, no. 2: 361–76.

———. 2013. "Ethnography on the Road: Infrastructural Vision and the Unruly Present in Contemporary Dakar." *Africa: The Journal of the International African Institute* 83, no. 2: 385–402.

Meyer, Birgit. 1998. "The Power of Money: Politics, Occult Forces, and Pentecostalism in Ghana." *African Studies Review* 41, no. 3: 15–37.

———. 2004. "Christianity in Africa: From African Independent to Pentecostal-Charismatic Churches." *Annual Review of Anthropology* 33:447–74.

Millar, Kathleen. 2014. "The Precarious Present: Wageless Labor and Disrupted Life in Rio de Janeiro, Brazil." *Cultural Anthropology* 29, no. 1: 32–53.

Miller, Daniel, ed. 2001. "Possessions." In *Home Possessions: Material Culture behind Closed Doors*, edited by Daniel Miller, 107–22. Oxford: Berg.

Mohan, Giles. 2006. "Embedded Cosmopolitanism and the Politics of Obligation: The Ghanaian Diaspora and Development." *Environment and Planning A* 38, no. 5: 867–83.

Molé, Noelle. 2010. "Precarious Subjects: Anticipating Neoliberalism in Northern Italy's Workplace." *American Anthropologist* 112, no. 1: 38–53.

Muehlebach, Andrea. 2013. "On Precariousness and the Ethical Imagination: The Year 2012 in Sociocultural Anthropology." *American Anthropologist* 115, no. 2: 297–311.

Mutongi, Kenda. 2006. "Thugs or Entrepreneurs? Perceptions of Matatu Operators in Nairobi, 1970 to the Present." *Africa: The Journal of the International African Institute* 76, no. 4: 549.

Myers, Garth. 2011. *African Cities: Alternative Visions of Urban Theory and Practice*. London: Zed Books Limited.

Naïr, Samir. 1997. *Rapport de Bilan et d'Orientation sur la Politique de Codéveloppement Liée aux Flux Migratoires*. Paris: Ministère des Affaires Etrangères.

Ndione, Emmanuel, and Mohamed Soumaré. 1983. "Growth and Evolution of the Dakar Suburbs: The Case of Grand-Yoff." In *Reading the Contemporary African City*, edited by Brian Brace Taylor. Singapore: Concept Media.

Nguyen, Vinh Kim. 2010. *The Republic of Therapy: Triage and Sovereignty in West Africa's Time of AIDS*. Durham, NC: Duke University Press.

Niane, Aminata, ed. 2010. *Rapport Annuel APIX S.A.* Dakar: Direction Générale d'APIX S.A.

Nielsen, Morten. 2011. "Futures Within: Reversible Time and House-Building in Maputo, Mozambique." *Anthropological Theory* 11, no. 4: 397–423.

Norberg, Carin, and Fantu Cheru. 2009. "Migration and Development." In *Newsletter from the Nordic Africa Institute*. Uppsala, Sweden: The Nordic Africa Institute. http://www .nai.uu.se/news/newsletter/newsletter_april_2009.pdf.

Notar, Beth. 2012a. "'Coming Out' to 'Hit the Road': Temporal, Spatial and Affective Mobilities of Taxi Drivers and Day Trippers in Kunming, China." *City & Society* 24, no. 3: 281–301.

———. 2012b. "Off Limits and Out of Bounds: Taxi Driver Perceptions of Dangerous People and Places in Kunming, China." In *Rethinking Global Urbanism*, edited by Xiangming Chen and Ahmed Kanna, 190–207. New York: Routledge.

Passaro, Joanne. 1997. " 'You Can't Take the Subway to the Field!' 'Village' Epistemologies in the Global Village." In *Anthropological Locations: Boundaries and Grounds of a Field Science*, edited by James Ferguson and Akhil Gupta, 147–62. Berkeley: University of California Press.

Pellow, Deborah. 2003. "New Spaces in Accra: Transnational Houses." *City & Society* 15, no. 1: 59–86.

Perry, Donna. 2005. "Wolof Women, Economic Liberalization, and the Crisis of Masculinity in Rural Senegal." *Ethnology* 44, no. 3: 207–26.

———. 2009. "Fathers, Sons, and the State: Discipline and Punishment in a Wolof Hinterland." *Cultural Anthropology* 24, no. 1: 33–67.

Peterson, Kristin. 2009. "Phantom Epistemologies." In *Fieldwork Is Not What It Used to Be: Learning Anthropology's Method in a Time of Transition*, edited by James Faubion and George Marcus, 37–51. Ithaca, NY: Cornell University Press.

Pieterse, Edgar. 2010. "Cityness and African Urban Development." In *Urban Forum* 21, no. 3, 205–19.

Piot, Charles. 1999. *Remotely Global: Village Modernity in West Africa*. Chicago: Chicago University Press.

———. 2010. *Nostalgia for the Future: West Africa after the Cold War*. Chicago: University of Chicago Press.

Povey, John. 1966. "Dakar: An African Rendez-vous." *Africa Today* 13, no. 5: 4–6.

Rafael, Vicente L. 1997. " 'Your Grief is our Gossip': Overseas Filipinos and Other Spectral Presences." *Public Culture* 9:267–91.

Ralph, Michael. 2005. "Oppressive Impressions, Architectural Expressions: The Poetics of French Colonial (Ad)vantage, Regarding Africa." *African Urban Spaces in Historical Perspective*, edited by Toyin Falola and Steven Salm. Rochester, NY: University of Rochester Press.

———. 2015. *Forensics of Capital*. Chicago: Chicago University Press.

Ratha, Dilip, and Zhimei Xu. 2008. *Migration and Remittances Factbook*. Washington, DC: World Bank Migration and Remittances Team.

République du Sénégal Ministère de l'Économie et des Finances, Direction de la Prévision et de la Statistique. 2004. *Rapport de synthèse de la deuxième enquête sénégalaise auprès des ménages (ESAM-II)*. Dakar.

Riccio, Bruno. 2005. "Talkin' about Migration: Some Ethnographic Notes on the Ambivalent Representation of Migrants in Contemporary Senegal." *Stichproben. Wiener Zeitschrift für kritische Afrikastudien* 8, no. 5: 99–118.

———. 2008. "West African Transnationalisms Compared: Ghanaians and Senegalese in Italy." *Journal of Ethnic and Migration Studies* 34, no. 2: 217–34.

Robben, Antonius. 1989. "Habits of the Home: Spatial Hegemony and the Structuration of House and Society in Brazil." *American Anthropologist* 91, no. 3: 570–88.

Robinson, Jennifer. 2002. "Global and World Cities: A View from Off the Map." *International Journal of Urban and Regional Research* 26, no. 3: 531–54.

Roitman, Janet. 2005. *Fiscal Disobedience: An Anthropology of Economic Regulation in Central Africa*. Princeton, NJ: Princeton University Press.

———. 2013. *Anti-Crisis*. Durham, NC: Duke University Press.

Salazar, Noel. 2010. "Towards an Anthropology of Cultural Mobilities." *Crossings: Journal of Migration & Culture* 1, no. 1: 53–68.

Sassen, Saskia. 1991. *The Global City*. Princeton, NJ: Princeton University Press.

———. 1998. *Globalization and Its Discontents*. New York: New Press.

———. 2001. *The Global City: New York, London, Tokyo*. Princeton, NJ: Princeton University Press.

———. 2003. "The State and Globalization." In *The Third Way: Transformation of Social Democracy*, edited by Oliver Schmidtke. Surrey, UK: Ashgate.

Scheld, Suzanne. 2007. "Youth Cosmopolitanism: Clothing, the City and Globalization in Dakar, Senegal." *City & Society* 19, no. 2: 232–53.

Schnitzler, Antina von. 2008. "Citizenship Prepaid: Water, Calculability, and Techno-Politics in South Africa." *Journal of Southern African Studies* 34, no. 4: 899–917.

———. 2013. "Traveling Technologies: Infrastructure, Ethical Regimes, and the Materiality of Politics in South Africa." *Cultural Anthropology* 28, no. 4: 670–93.

Scott, James C. 1998. *Seeing Like a State: How Certain Schemes to Improve the Human Condition Have Failed*. New Haven, CT: Yale University Press.

Senghor, Leopold Sedar. 1966. "Negritude: A Humanism of the Twentieth Century." In *Perspectives on Africa: A Reader in Culture, History and Representation*, edited by Roy Richard Grinker, Stephen C. Lubkemann, and Chirstopher B. Steiner, 629–36. West Sussex, UK: Wiley-Blackwell.

Sharp, Robin. 1994. *Senegal: A State of Change*. Oxford: Oxfam Publications.

Shaw, Rosalind. 2007. "Displacing Violence: Making Pentecostal Memory in Postwar Sierra Leone." *Cultural Anthropology* 22, no. 1: 66–93.

Sheller, Mimi, and John Urry, eds. 2006. *Mobile Technologies of the City*. London: Routledge.

Simone, Abdou Maliq. 2001. "On the Worlding of African Cities." *African Studies Review* 44, no. 2:15-41.

———. 2004a. *For the City Yet to Come: Changing African Life in Four Cities*. Durham, NC: Duke University Press.

———. 2004b. "People as Infrastructure: Intersecting Fragments in Johannesburg." *Public Culture* 16, no. 3: 407–29.

———. 2004c. "Uncertain Rights to the City." *Africa & Mediterraneo* 50:37–51.

———. 2006. "Pirate Towns: Reworking Social and Symbolic Infrastructures in Johannesburg and Douala." *Urban Studies* 43, no. 2: 357–70.

———. 2012. "Infrastructure: Introductory Commentary by Abdou Maliq Simone." Curated Collections, *Cultural Anthropology* Online. http://www.culanth.org/curated _collections/11-infrastructure/discussions/12-infrastructure-introductory-commentary -by-abdoumaliq-simone.

Smith, Daniel Jordan. 2001. "Ritual Killing, 419, and Fast Wealth: Inequality and the Popular Imagination in Southeastern Nigeria." *American Ethnologist* 28, no. 4: 803–26.

———. 2007. *A Culture of Corruption: Everyday deception and popular discontent in Nigeria.* Princeton, NJ: Princeton University Press.

———. 2014. *AIDS Doesn't Show Its Face: Inequality, Morality, and Social Change in Nigeria.* Chicago: University of Chicago Press.

Somerville, Carolyn. 1991. "The Impact of the Reforms on the Urban Population: How the Dakarois View the Crisis." In Delgado and Jammeh 1991, 151–73.

Sparkes, Stephen, and Signe Howell. 2003. *The House in Southeast Asia: A Changing Social, Economic and Political Domain.* London: Routledge.

Stoller, Paul. 1982. "Signs in the Social Order: Riding a Songhay Bush Taxi." *American Ethnologist* 9, no. 4: 750–62.

———. 2002. *Money Has No Smell: The Africanization of New York City.* Chicago: University of Chicago Press.

Tall, Serigne Mansour. 1994. "Les Investissements Immobiliers à Dakar des Emigrants Sénégalais." *Revue Européene Des Migrations Internationales* 10 , no. 3: 137–51.

———. 2008. "La Migration Internationale Sénégalaise: Des Recrutements de Main-d'oeuvre aux Pirogues." In Diop 2008, 37–67.

Tandian, Aly. 2008. "Des Migrants Sénégalais Qualifiés en Italie: Entre Regrets et Résignation." In Diop 2008, 365–87.

Telle, Kari. 2007. "Entangled Biographies: Rebuilding a Sasak House." *Ethnos* 72, no. 2: 195–218.

Thomas, Phillip. 1998. "Conspicuous Construction: Houses, Consumption, and 'Relocation' in Manambondro, Southeast Madagascar." *Journal of the Royal Anthropological Institute* 4, no. 3: 425–46.

Truitt, Allison. 2008. "On the Back of a Motorbike: Middle Class Mobility in Ho Chi Minh City, Vietnam." *American Ethnologist* 35, no. 1: 3–19.

Tsing, Anna L. 2004. *Friction.* Princeton, NJ: Princeton University Press.

UNCTAD (United Nations Conference on Trade and Development). 2010. World Investment Report. New York: United Nations.

Urry, John. 2007. *Mobilities.* Cambridge: Polity Press.

Van Der Geest, Sjaak. 1998. "Yebisa Wo Fie: Growing Old and Building a House in the Akan Culture of Ghana." *Journal of Cross-Cultural Gerontology* 13:333–59.

Venables, Emilie. 2008. "Senegalese Women and the Cyber Café: Online Dating and Aspirations of Transnational Migration in Ziguinchor." *African and Asian Studies* 7, no. 4: 471–90.

Verdery, Katherine. 2000. "Privatization as Transforming Persons." In *Between Past and Future: The Revolutions of 1989 and Their Aftermath,* edited by Sorin Antohi and Vladimir Tismaneanu, 175–97. Budapest: Central European University Press.

Verran, Helen. 2001. *Science and an African Logic.* Chicago: University of Chicago Press.

Waterbury, John, and Mark Gersovitz, eds. 1987. *The Political Economy of Risk and Choice in Senegal.* London: Frank Cass & Co., Ltd.

Waterson, Roxanna. 1990. *The Living House: An Anthropology of Architecture in South-East Asia.* Oxford: Oxford University Press.

Weber, Max. (1946) 2009. "Bureaucracy." In *From Max Weber: Essays in Sociology*, translated by H. H. Gerth and C. Wright Mills, 196–244. Oxford: Oxford University Press.

Weekley, Kathleen. 2004. "Saving Pennies for the State: A New Role for Filipino Migrant Workers?" *Journal of Contemporary Asia* 34, no. 3: 349–63.

Whittlesey, Derwent. 1948. "Dakar Revisted." *Geographical Review* 38, no. 4: 626–32.

Willems, Roos. 2008. "Les 'Fous de la Mer': Les Migrants Clandestins du Sénégal aux Iles Canaries en 2006." In Diop 2008, 277–303.

———. 2014. "Local Realities and Global Possibilities: Deconstructing the Imaginations of Aspiring Migrants in Senegal." *Identities* 21, no. 3: 320–35.

Wittmann, Frank. 2008. "Politics, Religion, and the Media: The Transformation of the Public Sphere in Senegal." *Media Culture Society* 30, no. 4: 479–94.

World Bank. 2003. "Senegal – Country Partnership Strategy for the Period FY13-17." Washington, DC: World Bank. http://documents.worldbank.org/curated/en/5275514 68103763222/Senegal-Country-partnership-strategy-for-the-period-FY13-FY17.

Zaloom, Caitlin. 2004. "The Productive Life of Risk." *Cultural Anthropology* 19, no. 3: 365–91.

Zeilig, Leo. 2009. "Student Resistance and the Democratic Transition: Student Politics in Senegal 1999–2005." *Social Dynamics* 35, no. 1: 68–93.

Zeilig, Leo, and Nicola Ansell. 2008. "Spaces and Scales of African Student Activism: Senegalese and Zimbabwean University Students at the Intersection of Campus, Nation and Globe." *Antipode* 40:31–54.

INDEX

Note: Page numbers followed by "f" refer to figures.

precariousness, 18n15; literature on, 18–20
predicament, *embouteillage* and, 17–18

remittance-driven development, 114–15
remittances, of transnational migrants, 38–39
remitting migrants, transforming, to entrepreneurs, 113–14
Riverside County, California/2007, *embouteillage* in, 163–66
road development, 12

"salaried man," 34, 36
selective migration policies, 63–64
Senegal: building of, by transnational migrants, 123–24; diaspora of, 118–19, 118n11, 118n12; economy of, 105; foreign direct investment inflows in, 112; inflows of FDI into, 112; liberalization in, 16–17; ministry system of, and APIX, 106; pirogues as symbol of vitality of, 136–37; system of government of, 106n5. *See also* Dakar
Senghor, Léopold Sédar, 33, 41
Set/Setal ("clean up") movement, 37
Sister Taxi program, 57–59; male drivers' opposition to, 60
spatial mappings, 98
state authority, erosion of, 105–6
state governance, *embouteillage* as device for thinking about, 128–29
strandedness, 18n14
structural adjustment policies: effects of, 36–37; effects of, on Senegalese fishing industry, 137; mobility and, 36–37
structural adjustment reforms, 16–17
"stuckedness," 18n14

taxicab drivers. *See* cab drivers; women cab drivers
Titanique (Titanic) pirogue, tale about, 131–32, 139, 143
Touba, Senegal, 114–15n8
Tout Petit Crédit program, 153–54
traffic bottlenecks, 50; context of, 51–52. *See also* cab drivers; *embouteillages* (bottlenecks)
transnational migrants: building of Senegal and Dakar by, 123–24; as central figure of success, 38; Dakar's housing landscape and, 83–84; as gendered figure, 39–40; home building and, 85–86; obstacles for, 63–65; remittances of, 38–39; small businesses and, 38. *See also* mobility
transnational migration, 142n9; discourse of loss and, 121–22; as economic strategy, 121–22; extent of, 43–44; as individualized activity or matter of luck, 141–42; masculine solidarity and, 142; as means to buttress household budgets, 37–38; narrowing or blocking channels of contemporary, 141. *See also* clandestine migration; mobility

unemployment, 17; urban, 36
Université de Cheikh Anta Diop (UCAD), 23–24; protests at, 46–48; student tensions at, 27–29

Wade, Abdoulaye, 1, 2, 41, 42–43, 72, 106, 120, 140n8
Wolof, 6, 6n4, 9
women cab drivers, 56–59. *See also* cab drivers
World Bank, 41, 82, 105